British Institute of Archaeology at Ankara

Monograph No. 14

TİLLE HÖYÜK 1

THE MEDIEVAL PERIOD

by

JOHN MOORE

Published by

THE BRITISH INSTITUTE OF ARCHAEOLOGY AT ANKARA

1993

British Institute of Archaeology at Ankara,
c/o British Academy, 20–21 Cornwall Terrace
London NW1 4QP

ISBN 1 898249 00 8

© British Institute of Archaeology at Ankara 1993

Typeset by Imprint, Oxford
Printed by the Alden Press, Oxford

Contents

Preface

The Turkish Government is proceeding with a series of dams downstream from the Keban dam, completed in 1973. One of the dams, the Atatürk, will produce an artificial lake some 250km in length. In 1977, the British Institute of Archaeology in Ankara was invited to participate in the Lower Euphrates Rescue Project. In 1978, the Institute was allotted, by the Project Committee, the site of Tille Höyük. Rescue excavation began in 1979.

The site has been visited by several scholars in the recent past. A plan was made by the Eski Kahta team under Professor F.K. Dörner. Since then, topographic and archaeological notes have been made by Özdoğan (1977) and Serdaroğlu (1977). A small group from the British Institute of Archaeology at Ankara under David French carried out a reconnaissance in November and December 1978. Excavation began in 1979. Work in the Medieval levels on the höyük started in 1980. Notes on the progress of the work have appeared in *Anatolian Studies* 1979-1981 under 'The Year's Work'. An interim report appeared in volume 32 (French, Moore and Russell 1982).

I was invited to take responsibility for the excavation and publication of the Medieval settlement on the höyük after the first season's work in 1980. I am grateful to David French for this opportunity and for his advice, help and criticism over the next four years.

I must also express my gratitude to the staff who worked on the Medieval levels over the seven seasons carried out in the years 1980-1983. Those taking part in the excavations have been: Gülriz Akdenizli (1983), Joanna Bailey (1982); Stuart Blaylock (1980–82); Stephen Clews (1980); Wayne Cocroft (1982); Esin Dal (1981); Anne Fahy (1982); Robert Halliday (1982); Jennifer Inkpen (1982); Ahmet İşçimen (1980–81); Berin Kuşatman (1981); Sara Langdon (1981); Decca Moore (1981–83); Charles Mundy (1982); Ann Murray (1981–83); Graham Philip (1983); Robert Philpott (1980–81); Andrew Pye (1982); Malcolm Reid (1981); Harry Russell (1981–83); Diana Russell (1981); Funda Z. Sabri (1980–81); Alun Sheen (1980); Valerie Shelton-Bunn (1980); Taciser Tüfekçi (1981); Cathy Tutton (1983); Susan Vaughan (1980); Robert Whieldon (1980–81); Brian Williams (1982).

Tuğrul Çakar (1981–83) was photographer; Pamela French (1980) and Robert Payton (1981–83) were conservators; Lynn Grant (1982) restored pottery. Finds-illustration was undertaken by Joanna Bailey (1982); Theresa Breznau (1981); Mark Duncan (1982–83); Brian Williams (1982). The original pottery drawings were made by many of the staff mentioned above and were reproduced in ink for publication by Decca Moore and Cathy Tutton. The published plans were drawn up by Stephen Clews, Mark Duncan, Decca Moore and myself. The patient typists were Maureen Midgley, Jan Mitchell, Canan Philips and Christal Türkmen.

The coins were identified by Bay İsmail Galip and Simon Bendall.

I am indebted to David French and Stuart Blaylock for their constructive criticisms of the text during its preparation.

Lastly, my thanks go to the representatives of the Ministry of Culture, Ali Zafer Çakmakçı (1980), Ahmet Bal and Baki Yiğit (1981), Vehbi Uysal (1982) and Ali Önder (1983), and to the Directors of the Adıyaman Museum, Hacı Ali Ekinci (1980–82) and Emin Yener (1983).

This volume was completed in January 1984 and delays in its publication were beyond the control of the author.

List of Figures

List of Plates

Bibliography

BRITISH MUSEUM
1921 *A guide to the Early Christian and Byzantine antiquities*, London.

ETTINGHAUSEN, R.
1965 'The uses of sphero-conical vessels in the Muslim East', *JNES* 24: 218–229.

FRENCH, D. H., MOORE, J. and RUSSELL, H. F.
1982 'Excavations at Tille 1979–1982. An interim report', *Anat St* 32: 161–187.

HALL, G., McBRIDE, S. and RIDDELL, A.
1973 'Architectural study. Avan 1968–1972', *Anat St* 23: 245–270.

IRAQ GOVERNMENT, DEPT. OF ANTIQUITIES
1940 *Excavations at Samarra 1936–1939*, Baghdad.

JOHNS, C. N.
1935 'Excavations at Pilgrims' Castle, Atlit (1932–3): stables at the south-west of the suburb', *QDAP* 5: 31–60.

KÖY İŞLERİ BAKANLIĞI
1967 *Köy envanter etüdlerine göre Adıyaman 02*, Ankara (Köy İşleri Bakanlığı Yayınları 47).

LANE, A.
1947 *Early Islamic pottery*, London.
1962 *Later Islamic pottery, Persia, Syria, Egypt, Turkey*, London.

MITCHELL, S.
1980 *Aşvan Kale*, Oxford. (BAR International Series 80.

OLDENBURG, E.
1969 'Les objets en faïence, terre-cuite, os et nacre', in Riis, P.J. et al. (eds) *Hama, Fouilles et Recherches 1931–1938, 4,3*: 107–141, Copenhagen.

ÖZDOĞAN, M.
1977 *Lower Euphrates basin survey*, İstanbul (Middle East Technical University, Lower Euphr. Proj. Publ. 1,2).

PLOUG, G.
1969 'Les objets en pierre', in Riis, P.J. et al. (eds) *Hama, Fouilles et Recherches 1931–1938, 4,3*: 89–106. Copenhagen.

PLOUG, G. and OLDENBURG, E.
1969 'Les objets en métal sauf les monnaies', in Riis, P.J. et al. (eds) *Hama, Fouilles et Recherches 1931–1938, 4,3*: 89–106, Copenhagen.

PORTER, V.
1981 *Medieval Syrian pottery*, Oxford (Ashmolean Museum).

POULSEN, V.
1957 'Les poteries', in Riis, P.J. and Poulsen, V. (eds) *Hama, Fouilles et Recherches 1931–1938, 4,2*: 117–283, Copenhagen.
1970 'Islamisk Fayence fra Syrien', in *Fjerde del Jubilaeumsskrift 1945–1970, C.L. Davids Samling*: 257–292, Copenhagen.

REDFORD, S.
1986 'Excavations at Gritille (1982–1984): the Medieval period, a preliminary report', *Anat St* 36: 103–136.

ROGERS, J. M.
1969 'Aeolipiles again', in Aslanapa, O. and Naumann, R. (eds) *Forschungen zur Kunst Asiens in memoriam Kurt Erdmann*: 147–158, İstanbul.

SERDAROĞLU, Ü.
1977 *Surveys in the lower Euphrates basin*, Ankara (Middle East Technical University, Lower Euphr. Proj. Publ. 1,1).

SEYRIG, H.
1959 'Flacons? grenades? ealipiles?', *Syria* 36: 81–89.

THALMAN, J.P.
1978 'Tell 'Arqa (Liban Nord) Campanges 1–3 (1972–1974)', *Syria* 55: 1–152.

WAAGÉ, F.O. (ed.)
1948 *Antioch on-the-Orontes 4,1. Ceramics and Islamic coins*, Princeton.

CHAPTER 1

The Setting

Tille Höyük is situated on the western bank of the Euphrates, beside the modern bridge that carries the Adıyaman–Urfa/Diyarbakır road across the river. The village of Tille, now named Geldibuldu, lies on the north side of the road c. 30km east of Kâhta. The village is small. Houses are built on the east, west and south sides of the mound (fig. 1).

The mound is located on the edge of a small ravine formed by a tributary stream flowing eastwards into the Euphrates. The mound covers an area of approximately 200m by 140m (if the terrace to the east is included) and on the south-west side of the site stands to a height of 26m above the level of the plain (Pl.1a). The diameter of the conical part of the mound is about 130m at the base. The flat top before excavation measured 40m by 33m; the surviving area covered by the earliest phase of the Medieval was 46m by 40m. The sides of the mound are steep, especially the northern (fig. 2; Pl.1a).

Tille village is situated in the Euphrates valley, above the flood plain of the river and on a fairly wide terrace, the first of several. The various terraces and slopes have different agricultural uses. South of the main road the flat, first terrace is given over almost exclusively to cereal cultivation, wheat and maize, but also to cotton. The lower slopes above the first terrace are used for cereal and some vegetables; higher up are orchards and vegetable gardens. Above this zone is another terrace, a rough area where chick peas, lentils, squash, peppers and other vegetables are cultivated. The uppermost slopes of the Euphrates valley are given over to vines and to grazing. The plateau above the valley, does not belong to Tille; it is used almost exclusively for cereals. On the floor of the ravine on the north side of the mound are grown wheat, lentils, chick peas and other legumes. The area to the north of the village, being reasonably flat, is used mainly for wheat. In the immediate area around the village are vegetable gardens and small fields used for growing cotton and hemp. Also close to the village are various fruit trees. Trees used for firewood grow beside the small stream that runs through the ravine on the north side of the mound. A threshing ground is located at the western foot of the mound.

A number of springs supply the village with water. Three (all located south of the mound, on the slopes facing the village) are used solely for irrigation purposes, the water flowing through concrete channels. Two springs (one at the foot of the mound on the north-east side, the other some 150m to the west of the village) are used for drinking and irrigation purposes; a third spring at the head of the bridge over the Euphrates is used only by travellers.

In 1985, there were seventeen houses in the village. These range in size from two to seven rooms. Four new houses were built after 1979, when the excavation team had moved into the village. In 1979 we rented the largest building for accommodation and one other building for a depot and for work space. Various other buildings are used by the villagers for the storage of food and for animals (Pl.1b).

The agricultural produce of the village includes wheat, lentils, chick peas, sesame, onions, tomatoes, cucumbers, aubergines, squash, peppers, watermelons, apricots, grapes, figs, pears, mulberries (red and white), pomegranates, walnuts, cotton and hemp. The products sold on the local market include wheat, lentils (important in 1982), sesame (important in 1983 after failure of the lentil crop), cotton, hemp and apricots.

Very few animals are kept. Until 1983 there was only one small flock of goats. Since then there have been three mixed flocks of sheep and goats. Every family has one to three cows or oxen. A few donkeys are found in the village. Most families have some hens; a few have ducks, geese and turkeys.

Some ploughing is still done by oxen but this practice has declined owing to the increasing number of tractors (from one in 1980 to four at the end of 1982). A machine was purchased by one family in 1982 to harvest lentils. Cereals are now harvested by hired machines. Several families spread large quantities of chemical fertilizer on their fields in 1981 but very little was used in 1982 and 1983.

The area close to Tille generally escapes the snow which falls elsewhere in the province, although early 1983 was an exception. Neither does the area suffer from many frosts. The average number of rain days for the Kâhta district is 55.3 and the average precipitation is 556.3mm. (Köy İşleri Bakanlığı Yayınları 1967: 18 Table 4).

1

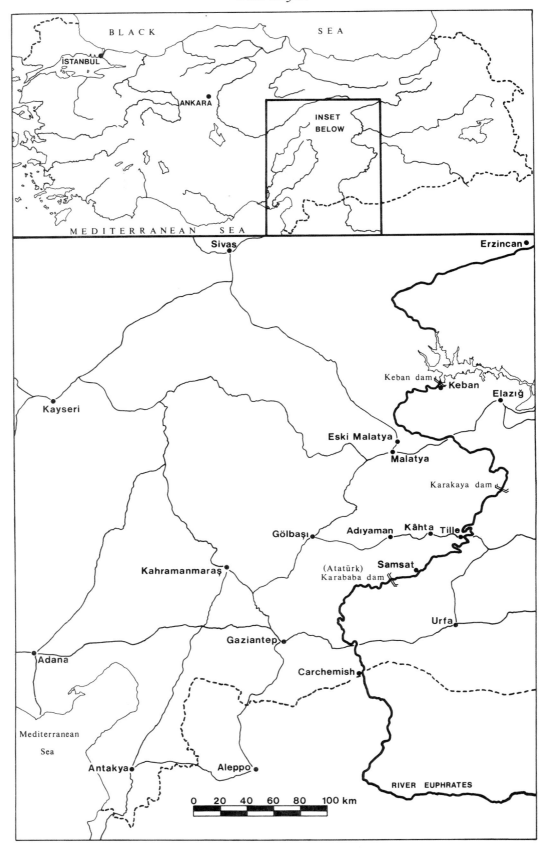

Fig. 1. Location of Tille

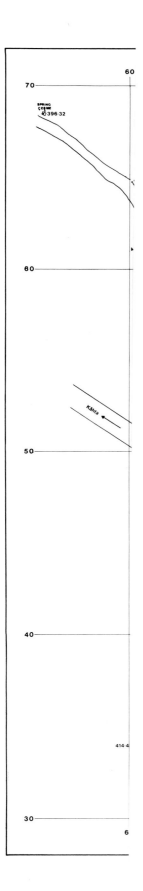

The village now lies beside the main road from Kâhta and Adıyaman to Urfa, Siverek and Diyarbakır. Before the bridge over the Euphrates was built in 1972, there was only a very rough road from Tille to Kâhta and Adıyaman. A track leads downstream from Tille to the hamlets (*mezraalar*) of Tilbe (now Tepecik) and Karatilbe (now Karatepe); a path goes upstream following the river side to the village of Hiniç (now Adalı). A track runs from the village north-north-westwards to the hamlets of Açoğlu, Kefiri (now Beşikli), Karsalah (now Akalan) and thence to Hiniç.

The approximate altitude at the bridge head is 379.30m.

CHAPTER 2

Historical Summary

The following is a brief history of south-eastern Anatolia (the region immediately on the south and east of the Taurus and Amanus mountains) during the eleventh to fourteenth centuries. The intention of this chapter is to provide, albeit briefly, an historical background to this period of occupation on the mound at Tille.

Early in the eleventh century, Tuğrul Beg, the real founder of the Seljuk Empire, invaded central Persia and became the protector of the Abbasid caliphates. Alp Arslan, his successor, invaded Armenia, which had been largely occupied by the Byzantines since 1021, and captured Ani (1064), before annexing the kingdom of Kars (1064). From here Seljuk bands and Turkoman nomads carried out raids and laid waste northern Syria a number of times (1067–68). They also penetrated into Cappadocia and Phrygia but there was no occupation of territory at this time.

During the same period, the Byzantine hold on south-eastern Anatolia (the area south and east of the Taurus and Amanus mountains) was limited to an area in the Urfa (ancient Edessa, modern Şanlıurfa) region. This area stretched about 80km to the north-east and included Siverek c. 40km east of Tille. Using Urfa as a base, the Byzantines carried out raids on the territories of Kisas, Harran (anc. Carrhae) and Suruç (Medieval Saruj). By the middle of the eleventh century Constantine Monomachos (1045-56) had retaken from the Arabs the cities of Melitene (mod. Malatya), Hisn Mansur (mod. Adıyaman), Keysun (mod. Çakırhöyük), Edessa and Samosata (mod. Samsat) which was the only safe link with the Christian territory to the west. Constantine resettled groups of Armenians in Cappadocia and Cilicia, Sivas (anc. Sebasteia) and Kayseri (anc. Caesareia) being the main centres of occupation. In the second half of the eleventh century, Seljuk bands and Turkoman nomads began to move into the area of northern Syria/south-eastern Anatolia; they captured Urfa, Malatya and Samsat but retired shortly afterwards. The Seljuks, indeed, followed the classic invasion route along the River Aras (anc. Araxes) and the Kara Su (the northern tributary of the Euphrates). They then fanned out to plunder an area from the Murad Su to the hinterland of Trabzon (anc. Trapezus, med. Trebizond) and reached Erzurum. Seljuk and Turkoman bands repeatedly raided the confluence of the two tributaries of the Euphrates; they advanced to Sivas in 1059, to the area below Malatya in 1062, to Urfa in 1064, to Kayseri in 1067 and to Konya (anc. Iconium) in 1068. Siverek was raided by Alp Arslan early in 1071.

Endeavouring to stop the raids into Byzantine Armenia, the Byzantine Emperor, Romanus Diogenes, went to Lake Van in 1071 with an army of 200,000 men. The Seljuks had just taken Malazgirt and soon after the capture of the stronghold, Alp Arslan feigned a retreat and drew the Byzantines into an ambush. The Emperor was taken prisoner and the greater part of his men killed. This victory opened the gates of the Anatolian plateau to the Seljuks, who then advanced as far as the region of İzmit (anc. Nicomedia). In 1078, Süleyman established the first Seljuk emirate in Anatolia with its capital at İznik (anc. Nicaea).

At about the same time, another Turkish tribe, the Danışmends, set up an emirate in the centre of Asia Minor around Kayseri, Sivas and Amasya (anc. Amasia) while the Menguçeks established a principality based in Erzincan. An Armenian, Philaretus Brachamius, formed an independent principality between Urfa, Maraş (anc. Germaniceia, mod. Kahramanmaraş) and Malatya. The Seljuks occupied the areas to the west and east.

During the second half of the eleventh century, quarrels between different groups of Armenians, on political and religious grounds, ruined the consolidation of the new Armenian kingdom, the approximate bounds of which were the Amanus mountains in the west, the upper reaches of the Euphrates in the north-east and the trans-Euphrates zone in the south-east. Thus Urfa, Maraş and Elbistan, together with Malatya, Keysun (now renamed Çakırhöyük; med. Crasson) and Gerger, were included in its territory. Before the death of Philaretus Brachamius in 1085, his territories were already breaking up and for the next six years the Sultan of Baghdad, Melik Şah, a Seljuk, controlled the area, until once again Armenian leaders regained bases in Malatya, Urfa, Maraş, Keysun and Araban (now renamed Altıntaş; med. Ra'ban).

On the eve of the First Crusade, in the last years of the eleventh century, the Seljuks commanded the southern route from the Taurus and Syria to the Sea of Marmara while the Danışmends, by holding Ankara, Kayseri and Sivas, controlled the northerly route and in particular central Anatolia and Cappadocia. An alliance between the Seljuks and the Daniışmends was formed during this crusade. In 1098, the citadel of Antakya (anc. Antiochia) fell to the Frankish force and Baldwin of Boulogne captured Urfa. Antioch was made an independent principality and the region of Urfa, including Samsat, Suruç and Birecik (med. Birtha), became a county. On Christmas Day 1100, Baldwin succeeded his brother Godfrey as King of Jerusalem. The County of Edessa now became a fief of the Kingdom of Jerusalem. Kılıç Arslan I was dispossessed of Nicaea by the Franks in 1097 and now attempted to extend his lands in central Anatolia to the east. Melik Şah, and later his brother Mesut, succeeded Kılıç Arslan I. Mesut enlarged his kingdom by seizing the lands of the Danışmends on the death of Danışmend Gazi, his former ally. The Second Crusade, 1146, was defeated by Mesut (in complicity with the Byzantines). A new power, the Seljuk Sultanate of Rum, and a new capital, Konya, then came into being. Kılıç Arslan II, son of Mesut, was intermittently at war with the Danışmends between 1156 and 1175; he succeeded in annexing Cappadocia and the Malatya area. In 1176, Manuel Comnenus was defeated by the Seljuk Sultan at the battle of Myriokephalon (near Yalvaç?).

The Sultanate of Rum was temporarily threatened by the Third Crusade which captured the town (but not the citadel) of the capital, Konya. After Frederick Barbarossa had crossed Anatolia, the Seljuks regained their former territories but they did not benefit, as much as they could have, from their victory over the Byzantines at Myriokephalon. The Fourth Crusade, the abdication of Kılıç Arslan II in 1188, the bitter fighting between his sons and his subsequent death in 1192, all disrupted the Seljuk state. The Byzantines themselves were unable to take advantage of the weak Seljuk state after the fall of Constantinople in 1204 to the Fourth Crusade.

An independent state, Lesser Armenia, came into existence in the region of Adana at the end of the twelfth century and under Leo II it began to expand. Several strongholds were captured from the Seljuks including Karaman and Ereğli (anc. Heraclia), although these towns had to be returned in 1216. Keykubad I enlarged the Seljuk state by seizing Alanya in 1220 and occupying Erzincan in 1230. The first outlet to the Mediterranean had been won by the capture of Antalya in 1207. Access to the Black Sea was achieved by the capture of Sinop in 1214. At this time, the Sultanate of Rum was at the height of its power and covered the whole of Anatolia with the exception of the Comnenid Kingdom of Trebizond and the lands of Lesser Armenia (in Cilicia), though both states recognized the Seljuks as their suzerains. At the battle of Köse Dağ, in 1243, the Seljuk army was completely routed by the Mongols aided by Georgians and Armenians. This defeat resulted in the creation of a client kingdom of the Mongols in eastern Anatolia, though it remained Seljuk in name until 1302.

Baghdad was captured by the Mongols under Hulagu in 1258. They invaded Syria and took Aleppo, Hama, Homs and Damascus. It must be assumed that the Adıyaman region also fell to the Mongols.

The middle of the thirteenth century saw a Mongol-Armenian alliance until 1268 when Cilicia was invaded by the Egyptian Mamelukes. In 1260 the Mamelukes under Baybars defeated the Mongols at the battle of 'Ain Jalut. Out of Syria and Palestine six provinces were created, each with its own governor. Aleppo was one of the six. At this stage it probably did not include the region of Adıyaman. Rum kale (on the Euphrates) fell to the Mamelukes in 1292 and in 1293 Maraş, Behesni (mod. Besni) and Til Hamdun (mod. Toprakkale) were captured from the Armenians. The earliest Mameluke inscriptions from Besni and Eski Kahta, however, date to the reign of Qalaun, 1279–1290. The kingdom of Lesser Armenia in Cilicia was finally annexed by the Egyptians in 1375.

In the first decades of the fourteenth century, the Ottoman dynasty started on the road to empire. After the initial seizure of Bilecik and İnegöl by Osman I and then the capture of Bursa in c. 1326, İzmit in 1330 and İznik in 1331, the Ottoman territory rapidly grew. In 1362, Murat I took Edirne which then became the capital of the Ottoman Sultanate until the capture of Constantinople in 1453. The Mameluke lands of Syria (which included the region of Adıyaman) and Palestine fell to Selim I after the battle of Marj Dabiq (north of Aleppo) in 1516.

Sources

Ashtor, E. *A social and economic history of the near east in the middle ages*, London, 1976.

Boase, T.S.R. (ed.) *The Cilician kingdom of Armenia*, Edinburgh, 1978.

Boulanger, R. *Hachette world guides: Turkey*, Paris, 1960.

Cahen, C. (trans. Jones-Williams, J.) *Pre-Ottoman Turkey. A general survey of the material and spiritual culture and history c.1071–1330,* London,1968.

Cambridge Medieval History1936 *4. The eastern Roman empire 717–1453,* Cambridge,1936.

Creswell, K.A.C. *A short account of early Muslim architecture,* London,1958.

Hazard, H.W. and Setton, K.M. (eds.) *A History of the Crusades: 3. The fourteenth and fifteenth centuries,* Wisconsin,1975.

Honigmann, E. *Die Ostgrenze des byzantinischen Reiches,* Brussels,1935.

Lang, D.M. *Armenia. Cradle of civilization,* London, 1970.

Manandian, H.A. *The trade and cities of Armenia in relation to ancient world trade,* Lisbon,1965.

der Nersessian, S. *Byzantine and Armenian studies 1, 2,* Louvain,1973.

Talbot Rice, T. *The Seljuks in Asia Minor,* London,1961.

Wolff, R.L. and Hazard, H.W. (eds.) *A History of the Crusades: 2. The Later Crusades 1189–1311, 2nd ed.,* Wisconsin,1969.*

CHAPTER 3

Method of Excavation

Excavation Techniques

The removal of the Medieval layers on the site took c. 4650 workman-days spread over seven seasons: June–July 1980, May–June 1981, September–November 1981, part of April–July 1982, October–November 1982, part of May–June 1983 and a few days of September–November 1983. The number of workmen employed at any one time varied from fifteen to forty-eight while the number of excavation supervisors and assistants varied from three to twelve. The optimum balance of excavation staff to workmen seemed to be three supervisors, three assistants and one planner to thirty-five workmen, a ratio of l:5, although in autumn 1983 with an experienced team, this ratio was reduced to four supervisors and an assistant to thirty workmen, i.e.1:6. These figures may give the impression of weighting the staff side. Nevertheless we tried to anticipate the unforeseen: illness, for instance, was predictable. At least half the time, one member (or more!) of the staff would be unavailable owing to sickness. Further, for most of the time, there was a struggle to keep abreast of recording and planning without holding up the progress of the work.

An arbitrary grid, comprising a kilometre square subdivided into 100m and 10m squares, was imposed on the territory of Tille village. Individual 10m squares are identified by the grid reference of the south-western corner, abbreviated to four figures e.g. the reference 76005800 refers to the south-western corner of the square known as 7658 (cf. Fig.24., on which all the squares excavated are identified). In this manner trenches opened anywhere in the area could be identified and plotted without difficulty. Two base lines were established on the top of the mound. From these the 10m by 10m squares which were to form the trenches for excavation were laid out. Diagonally adjacent trenches were excavated simultaneously in the manner of a chequer-board. Standing sections, or baulks, were not left between trenches. The sections exposed in the sides of the black squares were drawn before the excavation of the adjacent white squares commenced. Continuous section drawings have been compiled by joining together the section drawings along the desired line (e.g. Figs 25–27).

Approximately two metres of complex vertical stratigraphy was controlled by this system of ten metre square trenches. As each 10m square was excavated, sections were drawn before moving on to an adjacent square. Most squares were not dug continuously. Several squares were taken down to one single, contemporary level, in order to take area photographs or to understand the stratigraphy by reference to a wider area. Only one square (7557) was dug without a break from topsoil down to the earliest level of the late Medieval period. This square was, in fact, the very last to be opened.

The method of excavation by 10m square as opposed to open area was made necessary a) by the need for control sections and b) for the easier supervision and recording of stratigraphic units and finds.

a) The use of sections served as a control on the accuracy of excavation. As-dug sections were compiled as overlays on the as-drawn sections (the section left standing). An as-dug section is compiled from data recorded on trench plans, namely, the vertical and horizontal limits of units and the absolute levels or heights. The as-drawn section (i.e. the drawing of the section left standing) is recorded only along the edges of the squares. For complete reliability to be given to the unit sequence claimed by the trench supervisor, the as-drawn section must correlate absolutely, one-to-one as it were, with the as-dug section. The degree of reliability given to the materials recovered in the trench depends absolutely on the accuracy of the as-dug units. Without the information of an as-dug section, the as-drawn section must be accepted only as a record of perceived stratification: it does not confirm the accuracy of excavation. Interpretation of sequence and contexts cannot be based on the assumption that the as-drawn section is a record of precise excavation.

In many cases discrepancies occurred between these two types of sections. Usually more than one deposit or soil-unit had been removed in a single action: subsequently the as-drawn section showed the correct number of soil-units. When this happened, the adjacent square was then excavated correctly in order to give greater reliability to the finds recovered.

The as-drawn sections proved invaluable in

the top metre of dry deposits where several features, mainly robber trenches and floors, were not noticed during excavation. The weathering of these sections over a period of a few days or weeks produced answers to several problems e.g. discontinuities of floors, lack of floor surfaces. Again, once identified, these features could then be excavated in their proper sequence in the adjacent square.

b) The supervision and recording of excav-ation was found to be easier if carried out in well-defined areas. Each square had a trench supervisor and usually one or two trench assistants, the responsibility of the supervisor being, in general, the excavation and recording of soil-units and the responsibility of the assistant being the recording of the finds. The latter also assisted with planning and with supervision of the workmen.

Although separate recording in each square resulted in the multiple-numbering of some soil-units (which appeared in more than one square) this procedure was thought to be a better method of notation than the arbitrary allocation of soil-unit numbers to different supervisors. On an open-area excavation it is very easy for units to escape record as one supervisor often thinks that another has written down the necessary infor-mation. Furthermore, workmen can remove a lot of earth (and soil-units) without record when one supervisor thinks that another has overseen the operation. In one or two cases, this confusion arose even when an operation was carried out within the same ten metre square but not (happily) to any significant degree. The cross-referencing of notes and plans tends to be neglected, to a large extent, when several super-visors are acting within the same area.

The 10m square system allowed us considerable flexibility with the workmen. If we reached a stage (in one square) where no more material could be removed without immediate and extensive recording, the workmen could then be moved to another square. Our system enabled a supervisor or assistant easily to maintain con-tinuity after excavation had been temporarily halted. When the original square had been recorded, the workmen were moved back. By excavating three or four squares simultaneously, we found it easy to switch workmen according to the needs of a particular square. At one time, one square had thirty(!) workmen removing a destruction level while other squares were being recorded and planned.

The first work carried out in the layers of the Medieval period on the mound was the opening of the three squares 7559, 7658, 7759. As the topographers had not, at that time, laid out our grid, these trenches were started as eight metre squares; after three weeks they were enlarged to ten metres. The excavation of the strips around the eight metre squares caused problems of correlation between new units and those already excavated and removed. This difficulty was particularly acute on the west side of 7658 where part of what we thought to be stone footings and wall tumble are now interpreted as a stone pavement.

The first season's excavation, 1980, was carried out slowly and carefully. As we became familiar with the nature of the site and its deposits we were able to change our tactics and to conduct the work at a much faster pace. The presence of robber trenches of a recent date enabled us to gain a preview of the stratigraphy, although they (the robber trenches) had destroyed relationships across large areas. Cooking-pits (the Turkish word *tandır* is used here since there is no precise English equivalent: a cooking pit with a plastered clay lining, baked by use, and characteristically beehive-shaped in section; see Section 1, Fig. 25 [091a]) were perhaps the most useful indicators, as generally they lay inside rooms. They showed us the thickness of floor sequences which could then be removed to-gether. We found that, especially in the very topmost metre or metre and a half of deposits, the soil either was very dry or became dry within hours of exposure. The only method to distinguish floors from mud-brick walls was a careful brushing which usually (but not always) showed the interface between the two, i.e. floor and wall. Sometimes, individual bricks could be picked out in the wall. Only by immediate cleaning of newly exposed surfaces were we able to make a firm interpretation. When an area had been temporarily left because it was obscure and subsequently had became excessively dry there was very little chance of concluding a satis-factory interpretation.

The difficulty of detecting mud-brick in the dry, upper levels of the mound and the obser-vation that nearly all mud-brick was laid on stone footings, both led to our adopting the practice whereby the mud-brick was removed and the stone footings only were used for the plan and structural relationship of a wall. In the vast majority of cases the floors ran up to the stone footings. Only when the wall had a long life would the floors run up to the mud-brick. As work increased in pace in the seasons after 1980, the earth retained its moisture and discontinuities in units could be more readily observed. It then became easier to locate mudbrick lying on top of stone footings.

The lack of finds, in any sizeable quantity, from clearly definable stratigraphic contents contributed to the formulation of a strategy for subsequent seasons. Very few whole pots were found: even fewer were found lying on floor surfaces.

These factors brought us to an excavation policy designed to recover plans of the Medieval buildings as complete, and in as short a time, as possible. The first aim was to reconstruct the main structural elements of the different *levels*, in the hope that we could understand the secondary *phases* as work progressed. Any room-furniture that could be identified was regarded as a bonus. Although eagerly looked for, very few examples were noticed.

By the end of the second season—spring 1981— more than three-quarters of the top of the mound had been cleaned down to Medieval Level 2 Phase 2, by the use of the chequer-board method of excavation. The south-western part of the mound had not yet been touched.

In the autumn season of 1981 a small part of the south-western area on the mound was excavated: squares 7556 and 7457. Square 7557 was not then excavated. This square had been left as it was thought that its stratigraphy was complex and that lack of time would prevent its removal. It was excavated in 1982 in order to answer the problems unsolved by the examination of the surrounding squares. These problems mostly lay in the understanding of the walls and floors seen in the western section of square 7657 and in the lack of stratigraphy between the south wall (= 7558/128) in square 7558 and the east wall (= 7457/020) in square 7457. The excavation of square 7557 made it possible to reconstruct the whole of the various stages and phases of the major building located in this square.

During the third season—1982—the last of the Medieval occupation in the north-western corner of the site was exposed and removed. By working in adjacent squares, we were forced to leave thin baulks between them. The sections were drawn and the baulks subsequently removed.

In spring 1982 the deposits that we thought were the very last of the Medieval occupation were examined. Unfortunately, in 1983, after we had begun to excavate the latest Hellenistic levels on the south side of the mound, the earliest level of Medieval occupation was encountered. The first week of June 1983 saw the final clearance of the whole of the Medieval occupation on the top of the mound. In the autumn of 1983, some more Medieval deposits were found on the northern edge of the mound at a level slightly lower than those on the top of the mound. The examination of these was completed in autumn 1984.

Recording the Site

Soil-units within each square were given an individual number in a consecutive series (which began with 001). The amount of recorded detail for each individual unit varied according to the season in which the unit was excavated and to its assumed relative importance. These assumptions, however, were made only after two seasons of excavation. Even then firm assumptions became possible only after the re-occurrence of certain types of feature. To give two examples: unless exceptional, the beaten earth or mud-chaff floors were not colour-coded by Munsell chart and the types of fill of the *tandır* pits were not noted after the first two seasons work since the characteristics tended to be repeated.

Each unit was recorded on a pre-prepared printed sheet (Fig. 3) bearing a checklist of obligatory observations and a further section for non-obligatory observations and for description of items not covered by the check-list. After the first season, when the recording had been written in hard-backed trench-books which could only be used by one person at a time, a loose-leaf system was introduced.

During the first season, the planning of the site was carried out in two ways: either in the trench-book or on large pieces of plastic draughting film that covered the square at a scale of 1:20. These large plans generally were drawn when a level or phase was thought to have been completely uncovered. The system was found to be thoroughly impractical and in subsequent seasons all site planning was carried out on blue, millimetrically grided draughting film over-printed (in black) with metre-indicators and provided with boxes for the recording of plan numbers and relationships to other plans (Fig. 4). Each plan sheet covers an area 5m by 5m at a scale of 1:20. Four sheets thus cover the whole ten metre square. The advantage of these sheets on site is enormous. If necessary, four people can simultaneously plan in one ten metre square. The sheets are small and the support board used for the sheets is very light and easily manageable. A second advantage of this system is the ease with which a completed plan can immediately be laid over previous plans for that area. Errors can be instantly checked. All plans for one square are kept in a ring-binder which is convenient for consultation. The benefits of this system are also carried through to the stage of

Tille Höyük

SITE NAME		GRID No.		UNIT	

DESCRIPTION	
LOCATION	
DIMENSIONS	THICKNESS
COMPOSITION (MUNSELL)	
ABOVE	BELOW
CUT	CUT BY
ABUTTS	SEALED
PLAN	SECTION
LEVELS	PHOTO
FINDS - GENERAL	
FINDS - SPECIFIC	
RELIABILITY	D. D. B. W.
NOTES	

Fig. 3. Site Recording Sheet

12

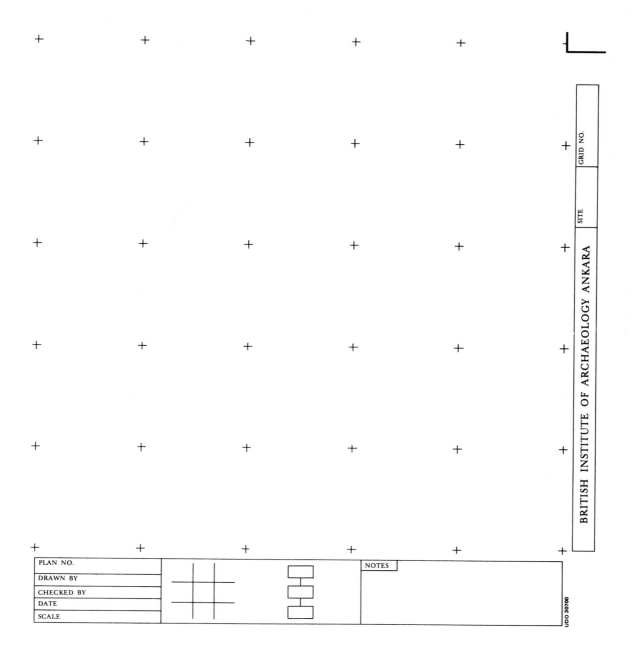

Fig. 4. Site Planning Sheet

information-processing. The plans are easily handled. A particular area can be isolated and the necessary plans can be overlaid in order to reconstruct the relationships and stratigraphy. Absolute heights on floors and the limits of general spreads of material were usually recorded on a sketch plan which was then inserted into the loose-leaf folder immediately after the notes on that unit.

The two types of drawn sections have already been discussed under *Excavation Technique*. These were drawn at a scale of 1:20 on plastic draughting film. Each section between adjacent squares has one as-drawn section and two as-dug sections (one for each square).

Three types of site photograph were taken. Firstly, general black-and-white negative and colour positive pictures were taken of the whole, or of large parts, of single levels or phases. These could be used for publication, display or lecture purposes. Secondly, daily record-shots (black-and-white negative) were taken (of the squares undergoing excavation) at the end of each working day, in order (1) to form a consultable archive which would then support and illustrate the written record and (2) to assist in interpretation if lacunae were found in the notes. Thirdly, detailed photographs, both negative and colour positive, were taken, when thought necessary, for publication, lecture purposes or for consultation as part of an archive supplementing the written and drawn record. Except for the first season, a photographer has been employed every year for this aspect of site recording.

Removal of Earth

Digging was mostly carried out with pick and shovel. The local workmen liked to work in groups of three: pickman, shovelman and barrowman. This practice we tried hard to discourage. We preferred larger teams: (for example) two pickmen, two shovelmen and three or four barrowmen (according to the distance to the spoil chute). In later seasons, only the minimum necessary trowelling was allowed. Floors and general spreads were cleared with hoes. We found that when given a trowel, the workmen took it as an excuse for a rest. They worked very slowly. They also like to work in a circle so that they could chat with each other. Many of them would move the trowelled earth away from themselves so that they walked on their freshly cleaned areas. For a time trowels were banned in an effort to speed up the rate of excavation. Finally, only selected workmen were allowed to use a trowel. Pits were very labour-intensive, generally two

men worked on each. The disposal of spoil in 1980 and 1981 was a large problem. The first area used at the north-western foot of the mound was unsatisfactory. Large stones tended to roll further than desired, into some of the fields, with consequent damage to crops and trees. Eventually, part of the ravine on the north side of the mound was rented and the spoil was deposited here, sliding down the northern face of the mound straight into the ravine.

Finds Recovery

The only method of finds retrieval employed during the five seasons work on the Medieval levels at Tille was that of see-and-pick-up. Generally, when areas were being worked by pick and shovel the workmen collected material haphazardly. Some days, if they felt in the mood or had been bullied, they would gather up every scrap of pottery, bone and other finds. Mostly they did not. This was due to laziness rather than lack of attention. If a particularly attractive sherd or an unusual object was uncovered, it was very quickly retrieved. Again, the level of material recovery varied according to the workmen on the job.

At times, when a lot of material was emerging from a particular unit, the workmen did sort through the wheelbarrows as they were filled. Higher proportions of recovered material resulted from the removal of floors and pits since this was generally a more controlled operation, in which floors would be trowelled or carefully hand picked. Pits limited both the speed and the method of soil-removal.

A decision had been taken, early in the excavation, not to over-emphasize the retrieval, study and publication of finds. We were not unduly worried, therefore, by this uncontrolled recovery of material.

Although at times the use of a sieve (wet or dry) would have been beneficial, especially for the recovery of animal bone in some deposits, this practice was not adopted. Basically it was the lack of time which precluded the systematic use of a sieve, and to have used it in only certain circumstances would have introduced a curious bias to material otherwise retrieved by manual collection only.

Finds Coding

Finds were collected by material. Each type of material being allocated a code-number. Within each material-code, a batch of finds (one piece or several) was given its own unique batch-number within each 10m excavation square. A number was assigned to every bag or bowl in a consecutive sequence so that 7658/107/31/056 identifies the batch (no.56 of the series) of metal objects (31) from trench 7658. The batch (no. 56) derives from unit 107. Two sets of lists were kept of the excavated material from each square:

1. *batch-lists* showing which batches came from which soil units (only used on site) (fig. 5).
2. *specific-lists*: site copy: brief description of each batch of each material code. (fig. 6). house copy: as above plus record of subsequent treatment and other relevant information e.g. registration, drawing and conservation numbers.

The following material categories were established at the beginning of work at Tille. The number of categories was extensive and was intended to cover all possible eventualities. Not all of the material codes instituted were used. The process of selection and the discarding of residue (for which, see below) led to the result that in some material codes no batches were retained although collections had been made during excavation.

Ceramic

01 sherds
02 whole pots (when enough of a pot has survived to allow its physical reconstruction)
03 fired clay objects
04 tile (mostly re-used Roman tile)

Skeletal

10 animal
11 human
12 fish
13 mollusca/shell
14 worked
15 objects

Samples

20 carbon
21 soil (pollen)
22 seed (botanical)
23 soil (geological)
24 soil (mollusca, etc.)
25 slag
26 other

Metals

30 coins
31 objects

Stone

40 epigraphic and architectural
41 chipped (mostly flints for threshing sledges in the Medieval levels)

42 objects
43 mosaic (a few Roman tesserae were recovered)

Other

50 glass fragments
51 whole glass
60 leather
70 textile
80 miscellaneous (very few, e.g. plastic from modern robber trenches)

The system has the disadvantage that objects of the same type but made from different materials are classified separately, e.g. glass and stone beads, bone and ceramic spindle whorls. The situation where one object was composed of different materials, e.g. a metal object with a bone handle, has not yet arisen.

At an early stage of the excavation it was decided (1) not to keep large amounts of material that would not be published, and (2) to publish only a few examples of each type of object. As the range of objects was so limited (many were fragmentary, few were from good stratigraphic contexts), it was decided not to devote too much time to the study of finds. From this decision was created a policy of selecting only complete or near-complete objects (or distinctive sherds) *in situ* on floors (or surfaces) or in pits: the rest was dumped into the river Euphrates. The material thrown away was not kept for posterity for another, non-theoretical reason: the problems of storage. The excavators did not want the responsibility of maintaining a depot full of material that probably would rarely, perhaps never, again be inspected. Furthermore, the local museum does not have unlimited space. Consequently, only the publishable finds have been preserved and sent for storage in the Adıyaman Museum. A selection of type-sherds has been maintained on site. This collection too will eventually be moved to the Adıyaman Museum. Thus the Medieval objects and pottery sherds that appear in this volume represent nearly all of those which were kept, with the exception of animal bone where a sample has been retained, in the hope that they will be published in a separate volume together with the bone from the other periods.

The policy for the selection of pottery sherds was to keep pieces that (1) could contribute to a broad dating of the occupational levels or (2) as examples of the range of pottery types that occurred on the site during the Medieval periods. As the majority of our pottery did not come from good, secure contexts and as there was always the chance that some sherds were residual strays, it was felt that

Fig. 5. Batch Sheet

SITE NAME					19	GRID		MATERIAL							CLEAN/READY
															MARKED
															STORED
UNIT	MAT CODE	NO.	ITE	INIT-IALS		OBJECT		TREATMENT/COMMENT						REG NO.	

Fig. 6. Specific Sheet

little time should be spent on processing and publishing the sherd material. Only whole pots found *in situ* on floors can unequivocally be assigned to those structure(s) with which the floors are associated. Individual sherds can always—unfortunately—be residuals or strays. Very few such pots were recovered.

The pottery published here (Chapters 6 and 9) is, as near as possible, a complete range of the types and fabrics that occurred on the site during the Medieval levels. I hope that as a comparative collection it will be useful in future for sites of similar date.

CHAPTER 4

The Structures

Introduction

Below is a description of the Medieval buildings on the mound. The evolution of the site from Level 1 Phase 1 through to Level 2 Phase 1b and then its decline from Level 2 Phase 2 to Level 3 Phase 5 (the last building on the top of the mound) is given in some detail. All the walls were built of mud-brick on stone footings. In the majority of cases, the stone footings were only one to two courses high but occasionally the number of courses increased to five or six. It is usually the stone footings that are mentioned in the description, for the reason that, during excavation, little time was spent on examining the layout of the mud-bricks. The stone footings were sufficient evidence for the phasing of the different walls.

In the following description the rooms and other structural divisions are identified by Roman numerals (Plans, Fig. 7ff). The description is in numerical order except in cases where sub-phases and minor alterations have necessitated the allocation of additional room numbers (e.g. Phases 1a and 1b of Level 2, Figs 14 and 15) when the description follows a logical structural order rather than a strictly numerical.

Traces of Earlier Settlement

Before the settlement on the mound was built, the top was flattened. Surviving Hellenistic walls were levelled and some earlier Medieval surface(s) and accompanying buildings were removed. The only traces of the early Medieval occupation ([?]eighth to ninth centuries) were two large pits, one in square 7547, the other in 7758 (see below, Chapter 9). The robbing-out of the stone footings of several Hellenistic walls probably took place at this time and large areas seemed to have been plundered for building material. A large amount of earth with small stone (rejected building material) was found under the prepared surface. The prepared surface was uneven and untidy and the western part of the mound seems to have been mainly an area made up of stone in various shapes and sizes. In general, small river pebbles up to 0.05m in diameter were found in densely compact patches all over the area but elsewhere the pebbles were more dispersed and less densely packed. In addition there was a significant number of larger limestone blocks and river pebbles either resting on the surface or protruding through it from below. The rest of the surface was made of clay and organic matter, fairly well compacted and trodden, with occasional patches of stone. Earlier wall footings appeared in places where the surface had been worn away.

Level 1 Phase 1 (Fig. 7)

The first settlement on the top of the mound during this period comprised a three-roomed dwelling, with an enclosed courtyard and associated buildings, and a range of outbuildings and courtyards on the south-western side of the mound. The main building in the northern half of the site was well built and regular in plan while those to the south were irregular and less well constructed. A perimeter wall was found along the northern edge of the mound but on the other three sides it had fallen away from the top; no trace of it survived.

The Perimeter Wall

The perimeter wall displayed two features: an outer mud-brick face on stone footings and an inner mud-brick bank. The footings were laid in a single course, in limestone, with the facing stones set with their longer axis at right angles to the orientation of the wall. Between the two rows of facing stones there was an in-fill of limestone ranging in size from small rubble to blocks as large as the facing stones. Where the latter occurred, the in-fill was laid in two rows. There was, thus, a total of four rows of stones across the width of the wall. The width of the stone footings varied between 0.90m and 1.10m The western end lay over a clay loam and rubble make-up that filled in and levelled off the underlying Hellenistic buildings, while the eastern part had been built directly over stone footings of Hellenistic walls, into which, at one point, the Medieval walls had been cut.

The inner mud-brick bank was not as regular in its width as the outer footing stone. The western section varied from 1.08 to 1.52m wide, the average width being 1.12m The eastern section of the bank was much wider, 2.40m to

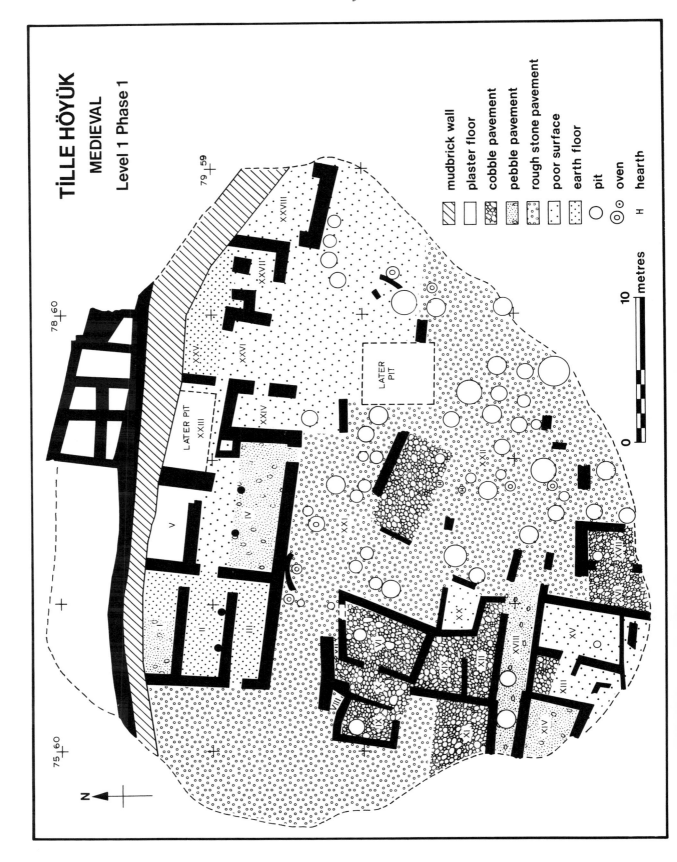

Fig. 7. Level 1 Phase 1, Plan

2.80m. The building of the bank was carried out in a somewhat peculiar fashion. The earlier Hellenistic remains, and any Roman remains which may have been present, were partially cleared; part of the resulting surface was then dug away, leaving a long, proud, upstanding strip. The bricks for the resulting bank were placed on top of, and between, surviving ruinous walls. Thus, although the stone foundations of the earlier walls acted as strengtheners or supports, the bank did not have a continuous stone footing. There are three possible uses of this bank: 1) to act as insulation by keeping out the cold, damp and rain from northerly winds, 2) to act as a support for roofing timbers for the buildings set against the outer wall and 3) as a walkway between the defensive wall and the buildings, in fact a parapet. A combination of the three is the most likely explanation. The base for the bank was mostly deeper than the foundations of the outer wall and would have helped to seal the point between the lower floor level and the bottom of the outer wall footings. The shape of some of the buildings, especially rooms XXV, XXVII and XXVIII, indicates that if these rooms were covered, then roof timbers would have had to have been supported on, or in, the mud-brick bank. If the bank was used as a parapet, the outer wall could be expected to have been c. 2m higher than the parapet, perhaps c. 6m in total height, since the main buildings were two-storeyed (pp. 33 and 36).

External to the perimeter wall there was a cellular construction of six small rooms. This structure had been built against Achaemenid and Hellenistic walls which had survived into the Medieval period and which were exposed on the side of the mound. The perimeter wall overlaid part of the construction. The cells thus became an integral part of the planned layout of the primary settlement in the Medieval period. The function of these small rooms was not apparent.

The Main Buildings, North Range

The main dwelling, rooms I–IV, was built against the perimeter wall and was cut down into the levelled surface of the mound. This building had three main rooms on the west side of a courtyard. Rooms I–III had internal dimensions of 3.80 to 4.10m north/south by 3.40 to 3.50m. For 3.20m at the western end of room I the floor was made from small pebbles, densely laid and set into a silty clay loam The floor over the rest of the room, and over rooms II–III, was a mud and chaff mix, laid in thin deposits, renewed regularly, so that the floor survived as a

series of thin layers. Near the north-western corner of room III was a doorway, 0.90m wide, leading into the 'backyard'. A short length of pavement, external to this doorway, was discovered. In the room there was an earth step which gave access onto the stone footings that formed the thresholds.

The doorways leading from rooms I and III to room II were 0.90 to 1.00m wide; the entrance to room II from the enclosed courtyard (IV) was 1.16m wide. The courtyard was divided into three parts. The northernmost, against the mud-brick bank, lay between the northern part of the dwelling and a length of reused Hellenistic wall. Soon after the initial erection of the buildings this northern part was partitioned, in order to form a separate room (room V, Level 1 Phase 1a) (shown on Level 1 Phase 1 plan, Fig. 7). This area had a patchy surface of loam and organic material. The southern area of the courtyard (south of the two northern post supports) was surfaced with densely packed pebbles set in clay, while the middle part of the courtyard was covered with clay only.

The northern two post-settings were practically equidistant from each other and the east and west limits of the courtyard. They were also aligned with the edge of the pebble surface which extended southwards for one-third of the north/south length of this courtyard. This alignment was continued westwards by a further two post supports in room II. Again, these posts were equidistant from each other and from the east and west limits of the room.

A stairway was built against the east wall of the courtyard, next to the entrance into the courtyard from room XXIII (Fig. 8; Pl.2a). The entrance to the stairway, at ground level, was from room XXIII. The threshold for the door-way into the staircase was made from two ashlar blocks laid between two others that were in-corporated into the flanking walls. The threshold had a rebate 0.09m wide, 0.04m deep in which the bottom of the door, when closed, would have been held. This recess was cut into the eastern flanking ashlar block, to a depth of 0.03m; presumably the door pivoted from this side. From the stair-foot, 0.80 by 0.90m, the stair climbed eastwards by means of two large stones set into the east wall. Where then the stair continued is uncertain; presumably the rest was made of wood although no post supports were found to indicate the direction of the stair. The stair-head, above the courtyard, must have given access to a veranda, over the middle third of the courtyard. The northern third of the court-yard could have supported a room above it while

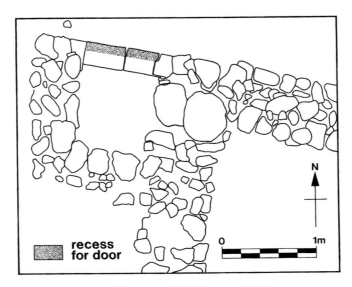

recess
for door

N

0   1m

Fig 8. Courtyard IV, Stairwell Plan

the two post supports in room II indicate that a second storey was built over rooms I–III.

South-western Range of Buildings

An entrance-way into the south-eastern corner of the courtyard (IV) gave access to the buildings on the south side of the mound. These were a collection of small structures, rooms and court-yards. Mostly they were poorly made. Walls were crooked. Corners were not right angles; in some cases the latter survived in a very fragmen-tary condition.

A narrow cobbled entrance-way, room VII, led to a further cobbled area, room X that gave access to rooms VI and IX. Room VI had a cobbled floor made from limestone, somewhat flat rubble mixed with river pebbles, as did room IX. The latter room contained a large pit, c. 1.40m in diameter and 0.50m deep. It is possible that room VIII formed the bottom of the stairway going up over room VII and leading to an upper floor above rooms VI, IX and X. If this was not the case, then the north wall of rooms VII and VIII fulfils no function.

To the south of room IX was a courtyard, XI, that had an entrance from room X. The southern half of this courtyard was paved with limestone, somewhat flat rubble mixed with river pebbles whereas the northern half had an irregular stone surface. The north/south length of the courtyard was 7.80m; the western side had been lost at the edge of the mound. To the east of the above courtyard were two rooms entered from path XVIII. Again, remnants of a stone pavement were found here, rooms XII and XIX. Further east, a small room XX had only a poor surface.

South of rooms XII and XI was a path (XVIII) that had several layers of gravel and small pebbles set in clay, thus forming a hard surface. This cobbling in room XIV, which was a well laid, river-cobble pavement on the south side and an irregular stone pavement on the north side, was a secondary surface; the original surface was a dark, fine-textured clay loam. Cut from the primary surface were two large pits. In one, 1.30m deep, the lowest 0.30m of deposit was a back-fill of dark brown, inclusion free loam; the rest was almost entirely filled with small to medium sized river pebbles in a c. 20 per cent matrix of the same very dark, very soft loam.

The northern part of room XIII was again cobbled while the area south of the entrance, from room XV, was floored with dark clay loam The remains of a wall with a right-angled corner was found in the room. This wall may have originally continued southwards to join a small piece of the south wall of this room These walls would have enclosed an area 0.70 to 0.90m wide, 2.00m long. Room XV lay between room XIII and rooms XVI and XVII. This room and room XIII had two surfaces during this period; a rough surface of loam that was replaced by a surface, some 0.15m higher, of dark well-compacted clay loam with some grit and small pebbles (lying on top). A small pit, (diameter 0.32m, straight sides 0.20m deep; a slightly dished bottom) had been cut from this later surface. It had been back-filled with a fine greenish sand.

East of room XV were the remains of a building of which only two rooms are definable. The floors of rooms XVI and XVII were both cobbled. Later pits had destroyed part of the north wall and also the partition wall between

22

the two rooms. The north wall of rooms XVI and XVII continued eastwards; it is thus possible that another room was located here.

Area XXII, in the south-eastern quadrant of the site, contained several short lengths of wall, twenty-seven pits, two *tandır* and two hearths. This area was composed of layers (or dumps) of material containing much stone and pebble. One area had a concentrated deposit of small river cobbles that ran up to two fragments of walling.

North-eastern Buildings

The majority of the buildings in the north-eastern corner of the mound must have been two-storeyed. The ground plan as recovered makes little sense; it probably constituted work and storage areas.

Room XXIII was entered from the north-eastern corner of courtyard IV. Very little of this room remained; a later pit had cut down through the greater part of it. The floor material was composed of fairly hard, compacted mud-mix with some pebbles. Room XXIV lay to the south and was open-ended on its south side. The room had a poor surface of fairly hard, compacted clay loam and a number of pebbles set into the surface. The eastern part of room XXV must have been roofed but it is not clear whether the rest of the room was also covered; no post supports were found during excavation. Room XXVII was curiously shaped and had supports for an upper storey. The east and south walls were re-used Hellenistic walls. The fragment of masonry abutting the west wall of room XXVII may well have been the foundation for a staircase. It was built of smallish stones laid in an irregular pattern. The floor of room XXVII was a very uneven surface of hard brown earth with some pebbles. Room XXVI seemed rather wide to have been roofed. Although the usual limit of the span appears to have been about 3.00m, this room was 4.00m east to west. The architectural study on the modern village at Aşvan found that direct spans were limited to a maximum of 3–3.5m (Hall, McBride and Riddell 1973: 257). The final room, XXVIII, was set between room XXVII and the mud-brick bank of the perimeter wall. A 0.55m wide entrance led through the west wall. The floor surface of this room was a hard light brown earth with limestone flecks.

Summary

If the top of the mound is viewed as a whole, the main dwelling, rooms I–IV, with its storage area, rooms XXIII–XXVIII, occupies the northern part of the settlement. The buildings in the southern part would presumably have been used for animals and for the storage of agricultural implements and food products that were not required daily. It is likely that a path led up the side of the mound to the path XVIII.

Level 1 Phase 1a

Within a short space of time, courtyard IV, east of the main building, was divided into two by the insertion of a wall. This wall joined the east wall of room II, as a butt joint 0.46m from the southern end. The short length further south was taken down to the bottom course of the stone footings. By this means, the width of the doorway of the building was enlarged to 1.60m.

North of this new wall, room V was floored with a concrete and plaster surface on a base of very small pebbles. During this sub-phase the floor was replaced by a compacted clay surface. The entrance from the courtyard into room V was in the south-eastern corner of the room where a single row of stones marked the threshold. The entrance was 0.90m wide, with a setting for a door post on the east side, i.e. inside the threshold.

A new surface of light grey-brown loam with small limestone flecks was laid down in room XXVI. At the same time, in room XXV, a short stretch of masonry was erected (not shown on the plan). This fragment of walling, only one stone wide and 0.70m long, was laid against the western part of the wall between rooms XXV and XXVI. Since it ran northwards, it may have served to divide room XXV into two.

While other floor surfaces must have been renewed during this sub-phase, it is impossible to distinguish them from those of the later period (Level 1 Phase 2). They are therefore discussed with that phase.

The immediate need for an extra room perhaps reflects the beginning of the expansion which is continued through to Level 2 Phase 1b.

Level 1 Phase 2 (fig. 9; Pl. 2b)

The main changes in this phase were the lengthening of the middle room of the main building, the division of the rooms to the north of the covered courtyard and the attachment of several rooms to the south of the main building. The range of small rooms and courtyards on the extreme west of the site disappeared. At the same

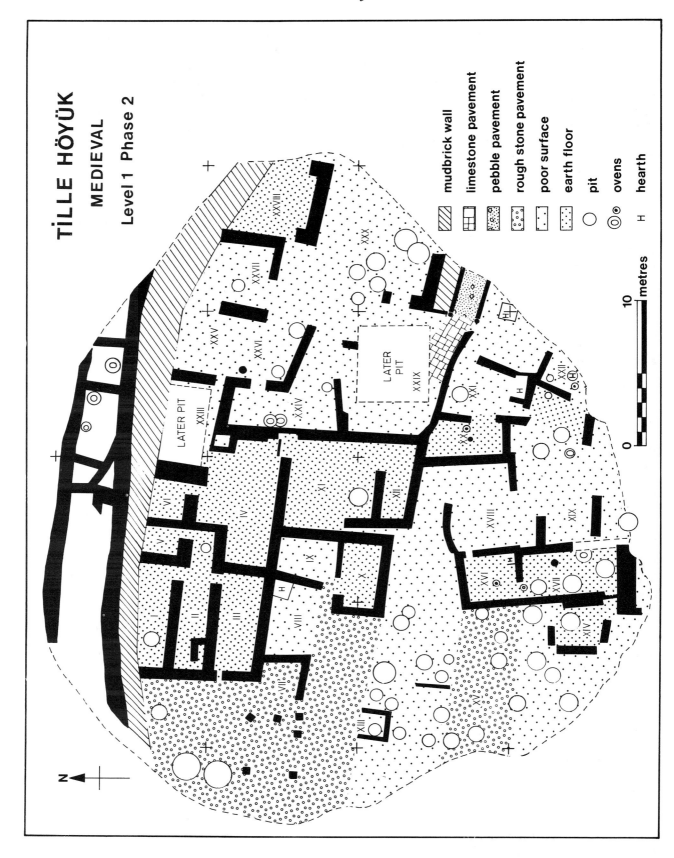

Fig. 9. Level 1 Phase 2, Plan

time, a small house (XVI and XVII) with a range of courtyards to the east, was built. A gateway was erected on the east side of the mound.

The cellular structure external to the perimeter wall was rebuilt in this phase. A revetment was built to stabilise the edge of the mound and to prevent the perimeter wall from slumping down the slope. Several walls, running between this revetment and the perimeter wall, divided the area into rooms. Within these rooms were three ovens.

Alterations to the Main Dwelling

In the main building the divisional wall between rooms II and III was rebuilt in a position slightly further to the north. The alignment of this wall was continued further eastwards into the covered courtyard. There it turned northwards, dividing room V of Level 1 Phase 1a into two new rooms. This east/west replacement wall was the start (on this alignment) of a wall that survived for several phases, in fact through to Level 3 Phase 4. This new building increased the length of room II to 9.10m. Within this room near the eastern end a pithos (0.70 to 0.78m in diameter, 0.30m deep) was cut into the floor. A small, stone-based feature had been built against the new wall in the south-western corner of room II. An L-shaped arrangement of limestone blocks left an area, 0.40–0.50m wide, between the south wall of the room and the inside edge of the north side (of the stone-based feature). The area was 1.50m long and there was a gap of 0.40m between the feature and the west wall of the room This stone-based feature is interpreted as an internal staircase to a second storey.

The floor of room I was now made of mud. A succession of mud surfaces made a 0.15 to 0.25m thick deposit. This build-up was similar to the new floor surfaces in rooms II and III (Section 1, Fig.25 [044, 043 and 041]). A circular pit, c. 1.30m in diameter at the top, was cut from near the top of the floor sequence in room I. The pit was 0.84m deep and had a bottom diameter of c. 0.95m.

The entrance into room I from room II was located in the same place as in Level 1 Phase 1. It is presumed that the entrance into room III from room II was also in the same place, although no evidence was found to confirm this suggestion. The room remained basically the same as in the previous phase.

As stated above, the room to the north of the covered courtyard was divided into two. The small room (V) to the west of the new wall measured 1.80m (east/west) by 2.30m while the other room (VI) was 2.65 by 2.10m Both rooms were floored with mud, 0.25 to 0.30m thick. The entrance into room VI from the courtyard was the original doorway into this area. At the same time, a new doorway into room V was constructed. This doorway was knocked through the Level 1 Phase 1a wall at the same time as the new north/south wall was built. Courtyard IV at this time had a mud surface. One may suppose that if the whole of this courtyard was not now covered, the floor surface would have been washed away by rain.

To the west and south of the building there was an untidy area perhaps representing a 'back-yard', storage or work-area. Abutting the south wall of the main residential building were three lean-to structures. The western one, room VII, had stone-footed walls for its eastern and for part of its southern wall. The western two-thirds of the building was represented by several post pads: three on the south side, two on the north side and one in the centre of the floor. This lean-to had overall internal measurements of c. 7.35m east/west by c. 2.55m. The floor of this building was the same as the irregular stone surface of the 'backyard' and it appears that this structure had been placed on top of the Level 1 Phase 1 surface.

Additions on the South of the Main Dwelling

Room VIII, added to the main building, shared a wall with room VII. In the north-eastern corner of the room was a hearth set into a floor of clay loam and cobble patches. It comprised a large flat slab of limestone—found broken when first uncovered—surrounded by small stones on the south and west and by flat disc-shaped river pebbles set on their ends against the walls to the north and east, in order to prevent scorching and therefore damage to these walls. The open-ended room/area formed by this three-walled structure might not have been roofed as there was no evidence of post-settings along the southern side. The span (5.00m) is large. It is possible that one of the stones lying slightly east of the midway point along this side could have served as a post support. The presence of a hearth suggests this area was used for a workshop rather than for a store.

Room IX was a small area left between rooms VIII, IV, XI and X. Partially filling this area was a pile of stones ([?]a store of building material) lying on a poor surface of compacted earth. An entrance to this area, 0.80m wide, lay between the end of the west wall and room X to the south. The wall forming the east side of this area separated the higher level of the so-called 'backyard' (see above) from the lower surface in room XI, a vertical difference of c. 0.40m.

Room X, 4.50 by 2.50m, was found to the south of the eastern lean-to building. This room seems to have been used for domestic purposes; it had a soft mud floor.

An area in the north of the backyard, west of rooms I and II, was surfaced with pebbles and, occasionally, with single large cobbles. This deposit, 0.12m thick, extended 4.00m alongside the base of the wall and 1.80m outwards. The purpose of this cobbling was perhaps to protect the surface from rain running off from the roof of the main residential building. A pit was found just inside the perimeter wall. It had a top diameter of 1.25 to 1.30m, narrowing to c. 1.00m at the bottom.

Just to the north of room VII two pits were found. One had a top diameter of 1.80 to 1.90m, increasing to 2.13m at the bottom (1.27m down). The other pit, 0.38m north of the last, had a top diameter of 1.80m and was 0.45m deep.

The open strip (of Level 1 Phase 1) that was found between the northern range of buildings and those on the southern part of the mound, had to a large extent been enclosed by various rooms and a courtyard in this later phase. Rooms XI and XII now occupied a large part of this area in the centre of the site.

Rooms XI and XII were located south of the courtyard, IV. The line of the east wall of the courtyard was continued southwards for a further 8.00m An entrance through this east wall of rooms XI and XII must have existed but the evidence for its position had been removed by the post-Medieval robber trench. The south wall of these two rooms had been built over the north-western corner of room XX. Rooms XI and XII were separated by a narrow wall. A doorway 1.80m wide led between the two. The western 0.80m of room XII had been partitioned off by a single row of stones (limestone) that stood 0.16m above the floor. This feature has been interpreted as a feeding area for animals. The original floor of these two rooms was a greyish-brown clay with very tiny pebbles set into the surface. Several later floors of very well compacted loam and organic matter were laid in these rooms. In the north-eastern corner of room XI, just south of the entrance into room IV, there was a stone platform extending 2.30m southwards from the doorway and 2.00m into the room from the east wall. It stood c. 0.14m above the original floor; it was level with the latest floor surface. This feature

was made from roughly squared limestone blocks and river pebbles which were embedded in a dark-brown, fine clay loam Presumably these stones were deliberately placed in order to prevent wear-and-tear of the floor next to this entrance. This same feature may also indicate the position of the entrance through the east wall. If the floor by one entrance was so protected, one would then expect the floors by other entrances also to have been protected. Nowhere else was there a cobbled surface. It is therefore reasonable to presume that the east exit from room XI was situated in this north-eastern corner.

New Buildings: West and South

On the western side of the mound the several small buildings and courtyards that had been knocked down were replaced by one small building (room XIII) and a large open area (XV) which contained several pits. The small building (XIII) was only partially preserved, as a later building in Level 2 Phase 1 had foundation trenches that partly destroyed the west wall and completely removed the north wall. A fragment of floor surface (a yellowish-brown clay loam) was found in the south-eastern corner of the room. In the south-western corner of this room is a pit. Its fill indicated that it had been used for rubbish; the material had accumulated spasmodically.

The large open area (XV) extended from the lean-to buildings (VII and VIII) at the north down to room XIV and the southern edge of the mound. Within this area were pits of all shapes and sizes. The in-fill of all eighteen pits was fairly uniform, mostly a dark-coloured clay loam. The fill had a moderate amount of limestone rubble and differing amounts of charcoal and brown clay. They were presumably rubbish pits. Near the centre of this area was a small revetment. This wall was formed by a single row of stones, 3.10m long, and effected a change in level, down from the west, of c. 0.30m. The area of XV was surfaced by a dark clay loam embedded with many pebbles. A lean-to (room XIV) was built against the small house (XVI and XVII) presumably some time after the house was built. Against the west wall of the house a long stretch of wall had been built. Although some of the stone footings of this lean-to were obviously missing, it is possible that the south-western and north-western corners were constructed of wood with mud-brick, though no evidence for this technique was found. The other two corners may have been open as entrances. In fact the south-eastern corner led into the entrance to room XVII. This small lean-to was floored with dark clay loam mixed with organic matter which had been burnt in the southern part of the area. Just south of this room was another irregularly shaped pit, 0.90 to 1.15m across, 1.12m deep.

The new house (XVI and XVII) was comparatively well constructed. Part of the east wall of room XVII was lost, probably because this part of the site lay very close to the pre-excavation level of the mound. Two entrances into the building were found. One led from the south-western corner of room XVII to the south-eastern corner of the lean-to building (XIV). This doorway was 0.80m wide and a threshold of small limestone blocks continued the line of the outside face of the wall. The threshold lay c. 0.28m above the floor of room XVII and c. 0.10m below the floor of room XIV. There was a second doorway through the east wall of room XVI near the junction with the north wall. The existence of a doorway was indicated by a swivel post-stone lying in the inside face of the wall. A rise of 0.18m from the level of the original floor onto the threshold stones occurred here. The entrance between the two rooms of the building was 1.00m wide. Both rooms were floored with mud. In the northern room three hearths were set into the floor. The one in the north-western corner was a near-circular pit, diameter 0.60 to 0.65m, 0.15m deep, filled with a large amount of charcoal. The hearth lying in the south-eastern corner of the room had a baked clay lining set in a circular pit c. 0.70m in diameter. The lining was 0.11m deep. There was a layer of ash over the bottom. The third hearth lay near the entrance to the southern room of this building. This hearth too had a baked clay lining, 0.04m thick and 0.60 to 0.65m in diameter. During this phase of occupation the room suffered a fire; a heavy burnt deposit of charcoal and ash was found covering the floor. A new floor was laid on top of the burning and two new hearths were built. Slightly off-centre to the room was a roughly circular oven, 0.40 to 0.45m in diameter and 0.18m deep. Against the south wall a hearth was built. To the west of the oven, just inside the doorway, two lamps were found (one similar to Fig.46 no.195, the other similar to Fig.46 no.185). While room XVII did not appear to have been affected by the fire, a new series of floors and ovens were constructed after the fire. Originally just one pit (1.00m in diameter, 0.35m deep) was located in this room During the remodelling of this room a post support was erected, a third of the length of the room from the north. Two *tandır* were built; one was set in the doorway connecting the two rooms. This

position had the effect of narrowing the access to 0.55m Three new pits were also dug.

The construction of the building containing rooms XVI and XVII was rather strange. The north wall, the east wall of room XVI and the northern part of the west wall had mud-brick clay footings (0.02 to 0.48m high) on which stone footings had been placed. The stones making up the footings of the north and east walls lay on their sides while those of the west and south walls were laid flat, all one course high. The floor of room XVI ran up to the bottom of the mud-brick clay footings.

Room XVIII was rather large (5.80m east/west by 3.50m from the northern edge to the northern partition wall) and may have been an enclosed area that was not roofed. The surface of this area was somewhat uneven; limestone rubble protruded through it. Through the south side of this area there was access to an open area (room XIX). This room was surfaced with a mid-brown clay loam mixed with some small pebbles. Cut into this surface were a number of pits and *tandır*, all found in the eastern half of the area.

New Buildings: South-east

The south-eastern block of buildings (rooms XX to XXII) were solidly built. Room XX had a mud floor which had been cut by several features. In the north-eastern corner of the room a large pot, of which only the base survived, had been sunk into the floor. To the south of it a group of stones had been placed against the pot as a support. Again in the north-western corner of the room, the base of a coarse ware pot was found set into the floor. Also in this room was a *tandır* next to the east wall. In the centre of the room was a well cut, circular limestone block, embedded in the floor material and standing 0.12m above it. This acted as a post support for the roofing of this room The presence of the *tandır* and the pot positions perhaps suggests that this room had a domestic use.

This group of rooms was constructed in Level 1 Phase 2 before the building of rooms XI and XII. When the latter two rooms were added the northern part of room XX was modified; the south wall of room XII was extended through the northern part of room XX before turning northwards. Prior to this modification a small *tandır* existed against and outside the north wall of room XX. A stone windbreak was built on its east side. When the rebuilding took place a new surface of mud was laid. No features were found in the room.

Room XXI had three exits: one to room XX,

one, 0.80m wide, in the north-eastern corner; and one, 0.44m wide, through the south wall to area XIX.

In the south-eastern corner was a chimney with an associated hearth. Just to the north of the hearth was a *tandır*. In the north-western corner a large pit, diameter 1.10m, depth 0.40m, had been dug and back-filled with a large amount of limestone rubble. To the east of this room was an open area of dark clay loam mixed with small pebbles. One hearth was found here.

The new room XXII was incomplete, as it lay on the present-day edge of the mound. A poor surface of pebbly material covered this area; a pit, a hearth and a *tandır* were located here. The pit was set in the north-western corner of the room and, although it had a diameter of c. 0.85m, it was only 0.15m deep. The hearth had decayed and part of the clay lining for it was found in a mass of grey ash. The depth of the hearth was 0.12m and the ash covered an area of 1.70 by 1.60m Next to the hearth was a well built *tandır* with a clay wall 0.05m thick, 0.50m in diameter and of the same depth. It had been set in a pit, c. 1.50m in diameter.

North-eastern Buildings

Very few changes took place in the buildings in the north-eastern part of the site. The floor of room XXIII was resurfaced with dark clay loam while room XXIV had a compacted mid-grey clay floor. This latter room was now made longer by a continuous west wall joined to the wall that formed the south side of the room. Within this room were two *tandır* (one replacing the other during the course of this occupation phase); against the southern wall was a small pit. Room XXV was refloored with dark clay loam and the small partition that had existed in Level 1 Phase 1a was not now in use. Against the perimeter wall a large cooking vessel was found sunk into the floor. No evidence for roof supports was found in room XXVII during this phase, although it is possible that mud-brick lay over the support of the previous phase and that this was not distinguished from the surrounding floor surface. Indeed it seems that the staircase in this room did not exist at this time. A small pit was dug in this room during this phase. Room XXVI now had a southern wall. A gap, 2.80m wide, was left between the end of the east and south walls. A post socket occurred near the west wall, 1.00m into the room. A small pit set in the south-western corner may possibly have been another post. Room XXVIII remained unchanged except for a further series of floors made of dark clay loam mixed with organic matter.

The new room XXIX occupied part of the open strip (of the previous phase) that lay between the main residential building and the small buildings to the south. The surface over most of the area varied between patches of dark clay loam (with or without pebbles) and pebbles. This area must have been a courtyard lying to the north of a path. The path was a pavement made of large slabs of limestone (average size 0.32 by 0.35m and 0.12m thick). Gaps between the slabs were packed with small pebbles. This pavement continued the pathway from the main gateway on the south-eastern side of the mound. The pavement extended c. 3.00m The rest was destroyed by the later Level 2 pit.

Area XXX was an open space on the east side of the mound; it was surfaced in a hard mid-grey to brown clay loam. Six pits were found here; their fill was similar. All contained plentiful pottery sherds and bone fragments. Evidently they were used as rubbish pits.

The Gateway

During this occupation phase, the gateway on the path was constructed. Only a short stretch of the path, 3.50m long, leading to the gateway was preserved; the rest has been eroded from the edge of the mound. The surface of the entrance-way was made from heavy cobbling (50 per cent river pebbles, 50 per cent limestone blocks). Along the north side the edging stones were set somewhat higher than the others. The path was slightly stepped in two places; the height of the first step was 0.05m and the second was 0.07m The distance between the two steps was c. 1.20m. Two moulded column bases were set at the western end of the cobbling. They had a double torus moulding on a square plinth (Fig. 89 no.204; Section 2, Figs. 26 [138]) and were set 1.60m apart. From the northern column base a wall ran along the north side of the path. The wall, which stood 0.72m above the surface of the path, had four courses of limestone blocks and formed a facing for a mass of mud-brick, 1.20m wide, that had been packed between the path and a wall further north. The southern entrance wall was a single row of roughly shaped limestone blocks held together by a stiff dark clay loam. Surviving 0.66m high above the path, the wall appeared to be free-standing. It is assumed that the pathway continued down the side of the mound in a series of zig-zags.

Summary

The main building in this phase was expanded by

the addition of storage areas and courtyards attached to the original range of rooms. A new house (XVI and XVII) was built; this structure had its own associated courtyard and work areas. Room XX seems also to have been a separate living area with courtyard and work areas on its eastern side. The location of the rubbish pits changed after the south-eastern corner of the mound had been built over.

The separate living areas may represent the houses of independent families, related perhaps to the family residing in the central structure.

Level 1 Phase 2a

Within Level 1 Phase 2 several building changes took place. These have been assigned to a subphase Level 1 Phase 2a. The lean-to building (room VII) was demolished and a *tandır* was built through the south-eastern corner of the building. A small building was erected in the open area XV. Only three walls (north, east and west) were discovered; the east wall had been mostly destroyed by later pits cut down from above. The surface of this little building was a dark clay loam containing a few small river pebbles. The building measured 1.90m east/west by at least 2.50m

Within the small house (XVI and XVII), the entrance between the two rooms was re-modelled and the original doorway was in-filled. Some mud-brick of the original cross wall was removed from the stone footings on the west side. These footings now acted as the threshold. An east wall was built for room XXIV in this subphase. This wall ran from the eastern end of the south wall of room XXVI southwards to the small section of wall in room XXIX.

Destruction of Level 1 Buildings

The end of Level I was brought about by an extensive fire that affected most of the northern part of the site. Rooms I–VI, XI, XII, XXIV–XXVIII and the small house (XVI and XVII) were found to be covered in a 0.20 to 0.50m thick deposit of ash, charcoal and burnt mud-brick (Section 1, Fig. 25 [046-048]). To the west of rooms I and II, a deposit of burning, extending c. 2.00m away from the building, covered the backyard. No evidence of burning was apparent in rooms VIII–X. The charcoal and ash particles found on the surface of area XV were probably fragments carried by the wind after the fire.

The thick deposit (0.20 to 0.38m) (Section 3, Fig. 27 [210]) in rooms XI and XII suggests two possibilities: either that this area was roofed with an upper storey that had collapsed onto the floor surfaces below or that during an extensive levelling operation this open area was in-filled in order to bring it up to a level consistent with the surrounding area. In this in-fill there were some large but fragile pieces of charcoal that would certainly have been broken up if moved in a clearing operation. There was also the presence of distinct layers within the burnt debris. It would appear that the former possibility, the presence of an upper storey, is the most likely explanation for this thick deposit.

It seems strange that the small house (XVI and XVII) also should have caught fire since there was a considerable gap between it and room XII, the nearest burnt room. One explanation could be that the fire was started deliberately with the intention of destroying the main buildings. If this was so, then the small house (XVI and XVII) would have been separately destroyed by fire.

Level 2 Phase 1 (Fig. 10)

This structural level saw a complete rebuilding of the site after the extensive fire of Level 1 Phase 2a. Some walls were rebuilt either on the same orientation as in the previous level or on very similar alignments. There was a marked increase in the number of rooms or areas, from thirty-one in Level 1 Phase 2 to forty-eight in Level 2 Phase 1.

Rebuilding of the Perimeter Wall

The perimeter wall was completely reconstructed with stone footings, along the line of the original Level 1 perimeter wall. The new stone foundations were partly built on top of the mud-brick bank of the original wall. For nearly 10.50m the southern face of the new wall corresponded with the alignment of the southern face of the bank. It was also partially built over the bottom of the mud-brick superstructure of the outer part of the original wall. At its western end the wall was 1.50 to 1.70m wide; probably it was c. 1.50m wide originally since the outside face of the stones appeared to have slipped slightly away from the main body of the wall. The facing stones were limestone blocks. The core was made from slightly smaller limestone blocks, up to four abreast, and river pebbles. The stones were closely packed and the footings were only one course high. This type of construction continued for 10.00m westwards along to 7640 east where the wall widened to 1.80m For the next 6.00m, from here up to the point where it was robbed by the large recent pit (Fig. 7), the wall had two rows of

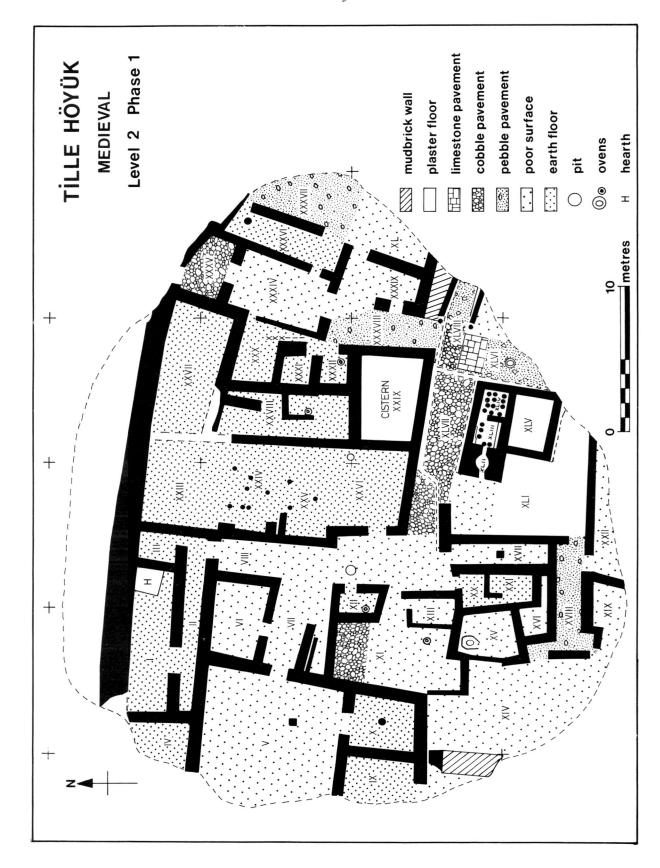

Fig. 10. Level 2 Phase 1, Plan

larger facing-stones, mostly with a row of slightly smaller stones inside them. The remaining space between the two sides was filled with mud-brick packing. The large recent pit destroyed a 5.30m section of the wall but for most of this length the outside edge of the wall could be determined from the position of the Level 2 Phase 1a tower. The stone footings then continued 1.40 to 1.55m wide. At grid reference 7824-5914 a limestone block, into which a circular hollow had been cut, lay in the row of inner facing stones. This stone was very similar to many examples of door sockets seen on the site. It may, therefore, have been a re-used door socket. There was, however, a gap just to the west, formed by a ([?]purposely) L-shaped block, possibly for a door frame. Two stones that would have been part of the threshold were worn. There is, therefore, a possibility that a small doorway through the perimeter wall existed at this point. The wall sloped down, west to east, following the natural slope of the mound. Nowhere were the outer wall footings more than one course high and no stepping of the foundations took place. The overall drop was 1.65m over a total length of 33.30m, a fall of 1 in 20.

Western Range Buildings

The north-western room (I) lay against the perimeter wall and was 9.60m long and 2.70m wide. The floor consisted of a series of thin deposits of mud. In the north-eastern corner of the room was a hearth, surrounded on four sides by limestone blocks. South of this room there was, it appears, a corridor (room II). The south wall of the corridor was a rebuilding of a Level 1 Phase 2 wall. The mud-brick superstructure had been dug out almost completely down to the single course of stone footing and a further three courses of stone had been added (Section 1, Fig.25 [065]). The floor of the corridor was a series of mud surfaces, 0.22 to 0.26m thick. The total length of the corridor was exactly 12.00m; its width increased from 0.85m at its western end to 1.20m at its eastern end. An entrance, 1.80m wide, led into room II; another, 0.80m wide, led into room III, a small room east of room I. Again the floor was mud, 0.25 to 0.30m thick. A doorway led from the corridor southwards into room VIII (the end of the path across the site from the main gateway). This entrance was 1.10m wide and was set 0.30m inwards from the corner of the room Room IV was a small area tucked between the perimeter wall, the main building and the continuation of the corridor south wall. This room had a surface of dark brown clay loam mixed with some pebbles.

Room V was a large open area with walls surviving on three sides. The west wall was lost over the edge of the mound. A surface of dark brown clay loam containing c. 10 per cent small river pebbles was similar to that in the courtyard VII. Two entrances, both 1.30m wide, led into the courtyard VII to the east and into room X to the south. While room VI was roofed (and was used for the storage of materials or animals?), the courtyard VII was probably open to the elements. This courtyard had patches of cobbling. The south-western part of the courtyard, south of the partition wall, was probably covered.

Room IX measured 4.50m north to south but its other dimension is unknown, as only part of this building had survived. The floor of the room was similar to that of room X, i.e. mud. The small rectangular room X measured c. 3.40 by c. 4.15m. This room was one of very few examples in the Medieval period where foundation trenches were dug for the walls. Usually stone footings were placed directly on the pre-existing ground level and the new surfaces were then laid up against the bottom of the footings. Centrally placed on the floor of the room was the top half of a rotary quernstone which presumably acted as a post support. Set into the north-eastern corner against the walls was a large flat-surfaced block of baked clay, 0.45 by 0.65m, possibly a hearth. Also set into the floor were two lines of stones, aligned east/west. These may have been intended to separate the southern (1.20 to 1.40m) room from the rest of the area. It was perhaps used as a sleeping area. The floor of the whole room was mud.

Area XI was most probably an open area with two small covered rooms (XII and XIII) in the north-eastern and south-eastern corners respectively. A strip, 2.00m wide, at the northern end of area XI was surfaced with a stone pavement (large limestone blocks and river pebbles with smaller stones between them); the rest was covered by a deposit of clay containing charcoal and scorched clay (probably derived from the burning of the previous phase). Near the south-eastern corner was an irregularly shaped *tandır*. The two covered rooms may perhaps have had different functions because they had different types of floor surface. Room XII had a mud floor with a *tandır* near the south-western corner. The floor of room XIII was a grey brown clay loam, well-compacted and able to resist heavy use. Was the structure used perhaps for animal stalls?

The south-western corner of the site was an open area (XIV). Most of the area had a compacted surface of dark clay with some cobbled patches lying in the western part. The west side of the area had been terraced. The revetment wall of mud-brick had been laid directly on top of the stone pavement of Level 1 Phase 1. The western face had been faced with limestone blocks standing two courses high. West of this revetment, the ground surface had been lowered 0.25 to 0.30m below the Level 1 Phase 1 pavement, c. 0.40m below the surface of the rest of area XIV.

It would seem that room XV was added after the main building work of this phase, to judge from the discontinuous remains of the south wall. We found no surfaces that had been external to room XVI before room XV was built. The west wall and the western part of the southern wall abutted the north-western corner of room XVI. Within room XV was an oven (Fig.11). Oval in plan, the oven had a stoke-hole or flue positioned at its southern end. The oven sides were composed of seven slabs of coarsely fired, gravelly clay, averaging 0.35 to 0.37m square. The sides sloped slightly inwards towards the bottom. The floor of the oven was made from a coarse, gravelly, white/grey substance similar to mortar. The slabs forming the sides were 0.04m thick. The internal dimensions of the oven were 0.82m east/west and 1.10m

north/south; it was 0.37 to 0.40m deep. The oven was filled with a mixed debris from the superstructure.

The areas, referred to as rooms XVI and XVII, have been interpreted as a staircase. The stairs were entered from the path (XLVII) through a 0.60m gap between the western stair support and the end of the east/west wall. The western end of the stairway broadened out to form an area 3.00–2.70m, east/west (XVI). This area represented the stair-head leading onto a first floor over rooms XV, XXI and XX. There must also have been an additional access to the stair-well as there was here a floor surface of compacted dark clay loam with numerous patches of burnt mud-brick on it. A pithos, 1.20m high, was found lying on the surface. Room XX appeared to be a small corridor leading from the main east/west path (XLVII) to a small room (XXI). Both rooms XX and XXI were floored with mud (which we interpret as a sign of a domestic function).

To the south of the stairway was a path (XVIII), surfaced with dark clay loam mixed with some pebbles. The path led from room XLI to area XIV and into room XXII to the south.

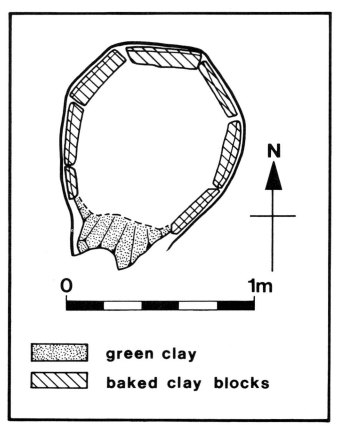

green clay

baked clay blocks

Fig. 11. Room XV, Oven Plan

Central Open Area

In the centre of the site was a long empty area (XXIII, XXIV, XXV and XXVI). Although no east wall to area XXIII was discovered (because of the large recent pit, see Fig. 7), a wall on that side must have existed because of the difference in height (a drop of 0.60m) between the surface of this area and the surface in room XXVII. The most likely position for this wall is on the line of the east wall of rooms XXIV, XXV and XXVI. The west wall of these areas (XXIII–XXVI) had stumps of an earlier wall protruding from it. Set in areas XXIV and XXV were various post-pads. Little coherent pattern can be made out of the distribution of the recorded supports but it is probable that several more were removed without being recognised as such (this area was excavated at speed by a large gang of workmen!). The post-pads suggest that at least areas XXIV and XXV were covered. The floor of these areas was mud. In the north-eastern corner of XXVI was a *tandır* 0.40m in diameter and 0.20m deep.

North-eastern Range

Room XXVII, east of the area (discussed above) and against the perimeter wall, also had a mud floor. This room measured 8.70 by 4.00m and it had a mud-brick bench against the perimeter wall. The bench ran from the east wall for 3.00m; it stood 0.30m high. In the north-eastern corner of room XXVIII there was a staircase which could be reached from room XXVII and from room XXX. The footings of the south wall of room XXVII provided the first steps while two worn stones in the eastern stair support-wall provided the top steps of the access to the stair from room XXX. Room XXVIII had a mud surface. Contained within this room was a small rectangular structure surrounding a *tandır*, 0.70m in diameter and 0.60m deep. Rooms XXX–XXXIII all had floors made of mud. Room XXXIII was a very narrow corridor linking rooms XXIV and XXX at the north with rooms XXXI, XXXII and XXXVIII to the south. Rooms XXVII, XXX, XXXI, XXXIII and XXXV suffered from a fire at the end of this occupation phase, as was shown by a burnt deposit lying on the floor.

Area XXIX was a large deep pit (7757.015), interpreted as a cistern (Figs. 7, 19 and 20 and Pl. 4b). At the time of writing the cistern had not been completely emptied. Its original depth exceeded 2.25m from the bottom of the stone footings of the surrounding wall. At a later date (indeterminable) the pit had been modified. The sides of the pit were lined with mud-bricks to a depth of 1.50m; below that level a new bottom of mud-brick was built. A thin layer of clay was then applied to the mud-bricks. The later pit was a flattened circle, with the larger axis east/west, 4.50 by 3.70m The pit was surrounded by a stone-footed wall forming a rectangle around it. The wall had partly collapsed into the pit.

Room XXXIV was a rectangular area, with entrances on all four sides. It was floored with dark clay loam and was probably a courtyard. To the north of this area was room XXXV, which was paved with large river pebbles and limestone blocks, set not very close together. A small doorway also led into this room through the perimeter wall. Room XXXVI had a floor of dark clay loam mixed with organic matter. A post pad was found central to the width of this long, narrow room, 0.70m from the perimeter wall. Leading from this room were two entrances into the area to the east (room XXXVII). The north and west sides of this latter area had not survived. The surface was composed of small river pebbles set in a dark brown clay loam.

Area XXXVIII was a path running between the cistern (XXIX) on the west and room XXXIX. The path led from the northern part of the settlement, on the east side of the site, down to the main east/west path beside the gateway. The surface of this path was small pebbles. Two rooms (XXXIX and XL) with poor-quality surfaces lay east of this path and north of the gateway.

The Bath-house

Located in the south-eastern corner of the site (to the south of the main east/west path through the settlement) was a bath complex (Fig. 12; Pl. 3a). West and south of the bath-building there was a courtyard (XLI). The western part of the courtyard measured 9.00m north/south and extended 4.00m from the furnace room or c. 5.50m from the (?)dressing room. The eastern part of the courtyard extended c. 2.30m south of the bath-building. The southern area of the courtyard for a distance of 5.50m had been plastered but the plaster had, to a large extent, decayed. In those places where it survived it was very patchy. The plaster floor had a foundation of cobbles. The northern part of the courtyard was floored with fairly well compacted loam.

The bath-building was constructed in three stages; firstly, a stone platform was laid down; secondly, the northern suite of rooms was built and, thirdly, the southern room was built up

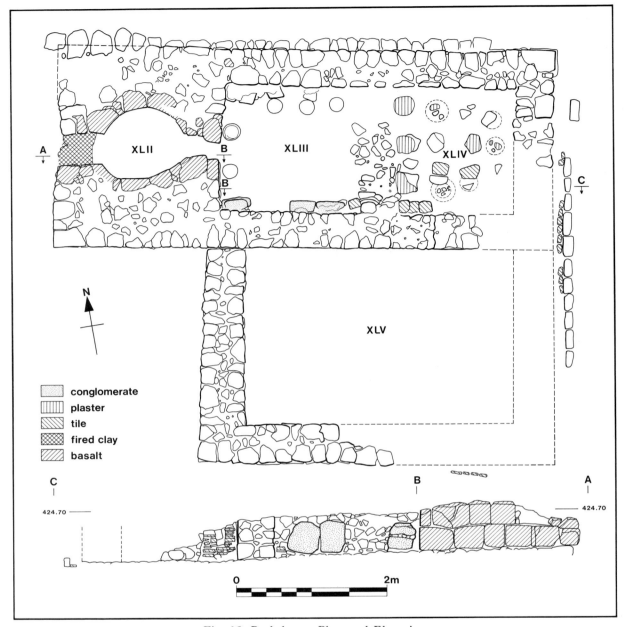

Fig. 12. Bath-house Plan and Elevation

against rooms XLIII and XLIV. The platform for the structure was made from a large number of small pebbles, with small pieces of limestone and river-cobble rubble, the whole held together by a gritty dark clay loam. The walls of the bath-building were c. 0.50m thick, built in two faces of limestone with a rubble and earth core bonded together by white concrete and orange mortar. Both the inside and outside face of the walls had been plastered with a grey mortar mixed with very fine limestone fragments (Pl. 3b). The plaster was generally c. 0.01m thick. The almost circular firing pit (room XLII) had a lining of basalt blocks mostly surviving to a height of 0.60m (2 courses high). The diameter

of the pit was 1.03 to 1.10m at the bottom, decreasing as the structure rose. At the top of the second course the overhang was 0.08m.

Parts of the top of a chimney were found in the in-fill of the cistern. They must belong to the bath-house as no other well-built circular structure was found on the site. The pieces gave a diameter of 0.70m for the top of the chimney (Fig. 88 no.201). The chimney top had nine projections. On two of the three and a half basalt pieces recovered were reliefs: a pregnant woman and a phallus (Fig. 88 nos 202–203).

The floor of the firing pit was built from medium sized blocks of limestone and small river pebbles, set on a foundation of heavy orange clay. The pit was surrounded by a mass of limestone rubble held together by white concrete and orange clay mortar and faced with large limestone blocks. The stoke-hole, 0.58m long and 0.42m wide, lay on the west side of the firing pit; it too was lined with basalt. The stoke-hole had an arched roof. The floor of the stoke-hole had been lined with a poorly fired brick, 0.41m long. The brick, 0.10m high in the middle, had been worn on both ends, the wear being greater on the eastern end where it tapered down to a thickness of 0.05m. Leading from the firing pit (XLII) into room XLIII was a 0.44m long flue, 0.35 to 0.41m wide at the bottom, again lined with basalt blocks. The upper stones were shaped to form an arch. Although the keystones of the arch had not survived, the height of the inside of the flue could be estimated to have been 0.65m. The under-floor areas of rooms XLIII and XLIV were divided by a wall that left a 0.50m wide gap between the end of it and the north wall. The surface of both these under-floor areas was formed by the platform for the bath-house and was thus very uneven. On top of this base surface were various settings for supports for the floor of the upper room. The supports themselves were cylindrical pots standing 0.45m high (Fig. 46 no.198). Five settings were identified in room XLIII and it is likely that others were removed by workmen during the cleaning of the room On either side of the flue was a setting formed by a concrete rim into which the pots were embedded. The northern one had two-thirds of its pot *in situ*. The other settings were in a line near the north wall. The western setting was formed by a specially made pot stand (Fig. 46 no.197). The other two settings were half circles of a stand embedded in concrete. In the north-eastern corner of the room was a drainage hole (diameter 0.10m at the top, narrowing to 0.08m) that went through the bath-house platform under the north wall into the drain that ran along the northern side of the bath-building. The drainage hole emerged c. 0.30m lower, 0.47m further west, i.e. upstream. Against the north and south walls of the room were further floor-supports, mostly made from conglomerate blocks. On top of one of the supports were traces of thick white concrete that ran up against the south wall; it would appear to be the same material by which the upper floor was held in place. The use of conglomerate was unusual as nowhere else throughout the Medieval period on the mound at Tille was this type of stone found. Limestone would have fractured across the middle under the (presumably) heavy weights to be supported and the floor would

certainly have collapsed. The eastern room (XLIV) contained many settings for floor supports. Four rows of four settings were found. These settings were patches of white concrete into which the pots had been sunk. One setting had the base of one of the pots still preserved in it, while another had an almost complete pot *in situ*. Built up against the south-western corner of the room was a vertical flue constructed from tile and concrete. Presumably this flue conducted the circulating hot air from room XLIV into the higher room XLV to the south. Built against the northern part of the bath-building was a room (XLV) 3.60 by 2.50m Although the east wall had been completely robbed out, the line was well preserved by the tile and stone drainage gully on the east and the edge of a later cobbled floor surface on the west. This room had a white mortared floor laid directly on the platform of the bath structure. On the south, east and north sides of the bath-building were drains that met at the north-eastern corner of the building where they flowed into a channel that ran under the path (XLVII). It seems logical to assume that the above-floor rooms reflected the layout of the under-floor rooms, i.e. that there were two above-floor rooms in the northern part: a hot room (XLIII) and a warm room (XLIV). The southern room (XLV) could have been a dressing room warmed to a certain extent by the air flowing through the flue from the under-floor part of room XLIV.

To the east of the bath-house lay an open area (XLVI). The floor of the southern part was a compacted clay with some small pebbles set into the surface. A *tandır* 0.80m in diameter and 0.20m deep, was constructed at this level. The northern part of the area had a cobbled surface formed mainly of medium and large sized river cobbles with a limestone kerb on the north, east and west sides. This platform formed a step-up, c. 0.30–0.35m, from the main east/west path (XLVII) into room XLVI.

Gateway and Street

The main path (XLVII) ran from the gateway (XLVIII) westwards for c. 18.00m before turning northwards to lead to the north-western corner of the settlement. From the gateway to the south-western corner of room XXVI and the entrance to the staircase (XVII) the surface of the path was made from large and medium sized cobbles. From the point where the cobbles stopped the surface of the path continued as a grey-brown clay loam containing a few small pebbles. The path rose 1.66m (east to west) over its 18.00m length; a gradient of almost 1 in 11. A drainage gully started near the entrance to the staircase (XVII). After running along the side of room XLI, it crossed the path diagonally and then ran along the south side of the cistern (XXIX) before flowing out through the gateway. A channel bringing waste water from the drains around the bath-building (XLII–XLV) ran from the north-eastern corner of the building. This channel was constructed to run under the path.

The gateway (XLVIII) of the previous building-phase remained in use but with the addition of a drainage gully along the north side and a bench along the south side (Fig. 13; Pl. 4a). The drain was constructed from small limestone blocks and white concrete. The narrow bench along the south side also was constructed from small limestone blocks and concrete. It formed a face behind which clay was packed. This work had the effect of narrowing the path through the gateway to 1.10m The surface of the path through the gateway was a deposit of gravel c. 0.10m thick. The entrance was closed by a gate in this phase. A recess, in the kerbing of the drainage gully, started on a line between the two column bases and would have held the gate

when it was open. Next to the southern column base were two limestone blocks; the end of the gate would have rested against them when the gate was closed.

Summary

The settlement was an integrated unit, well defended, with a large cistern and a bath house. There were three distinct living areas (similar to the situation in Level 1 Phase 2). The first (in the north-western corner) is, with its long rooms, once more the principal living area: a ground floor (rooms I–III) and an upper floor above rooms I–III (and probably also above rooms IV and VI). It is uncertain where the stair was situated but it is possible that part of corridor II ([?]west of the entrance to room I) was used for this purpose. The second area is near the south-western part of the site: a ground floor (rooms XX, XII and [?]XV) and an upper storey above XX, XXI, XV (and possibly also above XIII). The third area was in the north-eastern corner of the site: a ground floor (rooms XXX–XXXIII) and an upper storey above the same rooms (and possibly also above rooms XXIII–XXXV). A fourth area was also occupied but this was just a

Fig. 13. Gatehouse Plan

single unit (room X). The other rooms were either courtyards or storage rooms.

The settlement in this phase may perhaps have been occupied by an extended family group and the living area with its long rooms in the north-western corner utilized by the head of the house.

Level 2 Phase 1a (Fig. 14)

Some minor changes occurred in this sub-phase. The dividing wall between rooms I and III was removed, the courtyard (V) was divided into two; rooms XXIII to XXVI now became three distinct rooms. There was a slight rearrangement of the buildings in the south-western corner of the site. Very few changes occurred in the eastern half of the settlement. The strengthening of the perimeter wall has been assigned to this phase although it could belong to the next sub-phase, Level 2 Phase 1b.

Additions to the Perimeter Wall

Three tower-like structures were added to the perimeter wall (Pl. 5a). These structures were either an addition to the defensive character of the wall or a stabilization of the wall. More likely, they were a combination of the two. While uncovering the perimeter wall the excavators noticed that there had been difficulties in the construction; the wall had tended to slip outwards and to lean over. Slumping and earth slippage at the edge of the mound had caused the original mud-brick and stone footings to move further towards the edge. The outer face of footing stones at one point had slipped away from the core by as much as 0.15m. There had been various attempts to strengthen the mud-brick by the insertion of rows of limestone blocks into the north face. Some had tilted over at alarming angles and lay up to 0.60m north of the outside footing stones. In one area this strengthening of the mud-brick survived, in five courses, up to a height of 0.90m above the stone footings.

The three tower-like structures were constructed mainly from limestone blocks abutting the footings and the superstructure of the perimeter wall. They did not bond with the perimeter wall. The western structure was 5.50m long; it extended 1.50m away from the perimeter wall at its western end and 2.10m at its eastern end. To the west of this tower was a mass of limestone blocks placed up against the tower and the perimeter wall. These must have been intended to stabilize the edge of the mound. The middle tower was much smaller than the other two. It was only 3.50m long. It projected 1.50 to 1.80m

out from the defensive wall. To the east of this tower was another area of strengthening. The eastern tower was 4.50m long and extended 1.60m at its western end and 2.20m at its eastern end away from the perimeter wall. To the east of the tower was a further strengthening of the perimeter wall. Here the strengthening took the form of a double row of limestone blocks, in two courses, built up against the perimeter wall and bonded with the tower.

Western Buildings

Rooms I and III of Level 2 Phase 1 were formed into one room The intervening wall was stripped of its mud-brick superstructure and a new floor of dark clay loam was laid over the top of the footings. Room I was now 12.20m long. Between the different floor levels of this series (at least three were noticed, in a depth of 0.10 to 0.14m) were layers of ash and some charcoal. Two irregularly shaped pits were cut from these floor levels.

Room III of this sub-phase was a room west of room VI. It formed part of the former courtyard (V). A 2.10m wide entrance (although it may have been as narrow as 1.20m, since a later pit had cut down through the western part of the wall) led through the dividing wall into the courtyard. The floor of rooms III and V was a hard white, light-brown decayed mud and chaff material. In the eastern end of room III, for a distance of 1.40m, was an area of cobbling. In courtyard (V) there were several post-supports. They indicate that the courtyard was now covered. Against the eastern part of the dividing wall were a further two rows of post-supports. These may have been used as part of a staircase. A large hearth was located in this courtyard. It would seem that there had been considerable activity here, since a hollow had been worn around it. This hollow had been in-filled and had started again to wear down. Three pits were also found in this courtyard. An oven was discovered near the north-western corner of the area. Rooms V and III appear to have been damaged by a fire, to judge from the layer of burnt material, 0.05 to 0.30m thick, which overlaid the floors, hearth, oven and post settings. This debris contained decayed mud-brick with a high ash content and many charcoal fragments. The charcoal fragments made up c. 30 per cent of the total in the eastern half of room V and increased to 50–60 per cent in the western half. The percentage of charcoal in the debris in room III was 10–15 per cent. This difference may indicate that courtyard (V) had a wooden roof but no upper storey while room

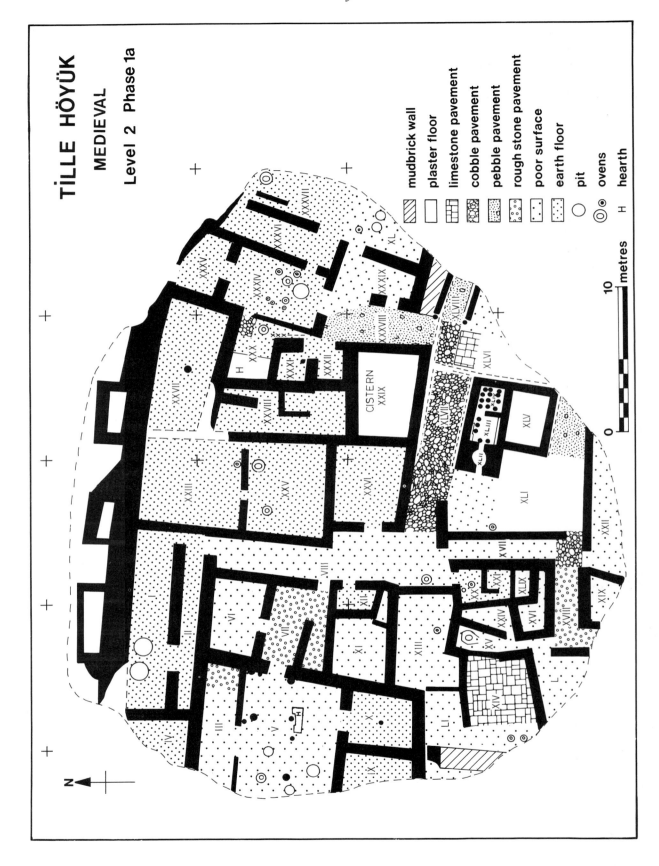

Fig. 14. Level 2 Phase 1a, Plan

III, with a much higher percentage of decayed mud-brick, did have an upper storey.

Several pieces of cylindrical stone roof-rollers were found during the excavation of the Medieval part of the site. They are exactly the same as those used today in the village. We may therefore accept that roofs were made of earth on a flat timber frame.

The eastern end of courtyard VII was separated off, for a distance of 2.10m, by a southward extension of the east wall of room VI. Between rooms VII and VIII there was an entrance 0.80m wide. An area of metalling extended from the entrance from room V for a distance of 1.60m into room VII while the rest of the room was surfaced with dark clay loam containing a high percentage of small stones, pebbles and large fragments of limestone blocks. It is likely that room VII was now roofed. Possibly there was a second storey above it, although there is no direct evidence for this proposal.

Room XI of this sub-phase was constructed in the northern half of room XI of the previous sub-phase and was separated from room XIII by a well-built wall. As the floors on either side of this wall were almost level with the top of the stone footings which were one course high, no door between the two rooms was discernible. In the strangely shaped area in the south-eastern corner of room XI a staircase may have been positioned. This staircase would have been entered at ground level from Path VIII. The stair-head would have been above room XII and would have led westwards to an upper storey above rooms XI, X and possibly IX, and northwards to the upper rooms above rooms VII, VI, III, II and I.

West of area XIII was a new room (LI). This was separated off from room XIV to which the area had formerly belonged. The greater part of room XIV was surfaced with a stone pavement formed mostly from limestone, somewhat flat blocks, forming an undulating but closely packed surface. The rest of the surface was made from dark clay loam into which two *tandır* were cut. The new room (L) was originally the southern part of area XIV in the previous phase.

Room XV of Level 2 Phase 1 was divided into two rooms (XV and XXIV). Room XV still contained the oven but surrounding it was a large deposit of ash and charcoal. Seen in the top of this deposit were two soil marks. These impressions, or 'ghosts', were circular and presumably represent organic containers. One was 0.10m in diameter, the other was larger, 0.45m in diameter. Room XXIV was accessible,

through its south-western corner, from room XV. This peculiarly shaped room must have been connected with the stairway which had been altered in this sub-phase. The west wall of room XVII was rebuilt almost exactly on top of the previous wall.

The path (XVIII) had a further deposit of dark clay loam with some cobbling in it. Running between the north-eastern corner of room XIX and the south wall of XVI was a line of stones forming a step 0.13m high. The path east of the step was cobbled.

In the centre of room XX was a *tandır*, 0.46m in diameter and 0.74m deep. Set against the north-western corner was a small oven formed from a semi-circle of fired clay, 0.04m thick, 0.24m across the open end and 0.08m deep. Room XXI was shorter than in the previous sub-phase. A single row of stones now partitioned off the southern end for a distance of 1.30m (the new room XLIX). The strange shapes and sizes of rooms XXIV and XLIX suggest that the stairs in this area had been altered. Instead of the stairs (which ran along room XVII) turning westwards and northwards over XVI, it seems more likely that the stairs started in room XXI, went over XLIX and then turned westwards over XVI and northwards over XXIV. It is possible that the part over XXIV led up to a third storey although the wall footings in this area were probably not substantial enough to support a second floor in addition to a first floor. If the first part of the stairs had been moved in this sub-phase, the consequence would be that room XVII was used as access from the main pathway (XLVII) to the smaller path (XVIII).

Central and Eastern Areas

Room XXIII was much longer, now 6.00m east/west by 6.60m The division between this room and the one to the south was formed by a rather untidy wall with two entrances through it. Along its length were a number of post-positions: a post pad and three post holes. Against the south wall, 0.80m from the eastern doorway, was a *tandır*. The floor of the room was of earth mixed with chaff. Room XXV, to the south, took up most of the rest of the rooms XXIV and XXV (of Level 2 Phase 1). The room contained two *tandır*. It also had a mud and chaff floor. The west wall of rooms XXIII and XXV must have been rebuilt in this phase, since part of the footings of the Level 2 Phase 1 wall were covered by the floors. The position of this new wall was marked by a recent robber trench as was the south wall of room

XXV. The positions of doorways into rooms XXIII and XXV are unknown because the alignments of most of the west, all of the south and most of the east walls were indicated only by modern robber trenches.

As a further evidence that room XXVII was roofed, a post support (an upturned stone mortar with its base worn through) was set in the middle of the room. Room XXX had a further series of mud and chaff floors while the surface around the entrance into room XXXIV was cobbled. The western end of room XXX, for a distance of 1.50m, was taken up by a hearth that extended from the north to the south sides of the room. In the eastern part of the room, south of the cobbles, was located a *tandır*. Against the north wall of room XXXI were stone footings for room furniture of some sort. The stones stood one course high and extended 0.90m along the north wall, from the north-western corner, and 0.70m away from the wall. Room XXXIV now had a mud and chaff surface. The room contained several ovens and *tandır*, most of them being replaced in the course of this sub-phase. Near the west wall were two small ovens, 0.45m and 0.34m in diameter, and 0.05m and 0.08m deep. These were later replaced by slightly larger ovens. Against the east wall of the room was a group of three *tandır*, the northern one being replaced by the pair slightly further south. Also in this room was a pit 0.90m deep and 1.00m in diameter at the top. During this sub-phase the cobbled surface of room XXXV was covered with a deposit of mud and chaff mix. The pebbled surface of room XXVIII also had a new flooring of the same material. The west wall of the latter room was supported by a brace, running from the northern end of the wall southwards for 2.20m. A *tandır* was found in this room. Room XXXIX had a dark clay loam surface; there was a patch of small stones in the south-eastern corner of the room. Within room XI, during this period, there was a small oven and two rubbish pits.

Bath-house

No later floor for room XLI was seen, since the plaster floor of the previous phase lay very close to the pre-excavation surface of the mound. It is possible that a further floor of plaster was laid down in Level 2 Phase 1a but had been broken up by worm and root action. The part of the room to the south of room XLV of the bath-house was re-surfaced with a make-up layer of cobbles capped by a pebbled surface. The southern part of room XLVI, to the east of the bath-house, received a mortar floor overlying the earlier pebble surface of which traces have survived.

All the rooms not mentioned had new floor surfaces but of a type similar to those of the previous phase.

Level 2 Phase 1b (Fig. 15)

Several minor changes occurred in this sub-phase: further modifications to the stairway (XX, XXI, XLIX, XVI), the removal of the partition between rooms XIII and LI (of the previous sub-phase) and the partitioning of rooms XXV and XXVI into several small areas. The use of some rooms was changed. The ovens found in room XXXIV in the previous sub-phase are now found in room XXXVI.

Between the western and middle towers a strengthening support in the form of mud-brick faced with stone was added to the perimeter wall. North of this reinforcement a *tandır* was built; it was partially screened on the northern side by a thin wall. East of the eastern tower a revetment in the form of a single row of stones, surviving up to three courses high was added to the outer face of the wall.

Western Buildings

During this period room I was floored with large, flat-topped, limestone slabs which formed a well-laid pavement. The pavement had not survived over the whole of the room; some areas of it were later robbed out. In the eastern part of the room was a hearth, roughly D-shaped with the straight edge to the east (Fig. 16). The lining was made of clay (which had naturally become baked hard) and was 0.08 to 0.10m thick. The bottom of the oven was 0.30m below the level of the pavement. At each end of the straight edge there was a socket of baked clay with an internal void, diameter 0.2 to 0.15m and c. 0.05 to 0.06m deep. Connecting the two sockets was a straight length of baked clay wall, 0.08m wide, built to the same height as the top of the southern socket but slightly lower than the northern. It seems likely that the oven was domed, with a door at the eastern end. The door would have been placed in the sockets when the oven was in use.

Room III had a harder floor than in the previous sub-phase; scattered river pebbles and many, very small stones were set into a dark brown clay loam. Room V also now had an uneven surface consisting of river pebbles and small stones; bone fragments and pot sherds were impressed into the surface. In the south-eastern corner was a somewhat higher area of good

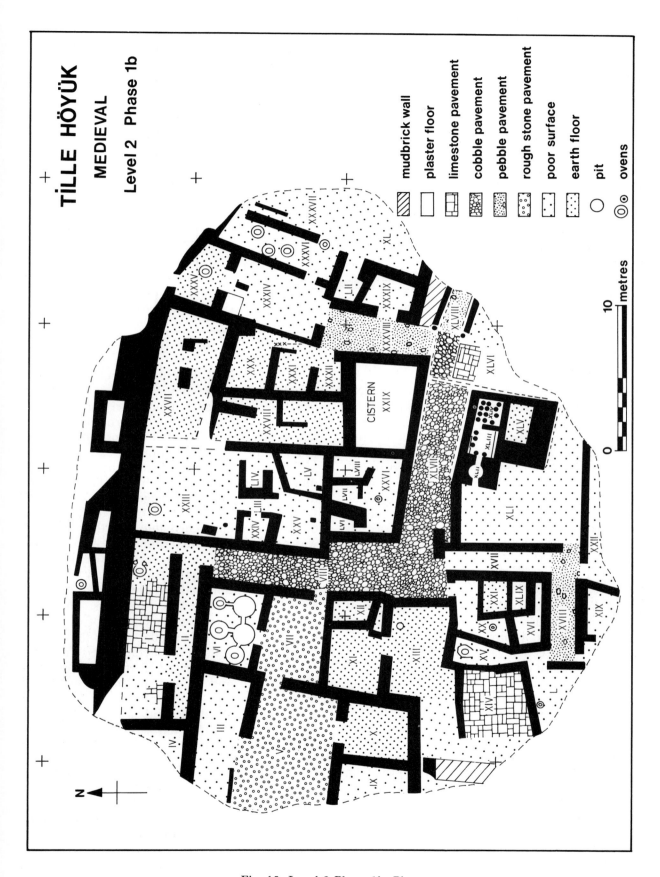

Fig. 15. Level 2 Phase 1b, Plan

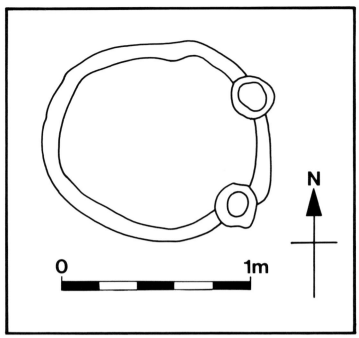

Fig. 16. Room I, Oven Plan

cobbling, a fact which suggests that the rest of the surface had been, to some extent, worn away. No evidence of any furniture or post supports were found in the room during this sub-phase. It is probable that the roof was not replaced after the fire in this area in Level 2 Phase 1a.

The function of room VI was changed in this period. The room now contained two stoking areas and three large ovens (Pl. 5b). The western stoking pit was a shallow hollow with a hard-bottomed surface. To the north of this stoking area was the best constructed and best preserved oven (Fig. 17). It was an approximately circular pit lined with limestone blocks and river pebbles. The pit had a maximum internal diameter of 1.20m, was 0.45m deep and contained a number of clay pillars. Two of these were found *in situ*; a third had collapsed into the pit. Their cross section varied from 0.12 by 0.09m to 0.15 by 0.10m; their length lay in the range of 0.24 to 0.35m The three pillars were placed on stone or tile pads and supported a floor of coarsely fired clay with a maximum thickness of 0.10m. The floor had been made in several discreet sections; the largest, surviving part was 0.65 by 0.58m. As the surface area of the surviving sections of the floor were not sufficient to cover the whole area of the oven, part of the oven must have been removed when the oven fell into disuse. A flue, 0.49 to 0.55m wide and 0.60m long, led from the stoking pit. To the west of the stoking pit was another oven with an internal diameter of 1.10m; its pit had a maximum depth of 0.30m Again, the pit was

lined with small limestone blocks and river pebbles. The flue contained ash and coarsely fired pieces of clay but no other furniture was recovered. The south-eastern corner of room VI had a stone facing placed against the walls in order to protect them from the eastern stoking pit. The facing was inserted during this sub-phase, since a layer of ash was found underneath it. The northern edge of the stoking pit was formed by a wall of baked clay, 0.10 to 0.26m wide; an arched flue run through it. It was not possible to determine any details of the oven in the north-eastern corner of the room.

In this sub-phase the courtyard (VII) lost its internal partition wall. Within the duration of this sub-phase there were two floors. There was an accumulation of earth on top of each. The earlier floor was very similar to the floor in the preceding sub-phase: hard compacted dark clay loam with a scattering of stones. Along the western wall and around the entrance through this wall the stone content of the surface became more concentrated. Several large river pebbles were laid to create a flattish surface. Lying on top of this surface was a better cobbled floor, basically constructed from river pebbles. It formed a fairly continuous surface. Dispersed above and between this primary surface were deposits of small river pebbles, partly filling the gaps between the larger pebbles, partly forming a compacted surface above them, in a manner similar to the surface of room V to the west. The surface contained many pot sherds and bone fragments. Lying over the southern part of

42

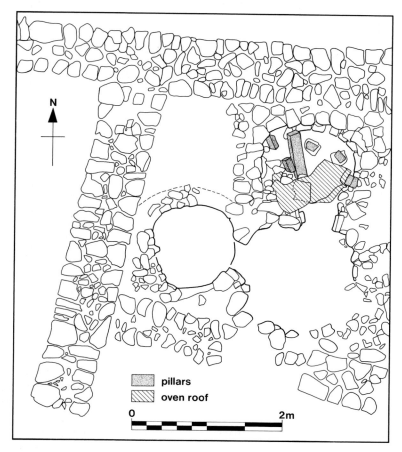

Fig. 17. Room VI, West Stoking Pit and Two Ovens Plan

the room, for a distance of 2.00 to 3.00m, was a deposit of burnt debris, 0.03 to 0.13m thick. As the south wall was replaced at the end of this sub-phase it seems likely that there was a localised fire in the southern part of the room.

The section of the path running northward (VIII) now had a cobbled surface, made mainly from medium-sized river pebbles and capped by very small pebbles, a feature similar to that in room VII. This cobbling of room VIII ran from the doorway into room II down to the east/west path (XLVII).

The south wall of XI was rebuilt and a doorway, 1.20m wide, opened through it into room XIII. The floor of the two rooms (XI, XIII) in this period was a dark clay loam mixed with organic matter (chaff?). The latter room now covered room LI of the previous sub-phases. The small partition wall went out of use, though a change in floor surface occurred here. West of this point the floor was made from dark clay loam. Near the north-eastern corner of room XIII a horse's skull was found in a shallow depression, 0.70 by 0.40m in diameter, 0.15m deep. Also contained in this pit were three iron nails and a small batch of pottery sherds.

While the surface of path XVII remained poor, the path XVIII was cobbled with densely packed small river pebbles.

Again there was a change in the layout of the rooms connected with the stairway in the south-western part of the settlement. Room XX now incorporated room XXIV of the previous sub-phase. The east/west partition between rooms XX and XXI was extended westwards; it now joined with the north/south wall to the west. North of this join the wall was knocked down. The floor of room XX was a dark clay loam with some pebbles (a change from the mud and chaff mix of the previous sub-phase). A *tandır*, 0.50m in diameter and 0.50m deep, was found in this room.

Central Area

In the centre of the site various alterations took place. Room XXIII had, in this sub-phase, a further series of mud floors, a *tandır* and some roof supports. Rooms XXV and XXVI of Level 2 Phase 1a were divided into small areas. The middle of these three areas was divided into five distinct parts. Room LIII was a small corridor between the two small rooms (XXIV and LIV). The rest of the area was taken up by two large rooms (LV and XXV). The walls for these small areas were not very tidily built. The stone footings and spaces for upright timbers were irregular. It may be that the superstructure of these walls was built either completely from timber or from timber with a little mud-brick. The southern area (XXVI of Level 2 Phase 1a) had three small rooms (LVI—LVIII) to the north of the larger area (XXVI). Contained within this latter area was a small *tandır*.

The appearance of these two areas with their small partitioned rooms suggests that they may have been used as animal pens.

Eastern Area

An internal partition was built in room XXVII during this sub-phase. The western end of this partition had been cut through by the later large pit (see Fig. 7) that had destroyed the west end of the room. Room XXX now had a floor of mud and chaff. A new east wall was constructed for room XXXI. The doorway from room XXX to XXXIV was now blocked. Room XXXIV had a short length of footings, central to the width of the room, just to the south of the entrance to room XXXV. A low platform was found in the northeastern corner of room XXXIV; it measured 0.80 by 1.00m and stood one course high. This room did not contain any ovens or *tandır* during this phase. Room XXXV, to the north, contained an oven, diameter 0.75m and a depth of 0.10m. The floors of rooms XXXIV, XXXVI and XXXVII were now all made from dark clay loam, not the mud and (?)chaff mix of the previous sub-phase. Room XXXVI contained three *tandır* while a fourth lay in the southern doorway between rooms XXXVI and XXXVII.

A new length of wall separated off the path (XXXVIII) from the rooms to the east. Room XXXIX of Level 2 Phase 1a was divided into two, a large and a small area (room LII). There was an entrance from room XL.

Bath-house

While the northern part of courtyard XLI still had a surface of dark clay loam the nature of the floor of the southern part is not known, since it lay very close to the pre-excavation surface. The area (XLVI) on the east side of the bath-house did have a white plastered floor set on a foundation of river pebbles and small pebbles. The southern room of the bath-house underwent a minor modification. The west and south walls

were thickened. The mud-brick superstructure was removed and a line of larger limestone blocks was laid down inside the room parallel to the walls; the intervening space was packed with small cobbles. These cobbles overflowed onto the top of the original footings. This thickening of the walls resulted in a reduction, to 2.60 by 1.60m, of the floor space of the room The floor was now a hard compacted dark clay loam.

Level 2 Phase 2 (Fig. 18)

Although some building alterations took place during this phase, the general shape of the settlement on top of the mound remained the same. The major change would appear to have been the dismantling of the staircase in the south-western corner of the site; thereby the rooms would be only single-storeyed.

Western Buildings

The oven in room I was replaced by a hearth, formed from a platform of stone and set against the eastern wall. Built into the south wall, halfway along its length, was a curious feature: a circular, limestone platform, 1.10m in diameter and two courses high, inserted into the mud-brick superstructure. The feature was slightly wider than the stone footings of the wall. The corridor (room II) was blocked at its eastern end by the insertion of a wall. A large stone mortar, internal diameter 0.47m at the top and internal depth 0.36m (Fig. 85 no.198), was positioned midway along the length of the room

Room III of this period was much smaller, owing to the building of a curved wall which separated off the western part of the room and thus formed a new room (XII). The floor of room III was a sandy loam mixed with many small pebbles; small patches of flat cobbles were set into it. The entrance from room III to room V was only c. 0.50m wide. The new room (XII) had a soft, dark clay loam floor containing very small stones and pebbles. The courtyard of room V of Level 2 Phase 1b was split into two large rooms, a (?)stairway and a further small room. Room V of this phase had a succession of dark clay loam surfaces. Room XXIV has been interpreted as a stairway. Its east wall stopped just short of the north wall; a door swivel stone was found here. It would appear that the stair was entered from room V through a door at this point. Further west was a small room lying on the edge of the mound. The floor was of a sandy loam. Room XVI occupied the southern part of room V (Level 2 Phase 1b). A stone facing was placed against the

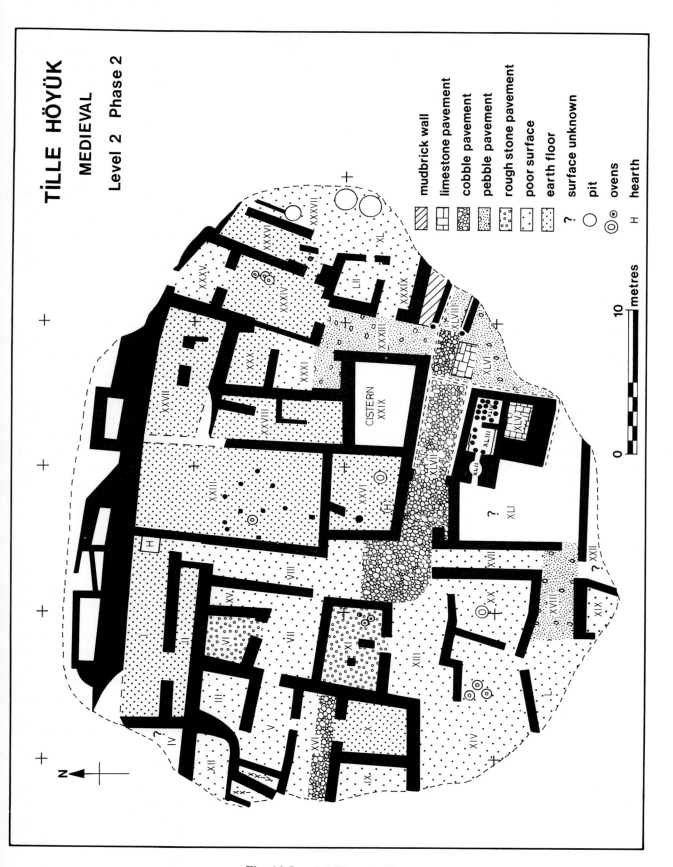

Fig. 18. Level 2 Phase 2, Plan

45

south and west walls (a strengthening for these two walls?). Projecting 0.70 to 1.00m away from this facing was a pavement of closely packed cobbles. The rest of the floor of room XVI was a very compacted, dark clay loam with a high proportion of small stones.

Room VI was remodelled during Level 2 Phase 2. When the doorway in the south wall was moved, a stone facing to the north side of the mud-brick was added to the lower levels. A new east wall was constructed, thus forming a further room to the east of room VI. The floor of room VI was originally a stone pavement. The north-eastern part was made from flat river cobbles but the rest was built from limestone blocks, with occasional river cobbles set into the sandy loam. At a later time this surface was replaced by a mud and chaff material which had a make-up layer of mixed composition. At the same time, the west wall was strengthened by an additional row of stone footings and mud-brick. Room VII had a succession of dark clay loam surfaces; many stones, pot sherds and bone fragments were compressed into the surfaces. North of the entrance into room V, the west wall had been strengthened by a further row of stone footings and mud-brick. Room VIII, the north/south path, now had a surface of dark clay loam mixed with some small pebbles; two long thin features were cut into it towards the southern end. Near the entrance into room VII the earlier feature was replaced by a later, second feature. The latter was 3.30m long with an internal width of 0.30 to 0.38m and a depth of 0.17m at the north and middle and 0.19m at the south. The sides and northern end of the feature were made of baked clay; the floor was hard baked earth. It was not straight but slightly curved, orientated north/south. The sides were vertical or near vertical; the northern end was rounded and the southern end open. Most of the sides were 0.04 to 0.05m thick; the sides of the southern end were 0.01 to 0.02m thick. The earlier feature had been cut through by the later. The earlier feature had a length of 2.30m and an internal width of 0.20m at it northern end. Its depth varied from 0.18m at the northern end, 0.15m in the middle, to 0.075m at its southern end. Its bottom was lined with baked clay. The purpose of these features is not known. Between rooms VI and VIII was a long, narrow room measuring 4.00 by 1.40m surfaced with a dark clay loam mixed with some small pebbles.

The north and east walls of room XI were replaced in this phase. The floor was dark clay loam; paved areas were paved. Two features were set into it. One was a large stone slab, in the form of a roughly rectangular limestone block, 1.00 by 0.60 by 0.145m (high), set flush with the floor. This slab had a recess in its upper surface, 0.44 by 0.24 by 0.05m (deep). The recess presumably acted as a mortice or socket to hold something standing on the stone. The second feature was a pit, 0.43m square, vertically cut to a depth of 0.05m The bottom was flat. In the south-eastern corner of the room was a group of three *tandır*; one of them had replaced an earlier *tandır*.

In this phase room XIII was an open area between the main path (XLVII) and, on the west, the modern edge of the mound. The surface of this area was a hard, dark clay loam with c. 30 per cent small pebbles compacted into the surface. Area XIV now included room XV of Level 2 Phase 1b and contained three *tandır*. Room L was no longer separated from the path (XVIII) but was an open area lying on the south-western edge of the settlement. The path (XVIII) was surfaced with a pebble pavement.

Room XX covered the area formerly under rooms XX, XXI, XLIX and part of XVI. This room measured 3.40 to 4.40m east/west by 4.40 to 5.00m The western end of the new south wall curved towards the north. The floor was a dark clay loam, well compacted, containing c. 20 per cent burnt clay fragments, some patches of charcoal and an even but light distribution of very small stones. Almost central to the room was a *tandır*, 0.64m in diameter and 0.50m deep, a replacement for one which had been in the same position earlier in the phase.

Central Area

The number XXIII is used to describe the area covered by rooms XXIII–XXV, LIII–LV in Level 2 Phase 1b. The southern half of this area contained several post supports. Though these do not make a coherent pattern, this part of the area must have been covered. These post supports took the form of stone pads. The floor of the whole of this area was of a mud and chaff mix. Cut into it was a small smelting pit. This shallow pit was approximately circular, diameter 0.46 to 0.53m and 0.09 to 0.12m deep. On the east side was a slot for the bellows, 0.15m long and 0.04m deep. Within the pit was a crucible, with an internal diameter of c. 0.20m and sides of thickness 0.02 to 0.05m at the top and 0.02 to 0.035m at the bottom. In it traces of copper alloy were found. Also in this area was a *tandır*.

In this occupation phase room XXVI had one small partition wall. One metre to the south of the end of this wall there was part of a re-used column that stood 0.67m above the floor of dark loam mixed with chaff. A *tandır* was cut into the floor and a hearth was found against the south wall. Near the north-eastern corner of the room the bottom half of a rotary quern was found. A long narrow block of limestone with a gaming board scratched on its surface came to light near the centre of the room (Fig. 87 no.200).

Minor Alterations to Eastern Buildings

Room XXXI now encompassed room XXXII of the previous phase. Part of the surface of this area was of dark clay loam; the rest was of gravel. Three *tandır* were found in the room XXIV, the southern one being a replacement for the northern. The floor of this room was of mud and (?)chaff (a change from the previous phase) as was the floor of room XXXVI. The southern part of the west wall was strengthened; a short length of partition wall existed near the southern end of the room A small oven was located just inside the doorway from room XXXIV. In this phase there was a large rubbish pit in room XXXVII and two in room XL. The south and east walls (room LII) were rebuilt. Its surface became higher than that of room XL. Between the two were two steps built from limestone and river pebbles.

The southern room of the bath-house (XLV) had a new floor made from flat, well shaped limestone slabs. To the east, room XLVI had a surface of hard, dark clay loam with many pebbles compacted into the top.

End of Level 2 Buildings

The end of this phase, and indeed of this Level, was brought about by a fire that destroyed the north-western part of the settlement. Rooms I and II seemed to have been extensively damaged. The upper storey collapsed onto the ground level floors. In room I a deposit of collapsed mud-brick (up to 0.40m deep) was excavated (Section 1, Fig. 25 [102]). Completely filling the room was a jumbled mass of tumbled mud-brick. Contained within the mud-brick were a number of charcoal patches, some of which were quite extensive. Some mud-brick was baked and had a tendency to form large lumps when moved. Immediately on top of the floor was a layer of charcoal, presumably the remains of a collapsed burnt ceiling. Similarly, in room II a large deposit of collapsed mud-brick was uncovered (Section 1, Fig. 25 [100]).

Level 3 Phase 1 (Fig. 19)

The settlement on top of the mound in this level bears a faint resemblance to the previous phase of the building. The central area of the western two-thirds of the site retained a similar pattern in the layout of the rooms. Only in two places did traces of a perimeter wall remain. Over most of the southern and south-eastern part of the site, the horizon for this level occurred too near the pre-excavation surface for much to have survived. The large, recent pit on the northern edge of the mound destroyed an area 11m by 5m.

For this level the rooms have been completely renumbered, even where rooms survive from the previous level. Room LII of Level 2 Phase 2 is now room XXIV, XVI is V, X is VI and VI is VII.

Western Range

Room I was an area in the north-western part of the site, to the north of the east/west wall (which had continued in use from the previous phase). The type of surface in this room could not be determined, since the floor material had been reduced to the consistency of soft, dusty top-soil. Room II lay to the south of a surviving section of the perimeter wall.

The perimeter wall was constructed with two faces, mainly from river pebbles, and with a core formed by small, limestone rubble. The footings for this wall were two courses high and had been cut down into the destruction debris after the fire of the previous phase (Section 1, Fig. 25 [114]). The floor of room II was of mud and chaff. The east side had been cut away by the recent, large pit; the line of the west wall was indicated only by a recent robber trench.

Room III seemed to form a courtyard with a surface of dark brown clay loam with some small stones and pebbles set into it. The north, east and south walls survived from Level 2 Phase 2. In the north-eastern corner of the courtyard was a small rectangular area (room IV). This room measured 2.80 by 2.20m. There was an entrance, 0.60m wide, through its south wall. The floor of room IV was a sandy loam; several large flat pebbles lay on the surface. Rooms V and VI were still in use during this level of occupation but with new surfaces: (1) dark clay loam with a lot of charcoal, limestone chippings, small stones and pebbles embedded in it for the earlier and (2) mud mixed with (?)chaff for the later.

Room VII did not alter except for the laying of a new floor surface of sandy loam. Within the room was a *tandır*, diameter 0.53m at the top and a maximum internal diameter of 0.90m at the bottom, a depth of 0.80m The *tandır* retained its old, 0.05m thick linings; a new, 0.06m thick lining was placed inside it. A long, narrow area

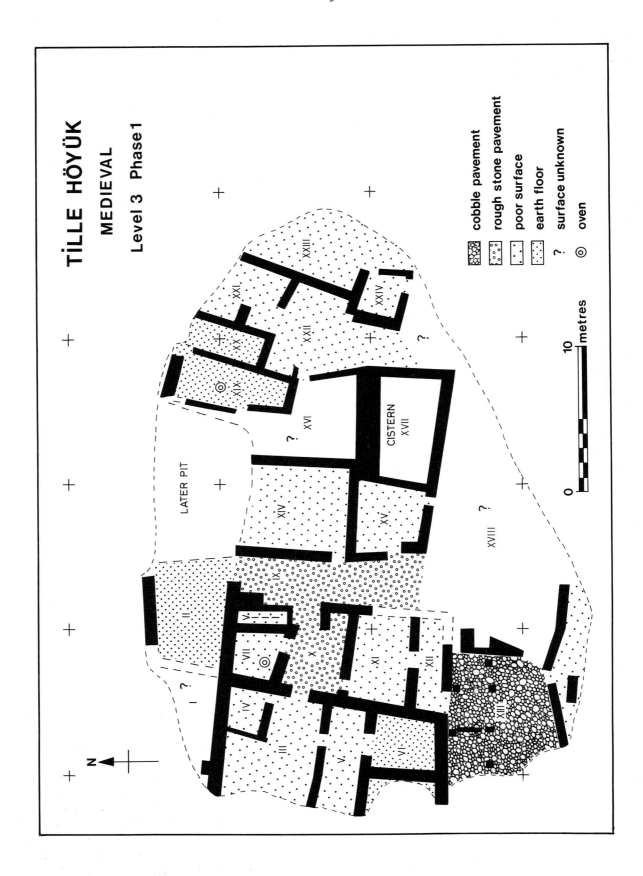

Fig. 19. Level 3 Phase 1, Plan

(room VIII) existed to the east of the above room. Owing to its strange east wall (built in two widths), it has been interpreted as a stair-way. Room IX formed a thoroughfare from room II southwards, between rooms VIII and XIV and rooms X, XI, XII and XV, to the open area on the south of the mound. It was surfaced with cobbles, tightly packed together, forming an uneven surface. There was access to room X from rooms IX, III, VII and XI. The south wall was a rebuild of a Level 2 Phase 2 wall on almost the same alignment. The west wall was also rebuilt; further courses of stone were placed on top of the original footings. The area (a courtyard) was surfaced with small pebbles, some larger river pebbles, pot sherds and tile fragments. The northern two-thirds of the area had a foundation of stone for the pebbled surface; this consisted mainly of river pebbles laid close together but very unevenly.

Room XI occupied almost the same area as room XI in Level 2 Phase 2. Only part of the east wall was identified. It was seen as a robber trench cut from top soil. The edge of the robber trench was very difficult to follow and its exact length is uncertain. It is probable that the robber trench extended southwards to meet the continuation of the south wall (also robbed out) of room XII. Room XI was surfaced with a dark clay loam deposit, 0.07 to 0.16m thick. Room XII was also surfaced with dark clay loam. It had an entrance, 1.50m wide, into area XIII.

Room XIII was a partially covered area. Six post-pads were identified in the northern half of the area. The south side of the covered area was defined by a line of four post-pads, two of which were opposite a further two that were positioned against the north wall. These pads took the form of large blocks of limestone set into and standing above the floor surface. A length of stone wall lay between the north-western pad and the second pad from the west (on the southern line). This feature, 0.30 to 0.40m wide, was interpreted as a base for a partition wall of mud-brick. The area of XIII had a cobbled surface in the form of patchy rather than continuous paving. The interstices were filled with small cobbles compacted with loam.

Central Area

Room XIV had a new west wall in this building phase. Lying on the east side of the robber trench (which represents the removal of the Level 2 wall) was a row of stones which must have been the eastern face of a new wall. The floor of this area was a dark clay loam. Room XV was rebuilt on three sides with two entrances. The first, 1.00m wide, was through the west wall, the second, 0.60m wide, through the south wall. The floor was a sandy loam.

In the western area, referred to as room XVI, the soil was so dry and so difficult to excavate with accuracy that it is impossible to say what might have occurred. The surface in the eastern part was rather broken and fragmentary but was recognised as a spread of limestone chips. Contained within this spread was a large quantity of bone, glass fragments and charcoal.

Cistern

The cistern (XVII) was probably still in use in this level, although the western wall must have been dismantled down to the ground level of Level 2 Phase 2. Between this west wall and the east wall of room XV was a feature lined with baked clay. The feature was rectangular; the western side was 2.60m long and 0.05m thick. The east wall only survived for its southernmost 1.00m, the rest being cut away by the later robber trench. Where measurable, the internal width was 0.54m. What remained of the eastern side was seen to have been built over the west wall (in Level 2 Phase 2) of room XXIX. The internal depth of the feature was c. 0.11m.

The area to the south of rooms XV and XVII and east of room XII and XIII, numbered XVIII, lay too close to the pre-excavation surface for any structures to have survived.

North-eastern Buildings

Room XIX was a long, narrow building, orientated north/south and joined to the perimeter wall. At this point, the northern face of the perimeter wall was mostly composed of river cobbles; its southern face was built mainly from roughly squared, limestone blocks. The core was formed from small limestone rubble. The width of the whole wall was 0.80m; the footings were only one course high. Room XIX probably represents a small house with a mud and chaff floor. Built in this room was a *tandır*, diameter 0.60m, a depth of c. 0.40m Room XX must also have abutted against the perimeter wall which did not survive in this area. The east wall remained in use from Level 2 Phase 2; the northern end was rebuilt. The room again had a mud and chaff floor; the area to the east (room XXI) had a dark clay loam surface.

Room XXII was, in part, a ramp leading up to a flat area on the northern side of a revetment that ran eastwards from the south-eastern corner of room XIX. The ramp, at its south end, was slightly cut down; in this process some footing stones of a Level 2 Phase 1b wall were removed. A Level 2 Phase 2 wall was stripped down to the footing stones which were then lightly concreted over and used as a step in the ramp. The ramp was kerbed on its east side and was surfaced with limestone chips and dark clay loam. This surface ran up to the revetment of the higher platform, then turned westwards and ran into room XVI. The higher platform had a surface of hard compacted dark clay loam with some areas of tiny pebbles. To the east was room XXIII, a large enclosed area with a floor of beaten loam. Room XXIV remained in use from Level 2 Phase 2. It had a dark clay loam surface.

Summary

There were probably three parts to the settlement on the mound. Rooms I and II continued the tradition of a residential area in the north-western corner and storage rooms and courtyards to the south. Room VI was still a living room with its associated buildings on the east and south and perhaps, additionally, on the west side (although these had not survived). The third living area was rooms XIX and XX with attendant buildings and areas on the eastern side of the mound.

Level 3 Phase 2 (Fig. 20)

The changes that occurred in this building phase are very minor and hardly revising the basic shape of the building. Room II is divided into two. The relative sizes of rooms III and V are altered. Room VIII of Level 3 Phase 1 disappears. Room XI and XII become one area and room XXIII is divided into two.

Western Range

The rooms in the north-western part of the site appear to have had the function of a living-area. Rooms II and VIII had mud and (?)chaff mix floors. Within room II was an oven, roughly oval in shape (1.00 by 0.60m), with its base at 0.20m below ground level. The remaining walls of the oven were 0.06 to 0.12m thick; the parts originally above ground have collapsed into the middle. In room VIII were five ovens. Two were saucer-shaped depressions of baked clay, 0.26m and 0.40m in diameter and 0.03m and 0.05m depth. A *tandır*, 0.40 to 0.50m diameter and 0.29m depth, was found just to the north of the two ovens described above. Two other *tandır* survived on the edge of the recent large pit. One was 0.75 by 0.65m, oval in shape; its walls were made of

baked clay, 0.03 to 0.04m thick. It had a depth of only 0.08m The other was similar; it measured 1.00 by 0.75m, walls c. 0.02m thick and 0.10m deep. Over the floor of these two rooms a layer of ash, 0.02 to 0.10m thick, was found; they may, therefore, have been damaged by a fire.

Room III appeared to be a storage room with a soft, dark clay loam surface. There was an entrance, 1.30m wide, from room V. The courtyard area of V increased to encompass most of the area of courtyard III (Level 3 Phase 1). This large courtyard was surfaced with dark clay loam containing a number of large stones together with very small stones and pebbles. The original surface of this area may have been a compacted pavement of very small pebbles such as survived, under the later surface, beside the entrance into room X.

In this phase, room VII had a new south wall with which was associated a sandy loam surface. Room IX of this phase now also covered the area of room VIII of the previous phase; it had a dark clay loam surface. The partial remains of an oven were found in this area. A small room (XII) probably a staircase, was built into the south-eastern corner of courtyard (X). A dark clay surface replaced the stone pavement in this courtyard. A small hearth was set against the north-western corner of the area. The hearth was formed by two intersecting bowl-shaped features.

A large courtyard (XI) was now found to the east of room VI. This courtyard had previously been two small areas but the dividing wall was no longer in use. A strengthening brace was built across the south-eastern corner. The brace had the effect of blocking off the original doorway; the later entrance must, therefore, have been through those parts of the walls which were later robbed out. In room XIII, against the south wall of room VI, a further section of wall was erected, surviving three courses high; it had a revetment of large blocks and a core of mud-brick and loose stones. On a line with the south end of the east wall of the rooms a revetment of a single row of stones, one course high, formed the southern limit of the new surface in this area. The surface, really an accumulation of debris on top of the cobbled surface, was made from clay with burnt clay, charcoal fragments and limestone chips. Many of the underlying cobbles protruded through this material.

Central and Eastern Areas

Room XIV had a new floor of dark clay loam. It was not established that room XV was standing in this phase but it seems likely that it was still in

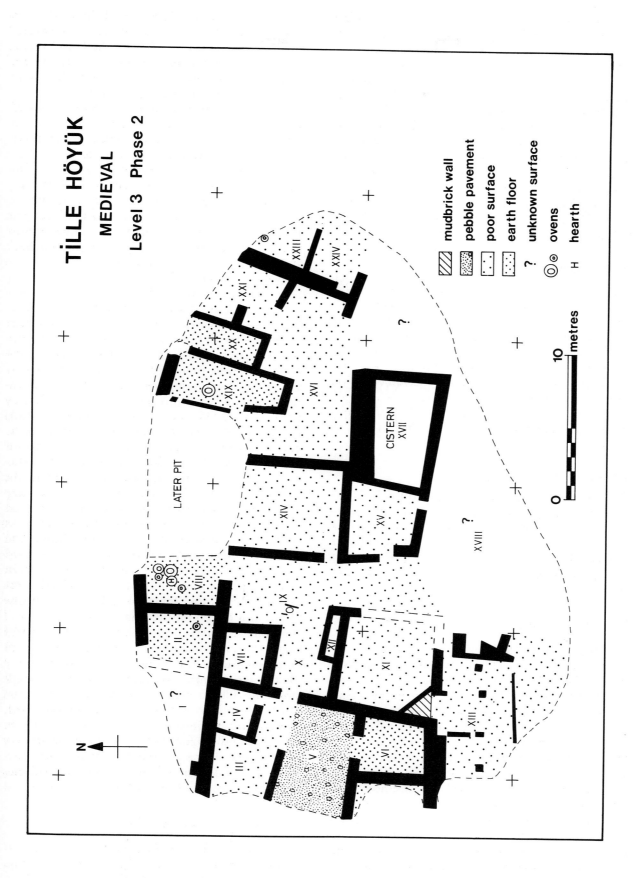

Fig. 20. Level 3 Phase 2, Plan

use. To the east, the surface of room XVI was an accumulation of rubbish, a dark clay loam containing many bone and charcoal fragments, pottery and glass sherds, and decayed organic material. It seemed, therefore, that this was an open space into which rubbish was thrown.

Rooms XIX and XX had a further series of thin mud and chaff floors; a new *tandır* was built in room XX. Room XXI did not change. Area XXII was now contiguous with area XVI and had an accumulation of rubbish similar to that in room XVI, although it contained more broken tile fragments and small pebbles. Room XXIII of Level 3 Phase 1 was divided into two areas during this phase of occupation. Before this division was made, the west wall was strengthened. Owing to the settling of the in-fill of a *tandır* (Level 2 Phase 1b), the wall had tilted over at an alarming angle. To prop up this wall, a second wall was built against its east side. Both room XXIII and room XXIV had surfaces of a loam material. An oven, 0.40m in diameter, 0.28m deep and walls 0.04m thick was built in room XXIII.

To the south of room XXII and XXIV it was impossible to disentangle any structural arrangements owing to the dryness (of the soil) which obscured stratigraphic differences.

Level 3 Phase 3 (Fig. 21)

By this phase the remaining structures had become very fragmentary, especially in the northeast where the walls of this and the following two phases are very flimsy. It would appear that in Level 3 Phase 3, the settlement had split into two discrete areas. The area on the west side was centred on the house (room II) and adjoining courtyard (room I) while the part occupying the north-eastern corner of the mound was centred on the house (room V) and adjacent outbuildings (rooms VI–IX).

Courtyard I covers the area of rooms III–V of Level 3 Phase 2; only one partition wall remained in use. The courtyard had a surface of dark clay loam containing a few stones and occasional charcoal lumps and limestone chips. Close to room II was a *tandır* which had a diameter of 0.86 to 0.98m and a depth of 0.35m On the east side of the courtyard, there seemed to be an entrance formed by room III. Extending 5.00m away from the courtyard were two narrow walls. Lying between them was a stone pavement made up of limestone blocks and large river pebbles; some smaller stones, used as packing between the two, were laid in a rather uneven fashion. To the north of room III was an open area (room IV) that

contained two small fragments of structures. Surrounding these two fragments was a spread of dark clay loam containing building debris.

Room II had its south wall repaired in this phase of occupation. A further two courses of stone were laid on top of the pre-existing stone footings and were inserted into the mud-brick superstructure of the east wall.

Room V had its northern end and the northern part of the east side rebuilt. This rebuilding involved the placing of new masonry inside the room against the original walls. In this phase the floor was a mud and (?)chaff material. A small hearth was located in the northern half; it was roughly circular (c. 0.48m in diameter) depression (0.05 to 0.08m) filled with ash and charcoal fragments.

Room VI was a modification of the northern part of the room XX of Level 3 Phase 2. A thin partition wall was erected; it abutted the west wall of the room An entrance, 0.90m wide, was left into room VII to the south. For room VII, the southern part of the west wall of room XX (Level 3 Phase 2) was pulled down in order to form a room measuring 3.80m east/west by 1.50m. The south wall was modified in order to create a doorway into the open area to the south. Both rooms VI and VII had mud and chaff floors. Room VIII was an area lying to the east of rooms VI and VII. Part of the surface of this area was a lime mortar floor with pebbles set into it. The floor survived in a very fragmentary state and, at one time, could well have covered the whole of this room. South of room VIII was an open area containing fragments of wall. The surface of the area south of rooms IX, V, VII and VIII was very mixed. It clearly derived from building destruction debris and contained a lot of rubbish in the form of pottery and glass sherds and bone and tile fragments.

Room IX, west of room V, contained several ovens. The west wall and most of the north and south walls were lost. There was a small doorway (0.80m wide), marked by a threshold of small limestone blocks, in the south-western corner. The ovens were of the shallow bowl-shaped, baked clay variety. The first was 0.26m in diameter and 0.02m deep. The second, 0.70m to the east of the first one, was 0.34m in diameter and considerably deeper, 0.17m. The third oven, lying close to the other two, was 0.42m in diameter and 0.15m deep.

Level 3 Phase 4 (Fig. 22)

In this phase, as in previous phases, the settlement on the mound comprised two separate

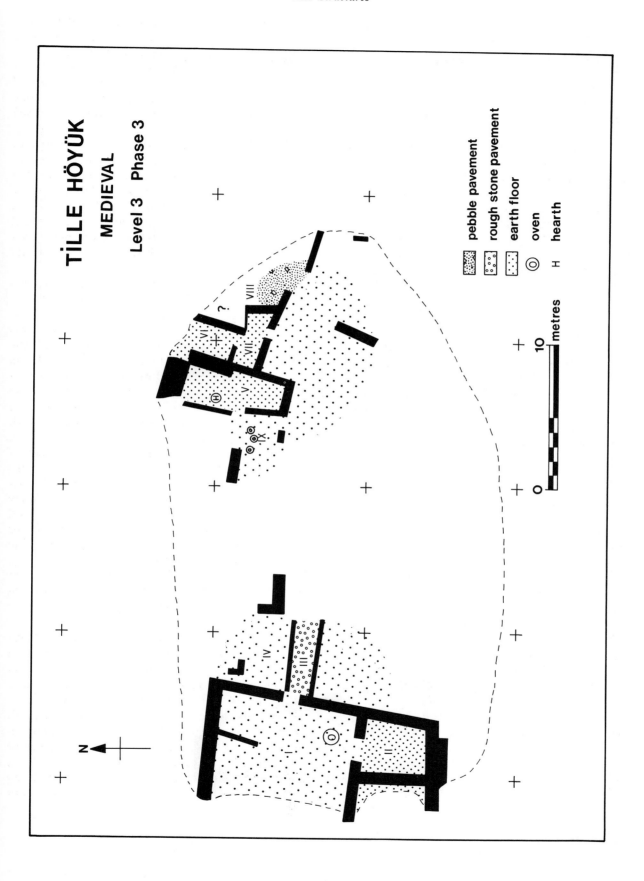

Fig. 21. Level 3 Phase 3, Plan

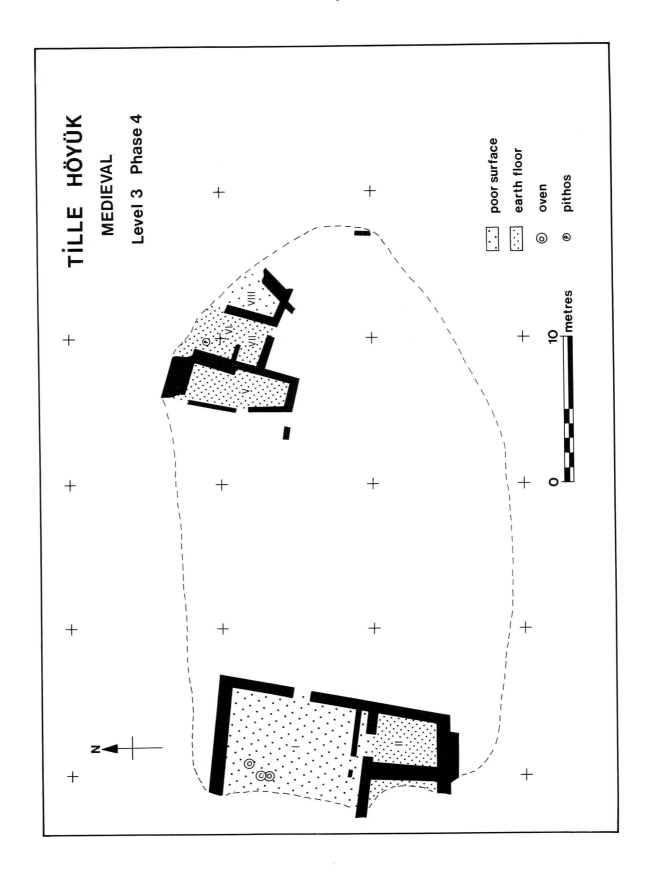

Fig. 22. Level 3 Phase 4, Plan

buildings. Minor changes took place in each. There were only six identifiable rooms.

The courtyard (I) lost the small partition wall in the north of the area. Three *tandır* were built very close to each other. The northern one was 0.53m in diameter and 0.74m deep. The second was 0.60m in diameter and 0.90m deep, the third one was 0.50m in diameter and 0.29m deep. The surface of the courtyard was dark clay loam with an even but sparse distribution of small stones and pebbles. The oven fragment (Fig.74 no.142) was recovered from this surface.

It seems that the north wall of room II was strengthened at this time. A row of limestone blocks, two courses high, was found abutting the east wall of room I, 0.45m north of the northern wall of room II. Between the two was more mud-brick. At the eastern end of the stone face there was a linear feature of clay which marked a sill or threshold for a doorway. To the east of this doorway was a further stretch of mud-brick continuing the new, widened line of the northern wall of room II. The original doorway into room II was blocked with mud-brick. The west wall of the room was also strengthened by the addition of an extra row of mud-brick, 0.40 to 0.50m wide, against the inside face of the wall. The floor was a mud and (?)chaff material.

Room V had a further series of mud and chaff floors laid down during this phase of occupation. Room VI was made wider by the construction of a new east wall. The floor was mud and chaff. A pithos cut into it. The pithos was found to contain eggshell, fragments of a drinking glass and a large jug (Section 2, Fig. 26 [181]). Room VII was made smaller by the construction of the new west wall of room VIII. A further series of thin mud and (?)chaff floors were laid down (Section 2, Fig. 26 [177]). The floor of room VIII was covered with a loam containing small pebbles.

Level 3 Phase 5 (Fig. 23)

As no further structural change occurred in the building on the west side of the mound it has not been included in this phase, although it could still have been in use.

Room I occupied the northern part of Level 3 Phase 4 room V. A new wall butted up against the west wall. It cut through the line of the east wall of the house of the previous phase. The new floor of mud and (?)chaff ran over the section of wall that had been inserted inside the east wall of the room. Hence, the original east wall must have been rebuilt after the inner one had been dismantled. The floor of room II was a lime mortar surface, 0.04 to 0.06m thick, laid over a foundation of cobbles. The foundation was composed of three layers of river pebbles; the edging stones were slightly larger size than those in the middle. This floor stopped at a point where the end of the west wall turned inwards. To the west of this area, there was a spread of dark clay loam, containing a large quantity of rubbish.

Room III had a new east wall. A doorway, 0.66m wide, was formed by a doorstep (a well dressed stone lying on its side); a small stone, on either side and set slightly lower, could have supported a wooden door frame. The floor was mud and chaff. Room IV may well have been a stairway into an upper storey. Between rooms III and VII was a small area (V). This area was separated off from the area to the south by a double row of stones, 0.45m wide, two courses high. The floor of area V was a compacted earth devoid of stones. Room VI was floored with a silty loam containing a few small river pebbles. Room VII had a surface of loamy material.

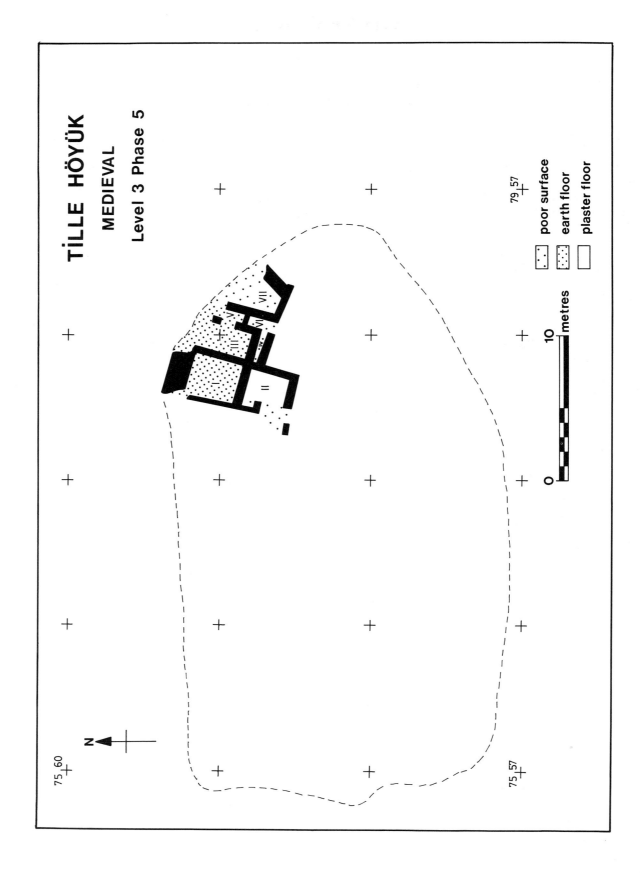

Fig. 23. Level 3, Phase 5, Plan

CHAPTER 5

The Stratigraphy

Three as-drawn sections are published here. They were chosen as the most informative. They run right across the site; one east-west, two north-south (fig. 24).

For each section a list is given showing (1) the period of each deposit, (2) the room in which each deposit was found and (3) any relevant comments. On the sections, the three levels of structures are separated by a thicker line. The original unit numbers are listed against the (unit) numbers used on the published section drawings.

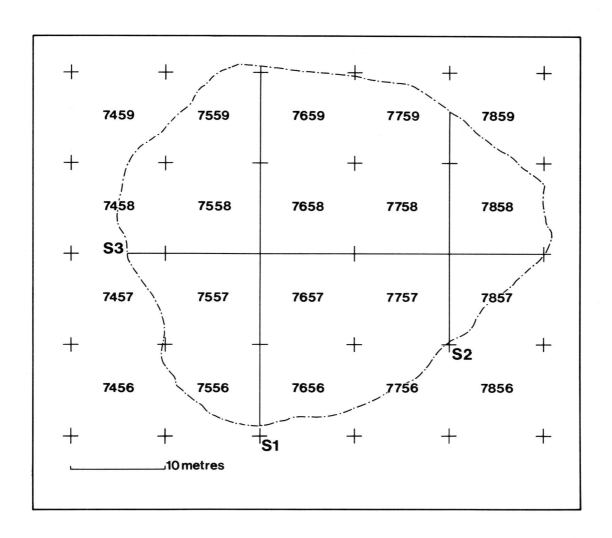

Fig. 24. Location of Sections

57

No.	Orig. Unit No.	Description	Room	Comments

Section 1 (Fig. 25, Plate 6)

Level 1 Phase 1

No.	Orig. Unit No.	Description	Room	Comments
001	7656/113	Surface, cobble	XVI	—
002	7656/096	Wall	XV/XVI	—
003	7656/124	Make-up	—	Late Hellenistic debris levelled to form pre-building surface
004	7656/094	Level 1.1 destruction debris	—	
005	7656/093, 7557/200	Path	XVIII	—
006	7656/091	Level 1.1 destruction debris	—	
007	7657/217	Wall	XII/XX	—
008	7557/225	Surface, poor	XX	—
009	7657/229	Wall	XX/XXI	—
010	7557/224	Pavement, cobble	XXI	Paved area external to rooms XX and VI
011	7557/222	Level 1.1 destruction debris	—	
012	7558/231	Wall	VI/XXI	—
013	7657/200, 7658/253	Level 1.1 destruction debris	—	—
014	7658/259	Small pit	XXI	—
015	7658/261, 7558/228	Surface, pebble	XXI	—
016	7658/220	Wall	III/XXI	—
017	7658/248, 7558/235	Floor	III	—
018	7658/249	Wall	III/II	—
019	7558/244	Post support	II	—
020	7658/251, 7659/137	Floor	II	—
021	7659/133	Wall	II/I	—
022	7659/136, 125	Floor	I	—
023	7659/113	Mud-brick 'bank'	I	Part of perimeter wall
024	7659/128	Perimeter wall	—	
025	—	Debris	—	Decayed material on side of höyük. No surface discernible.
026	7659/132	Revetment	—	Not fully sectioned.

Level 1 Phase 1a

No.	Orig. Unit No.	Description	Room	Comments
027	7557/151	Pit	XVI	Pit cut sometime in Level 1.1

Level 1 Phase 2

No.	Orig. Unit No.	Description	Room	Comments
028	7657/098	Wall	XVII	—
029	7656/083	Wall	XVII	—
030	7556/109	Pit	—	Cut late in Level 2.1 after house XVI/XVII had gone out of use.
031	7556/110	Surface	XIV	
032	7656/070	Wall	XIV	—
033	7656/069, 090 7657/188	Wall	XVII-XVI	Stone footings on mud-brick foundation.
034	7657/175, 154	Surface	XV	—

No.	Orig. Unit No.	Description	Room	Comments
035	7657/128	Wall	X/XV	—
036	7657/150	Level 1.2a destruction debris	—	—
037	7657/162, 163 7658/255	Floor	X	Includes make-up material for surface.
038	7658/149b	Wall	X/VIII	—
039	7658/244, 233, 222	Surface	VIII	Surface and accumulation of occupation debris.
016	7658/220	Wall	III/VIII	Constructed in Level 1.1
040	7658/231	Make-up	III	For floors 041
041	7658/227, 219	Floors	III	—
042	7658/085, lowest course	Wall	III/II	—
043	7658/224, 7659/123	Floor	II	—
021	7659/133	Wall	II/I	Constructed in Level 1.1
044	7659/117	Floor	I	—
023	7659/113	Mud-brick 'bank'	—	Constructed in Level 1.1
024	7659/128	Wall	—	Constructed in Level 1.1
025	—	Debris	—	As in Level 1.1
026	7659/132	Revetment	—	Constructed in Level 1.1

Level 1 Phase 2a

No.	Orig. Unit No.	Description	Room	Comments
045	7657/051	Debris	XVII	From fire at end of Level 1
046	7658/209 part	Debris	III	From fire at end of Level 1
047	7659/108	Debris	II	From fire at end of Level 1
048	7659/108	Debris	I	From fire at end of Level 1

Level 2 Phase 1

No.	Orig. Unit No.	Description	Room	Comments
049	7656/060 part	Surface	XIX	Did not show in section
050	7656/057	Surface	XVIII	—
070	7656/018	Wall	XIX/XVIII	—
051	7656/037	Wall	XVI/XVIII	—
052	7656/038	Wall	XVI/XXI	—
053	7656/030, 7557/121	Wall	XV/XXI	—
054	7656/035	In-fill	XVI	(?)Under stairway
055	?	Make-up	—	For wall 052; includes Level 1.2 mud-brick above wall 033
056	7657/087	Wall	XX/XIII	—
057	7657/150, 127	Floor and make-up	XIII	—
058	7557/115	Wall	XIII/XI	—
059	7657/150, 127	Floor and make-up	XI	—
035	7657/128	Wall	XI/XII	Constructed in Level 1.2
060	7657/131, 7658/252	Floor (part of Level 2.1a)	XII	—
075	7657/128	*Tandır*	XII	—
061	7658/149	Wall	XII/VII	—
062	7658/205	Surface	VII	—
063	7658/189, 111	Wall	VII/VI	—
064	7658/209 part	Floor (part of Level 2.1a)	VI	—
065	7658/085, 066	Wall	VI/II	Wall foundation cut down onto stone footings of wall 042
066	7658/152, 7659/105	Floor	II	—
067	7659/092	Wall	I/I	—
068	7659/099	Floor	I	Subsided into underlying fire debris

No.	*Orig. Unit No.*	*Description*	*Room*	*Comments*
069	7659/093	Perimeter wall	I	Note repair of north face of wall
Level 2 Phase 1a				
049	7656/060 part	Surface	XIX	Individual surfaces not identified
070	7656/018	Wall	XIX/XVIII	Constructed in Level 2.1
071	7656/027	Surface	XVIII	—
051	7656/037	Wall	XVIII/XVI	Constructed in Level 2.1
052	7656/038	Wall	XVI/XLIX	Constructed in Level 2.1
053	7656/030, 7557/121	Wall	XXIV/ XXXXI	Constructed in Level 2.1
056	7657/087	Wall	XX/XIII	Constructed in Level 2.1
072	7657/101 part	Surface	XIII	—
073	7657/101 part	Make-up	XIII	For surface 072 and wall 074
074	7657/074, 056	Wall	XIII/XI	—
076	Not numbered	Make-up	XI	In stairwell
035	7657/128	Wall	XI/XII	Constructed in Level 1.2
083	7657/100, 7658/153	Floor	XII	—
061	7658/149	Wall	XII/VII	Constructed in Level 2.1
077	7658/192	Surface, cobble	VII	—
063	7658/189, 111	Wall	VII/VI	Constructed in Level 2.1
064	7658/209 part	Floor (part of Level 2.1)	VI	—
065	7658/085, 066	Wall	VI/II	Constructed in Level 2.1
078	7658/089, 7659/060, 062	Floor	II	Division of floors for Level 2.1a and 2.2 seen in north section square 7658 (not published)
067	7659/092	Wall	II/I	Constructed in Level 2.1
079	7659/096	Floor	I	—
069	7659/093	Wall	I	Constructed in Level 2.1
088	7659/076	Wall	Tower	—
Level 2 Phase 1b				
049	7656/060 part	Surface	XIX	Did not show in section
070	7656/018	Wall	XIX/XVIII	Constructed in Level 2.1
080	7656/006 part, 7556/022	Surface, cobble	XVIII	Upper part belongs to Level 2.2
051	7656/037	Wall	XVIII/XVI	Constructed in Level 2.1
052	656/038	Wall	XVI/XLIX	—
053	7656/030, 7557/121	Wall	XX/XXI	—
081	7657/092	Floor	XX	Part has subsided
056	7657/087	Wall	XX/XIII	—
082	7657/042 part (that shown on sec.), 7557/077	Surface	XIII	—
074	7657/074, 056	Wall	XIII/XI	Now rebuilt; upper curse of stone footings added
075	7657/128	Stairwell	XI	Same as Level 2.1a
035	7657/128	Wall	XI/XII	Constructed in Level 1.2
093	7657/099, 7658/100	Floor	XII	Includes make-up
061	7658/149	Wall	XII/VII	Constructed in Level 2.1
084	7658/107	Surface, cobble	VII	—
063	7658/189, 111	Wall	VII/VI	Constructed in Level 2.1
085	7658/102	Oven surround	VI	—

No.	*Orig. Unit No.*	*Description*	*Room*	*Comments*
086	7658/195, 106, 110, 194	Debris	VI	In-fill of oven
065	7658/085, 066	Wall	VI/II	Constructed in Level 2.1
078	7658/089, 7659/060, 062	Floor	II	Part of this floor series belongs to Level 2.1a
087	7659/069	Pavement	I	—
069	7659/093	Wall	I	Constructed in Level 2.1
088	659/076	Wall	Tower	Constructed in Level 2.1a

Level 2 Phase 2

049	7656/060 part	Surface	XIX	Did not show in section
089	7656/060	Debris	XIX	Level 2.2 destruction debris
070	7656/018	Wall	XIX/XVIII	Constructed in Level 2.1
080	7656/006 part, 7556/022	Surface, cobble	XVIII	Lower part belongs to Level 2.1b
090	7656/017	Wall	XVIII/XX	—
091	7656/003 part, 7657/091	Surface and make-up	XX	—
091a	7657/047	*Tandır*	XX	—
056	7657/087	Wall	XX/XIII	Constructed in Level 2.1
092	7657/042 part, 7557/048	Surface	XIII	Did not show in section
074	7657/074, 056	Wall	XIII/XI	Constructed in Level 2.1b
108	7657/097, 098, 7658/070 part	Floor and make-up	XI	—
094	7657/137	*Tandır*	XI	—
095	7658/090	Wall	XI/VII	—
096	7658/137, 029	Surface	VII	Series of surfaces
097	7658/096	Destruction debris	VII	Make-up for Level 2.2
098	7658/064	Wall	VI/XV	—
065	7658/085, 066	Wall	VI/II	Constructed in Level 2.1
099	7658/088, 7559/041	Floor	II	—
100	7658/054, 055, 086, 087, 069, 132, 7659/012	Debris	II	From fire at end of Level 2
101	7559/011	Debris	II,I	From levelling of fire debris
102	7659/035, 037, 038	Debris	I	From fire at end of Level 2
103	7659/063	Floor	I	Not distinguishable in section from ash above
069	7659/093	Wall	I	Constructed in Level 2.1

Level 3 Phase 1

104	7656/006	Surface	—	—
090	7656/017	Wall	XIII	Constructed in Level 2.2
105	7656/003 part	?	—	Not distinguished during excavation
106	Not numbered	Robber trench (modern)	XIII/XII	Not noticed during excavation
107	7657/096	Floor	XII	—
074	7657/074, 056	Wall	XII/XI	Constructed in Level 2.1b
116	7657/094, 095, 7658/008	Floor	XI	—
109	7658/050	Wall	XI/X	—
110	?	?	—	Not distinguished during excavation

No.	Orig. Unit No.	Dexcription	Room	Comments
111	7658/070 part	Surface	X	—
112	7658/076	Wall	X	—
113	7656/136, 077 part	Surface	X	Lower part of this deposit
098	7658/064	Wall	VII/VIII	Constructed in Level 2.2
065	7658/085, 066	Wall	VII/II	Constructed in Level 2.1
114	7659/018	Perimeter wall	II	—

Level 3 Phase 2

No.	Orig. Unit No.	Dexcription	Room	Comments
115	7656/033	Surface	—	—
106	Not numbered	Robber trench (modern)	XI	For wall, constructed in Level 3.1
116	7657/094, 095, 7658/008	Floor	XI	Part of this series belongs to Level 3.1
109	7658/050	Wall	XI/XII	—
117	7658/051 part	Wall	XII/X	—
118	7658/052	Surface	X	Lower part of this deposit
098	7658/064	Wall	VII/IX	Constructed in Level 2.2
065	7658/085, 066	Wall	VII/II	Constructed in Level 3.1
114	7659/018	Wall	II	Constructed in Level 3.1

Level 3 Phase 3

No.	Orig. Unit No.	Dexcription	Room	Comments
119	7658/051 part	Wall	III	—
118	658/052	Surface	III	Upper part of deposit
120	7658/076 part	Wall	III/IV	—

Recent

No.	Orig. Unit No.	Dexcription	Room	Comments
106	Not numbered	Robber trench	—	Not seen in excavation
121	7658/134	Cut	—	Not seen in excavation
122	7658/128	Cut	—	Not seen in excavation
123	7656/001, 005, 7657/001,017, 023, 028, 016, 7658/001, 002, 004, 7559/001, 044, 007	Topsoil	—	Includes disturbed material on side of mound

Section 2 (Fig. 26)

Level 1 Phase 1

No.	Orig. Unit No.	Dexcription	Room	Comments
124	7857/095	Pit	XXII	—
125	857/089	Surface	XXII	Includes make-up for earliest Medieval surface
126	7857/086, 7858/185, 205	Surface	XII,XXI	Includes make-up for earliest Medieval surface
127	7857/093	Pit	XII	—
128	?	Debris	XXI	Medieval make-up
129	7858/224	Wall (Hellenistic)	—	—
130	7858/198	Wall	XXVI/XXVII	—
131	7858/203, 7857/043 part	Surface	XXV	—
132	7859/044	Mud-brick 'bank'	XXV	Part of perimeter wall
133	7859/045	Perimeter wall	—	—

Level 1 Phase 2

No.	Orig. Unit No.	Dexcription	Room	Comments
134	7757/095	Hearth	—	—
135	7857/088	Surface and make-up	—	Includes make-up for surface and gateway

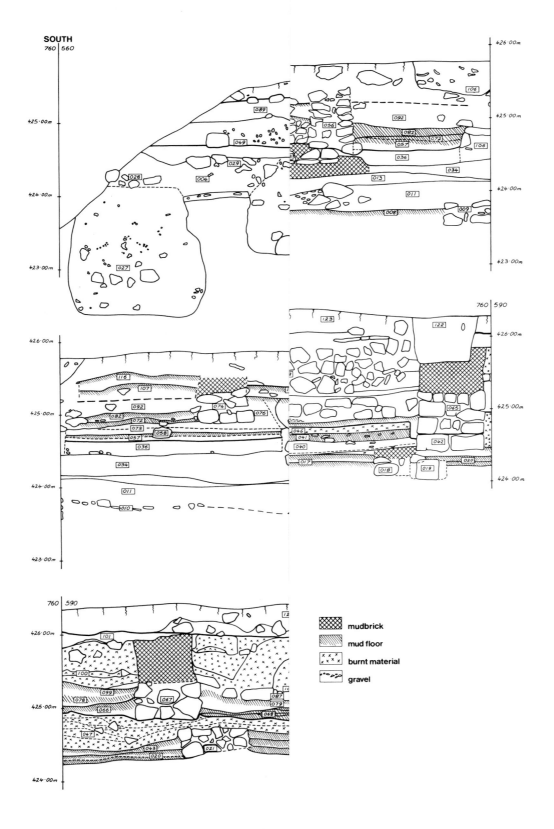

SOUTH
760 | 560

760 | 590

760 | 590

mudbrick

mud floor

burnt material

gravel

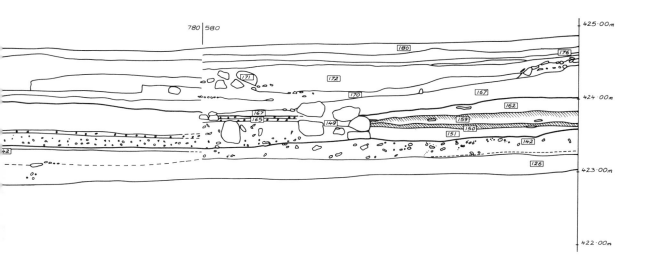

780 | 580

180
176
171
172
170
167
167
162
165
159
149
150
151
142
42
126

425·00m
424·00m
423·00m
422·00m

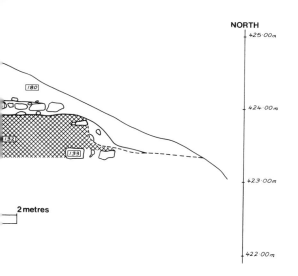

NORTH

180
131
133

2 metres

425·00m
424·00m
423·00m
422·00m

No.	Orig. Unit No.	Description	Room	Comments
136	7857/031	Wall	—	South side of gateway
137	7857/106	Surface	—	Path through gateway
138	7757/114	Column base	—	Part of gateway
139	7857/045	Make-up	—	For north side of gateway
140	7857/037	Wall	XXIX	—
141	7857/023	Wall	XXIX/XXX	—
142	7857/076, 084, 7858/162 part	Surface and make-up	XXIX,XXX	—
130	7858/198	Wall	XXVI/XXVII	Constructed in Level 1.1
143	7858/185, 7859/043 part	Surface and make-up	XXV	—
132	7859/044	Mud-brick 'bank'	XXV	Constructed in Level 1.1
133	7859/045	Wall	—	Constructed in Level 1.1

Level 1 Phase 2a

No.	Orig. Unit No.	Description	Room	Comments
155	7758/234, 7859/036, 037,038	Debris	XXV	From fire at end of Level 1

Level 2 Phase 1

No.	Orig. Unit No.	Description	Room	Comments
144	7857/043	Surface	XLVI	Part of this series of surfaces
136	7857/031	Wall	XLVIII/XLVI	Constructed in Level 1.2
145	7857/033	Surface	XLVIII	—
138	7757/114	Column base	XLVIII	Constructed in Level 1.2
146	7857/077	Drain	XLVIII	—
147	7857/046	Drain kerb and foundation	XLVIII	—
139	7857/045	Make-up	XLVIII	—
140	7857/037	Wall	XLVIII/ XXXIX	Constructed in Level 1.2
148	7757/022	Surface	XXXVIII	—
149	7858/126	Wall	XXXVIII/ XXXIV	—
150	7758/172	Surface	XXXIV	—
151	7858/162 part	Make-up	XXXIV	For 150
152	7758/155	Wall	XXXIV/XXX	—
153	7758/196, 192	Surface	XXX	Includes overlying burnt deposit and make-up for floor and wall 152
154	7758/104	Wall	XXX/XXVII	—
156	7858/152, 7859/035	Floor	XXVII	—
157	7859/011	Bench	XXVII	—
158	7859/020	Perimeter wall	XXVII	—

Level 2 Phase 1a

No.	Orig. Unit No.	Description	Room	Comments
144	7857/043	Surface	XLVI	Part of this series of surfaces
136	7857/031	Wall	XLVIII/XLVI	Constructed in Level 1.2
145	7857/033	Surface	XLVIII	Laid in Level 2.1
138	7757/114	Column base	XLVIII	Erected in Level 1.2
139	7857/045	Make-up	XLVIII	Deposited in Level 1.2
140	7857/037	Wall	XXIX	Constructed in Level 1.2
148	7757/022	Surface	XXXVIII	Part of series of surfaces
149	7858/126	Wall	XXXVIII/ XXXIV	Constructed in Level 2.1
159	7758/156	Floor and make-up	XXXIV	—
152	7758/155	Wall	XXXIV/XXX	Constructed in Level 2.1

No.	Orig. Unit No.	Description	Room	Comments
160	7758/173	Surface, cobble	XXX	—
154	7758/104	Wall	XXX/XXVII	Constructed in Level 2.1
161	7758/116, 7759/031	Floor	XXVII	—
157	7859/011	Bench	XXVII	Constructed in Level 2.1
158	7859/020	Wall	XXVII	Constructed in Level 2.1

Level 2 Phase 1b

No.	Orig. Unit No.	Description	Room	Comments
144	7857/043	Surface	XLVI	Part of this series of surfaces
136	7857/031	Wall	XLVIII/XLVI	Constructed in Level 1.2
145	7857/033	Surface	XLVIII	Laid in Level 2.1
138	7757/114	Column base	XLVIII	Erected in Level 1.2
139	7857/045	Make-up	XLVIII	Deposited in Level 1.2
140	7857/037	Wall	XLVIII/ XXXIX	Constructed in Level 1.2
148	7757/022	Surface	XXXVIII	Part of series of surfaces
149	7858/126	Wall	XXXVIII/ XXXIV	Constructed in Level 2.1
162	7758/154	Surface	XXXIV	?
152	7758/155	Wall	XXXIV/XXX	Constructed in Level 2.1
163	7758/158	Blocking of doorway	XXXIV/XXX	—
154	7758/104	Wall	XXX/XXVII	Constructed in Level 2.1
164	7758/108, 7759/026, 058	Floor	XXVII	Series of surfaces
157	7859/011	Bench	XXVII	Constructed in Level 2.1. Goes out of use during this phase.
158	7859/020	Wall	XXVII	Constructed in Level 2.1

Level 2 Phase 2

No.	Orig. Unit No.	Description	Room	Comments
144	7857/043	Surface	XLVI P	art of this series of surfaces
136	7857/031	Wall	XLVIII/XLVI	Constructed in Level 1.2
145	7857/033	Surface	XLVIII	Laid in Level 2.1
138	7757/114	Column base	XLVIII	Erected in Level 1.2
139	7857/045	Make-up	XLVIII	Deposited in Level 1.2
140	7857/037	Wall	XLVIII/ XXXIX	Constructed in Level 1.2
165	7758/145	Surface	XXXVIII	Only recorded in part
149	7858/126	Wall	XXXVIII/ XXXIV	Constructed in Level 2.1
162	7758/154	Surface	XXXIV	Part of this deposit
152	7758/155	Wall	XXXIV/XXX	Constructed in Level 2.1
163	7758/158	Wall	XXXIV/XXX	Constructed in Level 2.1b
154	7758/104	Wall	XXX/XXVII	Constructed in Level 2.1
166	7758/106, 7759/046, 058 part	Floor	XXVII	—
158	7859/020	Wall	XXVII	Constructed in Level 2.1

Level 3 Phase 1

No.	Orig. Unit No.	Description	Room	Comments
167	7758/095, 079, 126	Surface	XXII	Includes make-up from Level 2 destruction
168	7758/012	Wall	XXII/XX	—
169	7758/096	Floor	XX	—

Level 3 Phase 2

No.	Orig. Unit No.	Description	Room	Comments
170	7758/129, 094, 072	Surface	XXII	—

No.	Orig. Unit No.	Description	Room	Comments
168	7758/012	Wall	XXII/XX	Constructed in Level 3.1
169	7758/096	Floor	XX	(Part of a series)

Level 3 Phase 3

No.	Orig. Unit No.	Description	Room	Comments
171	7758/136	Wall	—	—
172	7758/078, 069, 061	Surface	—	—
168	7758/012	Wall	—	Constructed in Level 3.1
173	7758/096 part	Floor	VII	—
174	7758/098	Floor	VI	—
175	7758/059	Wall	VII/VI	—

Level 3 Phase 4

No.	Orig. Unit No.	Description	Room	Comments
172	7758/078, 069, 061	Surface	—	As in Level 3.3
168	7758/012	Wall	—	Constructed in Level 3.1
176	7758/067, 032	Floor and make-up	VII	—
177	7758/028	Floor and make-up	VI	—
181	7759/052	Pot	VI	—

Level 3 Phase 5

No.	Orig. Unit No.	Description	Room	Comments
176	7758/067, 032	Surface	—	—
168	7758/012	Wall	IV	Constructed in Level 3.1
177	7758/028	Robber trench (modern)	IV/III	—
178	7758/037	Floor	III	—

Recent

No.	Orig. Unit No.	Description	Room	Comments
179	7857/025	Debris	—	Post Level 2.2
180	7857/001, 002 7758/001, 011, 7759/001, 002	Topsoil	—	—

Section 3 (Fig. 27)

Level 1 Phase 1

No.	Orig. Unit No.	Description	Room	Comments
182	7458/010	Surface	—	—
183	7557/209	Wall	IX	—
184	7557/212	Wall	X	—
185	7557/213	Surface, cobble	VI	—
186	7558/no number	Surface, cobble	VI	—
187	7658/no number	Wall	—	Includes make-up and accumulation of occupation debris
188	7658/283, 253, 281, 291, 337, 338, 333, 253, 7558/244, 294, 281, 278, 260	Surface	—	
189	7658/339	Pit	—	—
190	7658/332	Pit	—	—
191	7658/299	Pit	—	—
192	7758/247	*tandır*	—	—
193	7757/127, 7758/282	Pit	—	—
194	7757/119, 7858/214 part, 211 part, 209	Surface and make-up	—	—

No.	*Orig. Unit No.*	*Description*	*Room*	*Comments*
Level 1 Phase 2				
195	7458/053, 065, 084, 079, 7558/198	Surface	—	Includes Level 1.1 destruction debris
196	7558/262	Pit	—	—
197	7558/191	Wall	X	—
198	7558/201 part, 7658/244	Floor	X	—
200	7658/239	Wall	X	—
201	7658/218	Wall	XI	—
202	7658/237	Floor	XI	—
203	7758/026	Wall (mod. robber trench)	XI/XXIX	—
204	7758/230	Surface and make-up	XXIX	—
205	7758/249	Wall	XXIX/XXX	—
206	7858/162 part, 185, 214, 205, 207, 190	Surface	XXX	Includes make-up and accumulation of material
207	7858/179	Pit	XXX	—
208	7858/178	Pit	XXX	—
209	7858/171	Debris	XXX	Part of make-up
Level 1 Phase 2a				
199	7558/210 part, 7658/232	Destruction debris	X	—
210	7658/203, 204	Fire destruction debris	XI	—
Level 2 Phase 1				
211	7457/012 part	Floor	IX	—
212	7458/080, 7558/207, 206	Wall	IX/X	—
213	7558/188, 7557/068, 069	Floor and make-up	X	—
214	7558/128, 147	Wall	X/V	—
215	7558/045	Wall	V/XI	—
216	7558/186	Surface	XI	—
197	7558/191	Wall	XI/XII	Constructed in Level 1.2
217	7558/186, 7658/205	Floor	XII	—
218	7658/148	Wall	XII/VIII	Cut down into Level 1.2 debris
219	7658/205	Surface	VIII	(Lower part)
220	7658/146	Wall	VIII/XXVI	Built on top of Level 1.2 wall
221	7658/202	Floor	XXVI	—
203	7758/026	Wall	XXVI/ XXVIII	Constructed in Level 1.2
222	7757/053	Cistern	XXIX	Slightly over-cut near bottom, some earlier stratigraphy shown. Not bottomed.
223	7758/168	Wall (mod. robber trench)	XXIX/XXVIII, XXXIII	—
224	7758/162	Wall	XXII/ XXXVIII	—
225	7758/187	Surface and make-up	XXXVIII	—
226	7858/125	Surface and make-up	XXXIX	—

No.	Orig. Unit No.	Description	Room	Comments
227	7858/073	Wall	XXXIX/ XXXVI	—
228	7857/034	Surface	XXXVII	—

Level 2 Phase 1a

No.	Orig. Unit No.	Description	Room	Comments
229	7457/012 part	Surface	IX	—
212	7458/080, 7558/207, 206	Wall	IX/X	Constructed in Level 2.1
230	7557/034	Floor	X	—
214	7558/128, 147	Wall	X/V	Constructed in Level 2.1
215	7558/045	Wall	X/XI	Constructed in Level .1
231	7558/144, 136	Surface	XI	—
197	7558/191	Wall	XI/XII	Constructed in Level .2
217	7558/186, 7658/205	Floor	XII	Part of this series belongs to Level 2.1
218	7658/148	Wall	XII/VII	Constructed in Level 2.1
219	7658/205	Surface	VII	Part belongs to Level 2.1
220	7658/146	Wall	VIII/XXVI	Constructed in Level .1
221	7658/202	Surface	XXVI	Part of this series belongs to Level 2.1
203	7758/026	Wall	XXVI/ XXVIII	Constructed in Level 1.2
222	7757/053	Cistern	XXIX	Constructed in Level 2.1
223	7758/168	Wall	XXIX/XXVIII XXXII	Constructed in Level 2.1
224	7758/162	Wall	XXXII/ XXXVIII	Constructed in Level 2.1
225	7758/187	Surface	XXXVIII	Part of this series belongs to Level 2.1
226	7858/125	Surface	XXXIX	Part of this series belongs to Level 2.1
227	7858/73	Wall	XXXIX/ XXXVI	Constructed in Level 2.1
228	7857/034	Surface	XXXVII	Part of this series belongs to Level 2.1

Level 2 Phase 1b

No.	Orig. Unit No.	Description	Room	Comments
232	7558/116	Surface	IX	—
212	7458/080, 7558/207, 206	Wall	IX/X	Constructed in Level 2.1
230	7557/034	Floor	X	Part of this series belongs to Level 2.1
214	7558/128, 147	Wall	X/V	Constructed in Level 2.1
215	7558/045	Wall	X/XI	Constructed in Level 2.1
232	7558/116	Floor	XI	—
197	7558/191	Wall	XI/XII	Constructed in Level 1.2
233	7658/153	Floor and make-up	XII	—
218	7658/148	Wall	XI	Constructed in Level 2.1
234	7658/107	Surface	VIII	—
220	7658/146	Wall	VIII/LVI	Constructed in Level 2.1
235	7658/184	Surface	LVI	—
236	7658/147, 155, 188	Wall	LVI/LVII	—
237	7658/186	Surface	LVII	—
238	7658/183	Wall	LVII/LVIII	—
239	7658/187	Surface	LVIII	—

No.	Orig. Unit No.	Description	Room	Comments
203	7758/026	Wall	LVIII/XXVIII	Constructed in Level 1.2
222	7757/053	Cistern	XXIX	Constructed in Level 2.1
223	7758/168	Wall	XXIX/XXVIII XXXII	Constructed in Level 2.1
224	7758/162	Wall	XXIX/XXVIII XXXII	—
225	7758/187	Surface	XXXVIII	Part of this series belongs to Level 2.1a
240	7858/117	Wall	XXXVIII/LII	—
241	7558/153	Surface	LII	—
227	7858/073	Wall	LII/XXXVI	Constructed in Level 2.1
228	7857/034	Surface	XL	Part of this series belongs t to Level 2.1a

Level 2 Phase 2

No.	Orig. Unit No.	Description	Room	Comments
232	7558/116	Surface	IX	Part of this series belongs to Level 2.1
212	7458/080, 7558/207, 206	Wall	IX/X	Constructed in Level 2.1
230	7557/034	Floor	X	Part of this series belongs to Level 2.1a
241	7558/153	Threshold	XVI/X	Raising of floor height of Level 2.1–2.1b doorway
214	7558/128, 147	Wall	X/XVI	Constructed in Level 2.1
215	7558/045	Wall	X/XI	Constructed in Level 2.1
242	7558/117, 118, 7658/100	Surface	XI	Includes room furniture and floor make-up
243	7558/123	Brace	XI	Strengthening of NW corner of room
244	7558/104 part, 7658/070	Debris	XI	Level 2 destruction debris
245	7658/091	Wall	XI/VIII	—
246	7658/029	Surface	VIII	—
247	7658/031, 082	Clay feature	VIII	—
220	7658/146	Wall	VIII/XXVI	Constructed in Level 2.1
248	7658/150	Floor	XXVI	—
236	7658/147, 155, 188	Wall	XXVI	Constructed in Level 2.1b
249	7658/150	Floor	XXVI	—
250	7658/151	Destruction debris	XXVI	—
203	7758/026	Wall	XXVI/XXVIII	Constructed in Level 2.1
222	7757/053	Cistern	XXIX	Constructed in Level 2.1
223	7758/168	Wall	XXIV/XXVIII, XXXI	Constructed in Level 2.1
224	7758/162	Wall	XXXI/XXXVIII	Constructed in Level 2.1
251	7758/145	Surface	XXXVIII	—
240	7858/117	Wall	XXXVIII/LII	—
252	7858/092	Surface	LII	—
253	7857/011	Surface	XL	—

Level 3 Phase 1

No.	Orig. Unit No.	Description	Room	Comments
254	7458/004	Surface	—	—
212	7458/080, 7558/207, 206	Wall	VI	Constructed in Level 2.1

No.	Orig. Unit No.	Description	Room	Comments
255	7559/208, 209, 7558/104 part	Floor	VI	—
241	7558/153	Threshold	VI/V	Constructed in Level 2.2
214	7558/128, 147	Wall	VI/V	Constructed in Level 2.1
215	7558/045	Wall	VI/XI	Constructed in Level 2.1
256	7558/104 part, 7658/008	Surface	XI	—
257	7658/130	Wall (mod. robber trench)	XI/IX	—
258	7658/056	Surface	IX	—
259	7658/046	Wall	IX/XV	Modern robber trench for part of 260
260	7658/013	Wall	IX/XV	—
261	7657/013	Surface	XV	—
262	7758/146	Wall	XV/XVII	—
222	7757/053	Cistern	XVII	Constructed in Level 2.1
223	7758/168	Wall	XVII/XVI	Constructed in Level 2.1
263	7758/130	Wall	XVI/XXII	—
264	7758/095	Surface	XXII	—
240	7858/117	Wall	XXII/XXIV	—
265	7857/021	Surface	XXIV	—
266	7857/018	Threshold	XXIV	—
267	7857/010	Surface	XXIII	—

Level 3 Phase 2

No.	Orig. Unit No.	Description	Room	Comments
254	7458/004	Surface	—	—
212	7458/080, 7558/207, 206	Wall	VI	Constructed in Level 2.1
268	Not numbered	Floor	VI	—
241	7558/153	Threshold	VI/V	Constructed in Level 2.2
214	7558/128, 147	Wall	VI/V	Constructed in Level 2.1
215	7558/045	Wall	VI/XI	Constructed in Level 2.1
269	7558/044	Surface	XI	—
257	7658/130	Wall	XI/IX	Constructed in Level 3.1
259	7658/046	Wall	IX/XV	Constructed in Level 3.1
260	7658/013	Wall	IX/XV	Constructed in Level 3.1
262	7758/146	Wall	XV/XVII	Constructed in Level 3.1
222	7757/053	Cistern	XVII	Constructed in Level 2.1
223	7758/168	Wall	XVII/XVI	Constructed in Level 2.1
270	7758/129	urface	XVI	—
271	7758/079, 121	Make-up	XVI	—

Level 3 Phase 3

No.	Orig. Unit No.	Description	Room	Comments
212	7458/080, 7558/207, 206	Wall	II	Constructed in Level 2.1
268	Not numbered	Floor	II	Part of this series belongs to Level 3.2
241	7558/153	Threshold	I/II	Constructed in Level 2.2
214	7558/128, 147	Wall	II/I	Constructed in Level 2.1
215	7558/045	Wall	II	Constructed in Level 2.1
272	7758/136	Wall	—	—

Level 3 Phase 4

No.	Orig. Unit No.	Description	Room	Comments
212	7458/080, 7558/207, 206	Wall	II	Constructed in Level 2.1

No.	Orig. Unit No.	Description	Room	Comments
273	7557/009	Wall	II	Strengthening of 212
214	7558/128, 147	Wall	II/I	Constructed in Level 2.1
215	7558/045	Wall	II	—

Recent

No.	Orig. Unit No.	Description	Room	Comments
274	7458/001, 7558/001,002, 017, 7658/001, 002, 004, 008, 007, 010, 7758/001, 032, 071, 075, 078, 7857/001, 002, 003, 016, 005	Topsoil	—	—
275	7558/145	Pit	—	—
257	7658/130	Robber trench	—	—
259	7658/046	Robber trench	—	—
203	7758/026	Robber trench	—	—
276	7758/166, 276, 071, 075, 032, 001	Robber trench	—	(Excavated spits drawn at this point before feature was recognized.)

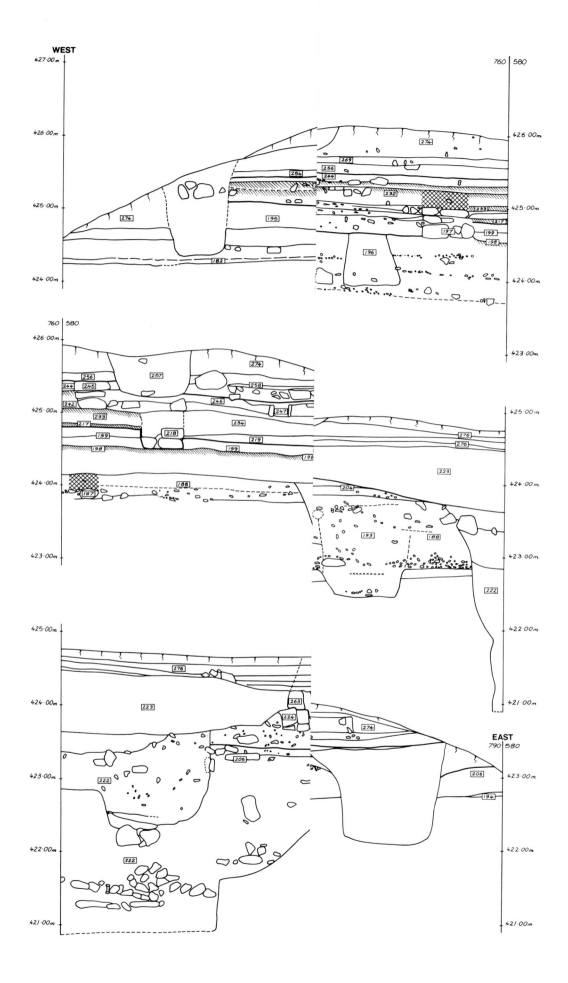

CHAPTER 6

The Pottery

The choice and range of pottery as published here is a consequence of a policy decision taken early in the excavation (outlined above, pp.14 and 15). No attempt has been made to divide the pottery into the different architectural levels. The coarse-ware has been grouped according to form while the glazed wares have been divided according to technique and colour. Although there is very little published material of this date in our area, certain parallels were found with the pottery at Aşvan, Hama and Antakya (Antioch). It is our belief that the pottery presented in this volume will be of greater use when the Medieval material from other sites in the Lower Euphrates Project is published. A detailed study of the Medieval pottery of the area may then be made. More important, we hope, from other sites will be the coin evidence which can be used for an area study.

It is presumed that the bulk of the pottery was of local origin although not made at Tille and that the imported wares came from the major site ([?]market) at Samosata where identical types have been found. Three glazed wasters or, more likely, seconds, were noticed: nos 275, 301 and 357 (below p.74).

Local Ware

Large Jars

The large one- or two-handled, tall, narrow-necked jars (nos 3-15) were very common. These often had an orange or dull red slip with or without orange to red paint decoration. Similar jars were found at Aşvan (Mitchell 1980: nos 1175, 1179, 1216, 1220, 1261).

Jars and Jugs

There was a wide range of jars including narrow tall-necked shapes both with flaring and with straight mouths. Some of the trefoil- and quatre-foil-mouthed jars (e.g. nos 25, 28) had applied 'eyes' on either side of the spout. These 'eyes' were found on two of the coarse lamps (cf. type 186 and 187). There were numerous squat wide-mouthed jugs. The decoration on the jugs varied enormously: incised lines, impressed marks, combed decoration, applied pellets and painted vertical streaks and spots. The cross-section of the handles again varied: rounded, oval and square. On the top of (at least) half the handles were applied knobs, ridges or occasionally 'worms' (nos 31, 36).

Cooking Pots

There were two very common types of cooking pots. One was made in an orange, very gritty fabric (nos 49, 54, 55, 58, 60, 80–84). The majority of these had orange to red painted decoration, mostly in the form of vertical streaks and spots. The painting was combined with combed decoration, incised lines and impressed marks. The other form of cooking pot, which was more common than the above, had a granular fabric, either reduced or oxidized (mostly reduced), with numerous inclusions (nos 85–96). These pots generally had applied decoration in the form of horizontal lines, wavy lines or inverted 'V's. Usually there was impressed decoration at the base of the neck. Occasionally the lower edge of the rim was notched. In the majority of cases there was a ridge on the top of the handle, sometimes with an applied 'worm'.

Red Burnished Ware

In a red ware, with or without a bright red slip, the common shape was a bowl; some of these were burnished on the exterior. These common bowls mostly came from the later Level 2 and Level 3 deposits. The bowls nos 266–268 were not a common shape.

Coarse Ware

Bowls in this ware did not seem to be very common on the site. Probably over half of them had handles (nos 104, 106, 109, 111–116, 122).

White and Buff Ware

The white wares (nos 130-136) were somewhat rare although several small pieces of the highly decorative moulded type (no.132) were found in the Level 3 deposits. The highly decorative buff sherd (no.137) was the only example found; only a few sherds with stamped design (nos 146, 150) were discovered.

Glazed Wares

Of the five sherds (found at Tille) with a rich

brown glaze, three (two jugs and one bowl) are published here (nos 210-212). Although the sherds came from contexts throughout the Medieval occupation it is likely that they originate in Level 1 and that the others are strays—indeed no.210 came from the stone footing of a wall. The vessels (jars and bowls) (nos 213–219) all had a very poor turquoise glaze that in most cases had decayed and had flaked off in patches from the fabric.

There are a few sherds with an all-over glaze without a slip (nos 274–277, all bowls); those with an all-over glaze on a white slip (nos 278–285, all bowls) came only from the back-fill of the cistern (Level 3.3–3.5).

Cups

The glazed cups (nos 220–238) came in a variety of colours, turquoise-blue being the most common. The other colours of the glazes were dull red, white, clear, black to brown, dull blue, bright blue and green. Similar cups were found at Aşvan (Mitchell 1980: nos 736, 737, 739, 744). The cups (nos 241–243) were mostly covered with a bright blue glaze but were also found in a patchy blue and white glaze. Again this type was found at Aşvan (Mitchell 1980: nos 731, 732, 734, 738, 740).

Bowls

The common bowls (nos 245–265) had several different finishes. The most common finish was a dark brown to black glaze, on a white slip, on the interior and also on the outer rim where the glaze had sometimes dripped down the outside. Many of these bowls had a turquoise or green glaze; some of them had various coloured slips (light grey, reddish brown, brown) over the interior and upper exterior. The potter's mark, found on two examples only (nos 272–273), is associated with the bowls nos 245–265. These bowls are similar to some found at Aşvan (Mitchell 1980: nos 789, 808, 1063, 1065, 1067, 1073, 1075, 1079, 1081, 1224–1240).

Sgraffiato Ware

The sgraffiato wares (nos 286–299, all bowls) mostly came from the back-fill of the cistern (Level 3.3–3.5) but others were present in the final Medieval deposits (Level 3.3–3.5). The absence of this type of pottery from the occupation deposits at Tille Höyük is one of the more puzzling aspects of the site. From observations of the Medieval levels underlying the present village, the sgraffiato wares are there very common. The back-filling of the cistern appears to have

been deliberate. The material for this operation, therefore, was brought from the foot of the mound. For a comment on the distribution of sgraffiato wares in the area, see Mitchell 1980: 75. While Tille did not produce enough sgraffiato wares to make a worthwhile comment, our piece no.288 is very similar to Aşvan no.676.

Syrian Glazed Wares

The other glazed pottery seems mostly to have come from Syria, 'la faience locale ancienne' of the Hama report and Raqqa. The blood-red (manganese) wares (category B VI f from Hama) are generally over-painted in lustre (nos 300–303). In several cases the lustre is very worn making it difficult to detect and to identify the pattern (no.303).

Double Glaze Ware

There are several sherds that appear to be decorated and to have a double glaze: a sandwich glaze painted ware. This possibility is mentioned at Antioch on the Orontes (Waag 1948: 92) in connection with the blue-and-black decoration under a colourless glaze. There it is said that the designs 'lay on a vitrified layer' (whether this is a slip, a lower layer of glaze or simply the vitrified surface of the body is not apparent). In our cases a slip is unlikely but the possibility remains that it is the vitrified surface of the fabric, although we favour a lower layer of glaze, especially in nos 305, 346. We have not been able to make tests in order to resolve the problem. Two pieces appear to have polychrome decoration between two layers of clear glaze. One (no.346) is decorated in black, blue and red. A second (no.305) also has traces of a fourth colour, green. While the decorative style of the latter is similar to the Raqqa wares found at Hama (Figs 540–542) (flowers reserved in white against a dark background), the use of three and four colours is more akin to the late thirteenth century wares whose production centre has not been identified (Porter 1981). The other double glazes are all of the black-under-blue style (black or dark blue under turquoise glaze). There seems to be a layer of all-over clear glaze covering the vessels before the decoration was applied; a blue glaze was then added on top. While one sherd (no.308) has only a partial blue glaze, perhaps the result of wear, several sherds (nos 309–313, 315–317) have an all-over blue glaze. Although this all-over blue glaze is generally a very thin layer, one example (no.312) is covered with a thick coating of the blue glaze. Other pieces in the black-under-blue style do not have this lower layer of glaze, the black being painted directly onto the fabric of the vessel (nos 314, 318). This style of decoration is very similar to pieces found at Antioch on the Orontes (Waag 1948), cp. Tille no.314 with Antioch Fig.51 no.8, Tille no.316 with Antioch fig. 51 no.10.

Under-Glaze Ware

The under-glaze decorated wares come in a variety of colours: lustre under clear glaze (nos 319 and 338); two-tone green under clear glazed (no.320); brown under pale green to clear glaze (nos 321 and 322); cobalt-blue under clear glaze (no.342) and reddish brown, light blue and dark blue (the light blue being applied over the reddish brown) under a clear glaze with blue tinge (no.345). The last has a decorative style similar to Aşvan no.880 (Mitchell 1980). Three sherds illustrated have under-glaze decoration: green under clear glaze (no.323) and cobalt-blue under clear glaze (nos 330, 337) but have lustre decoration painted near the glaze.

'Tell Minis' Ware

The so-called 'Tell Minis' wares, characterized by a frit body, tin or plain alkaline glaze and lustre painting (Porter 1981) are represented at Tille Höyük by several pieces (nos 324–327, Pl. 7). One example (no.324) (Pl.7a) has the characteristic leaves with a roundel in the well. Another (no.325) (Pl.7b), although the lustre is rather worn, has crescent moons separated by triangles. On both these sherds, fine details have been scratched through the lustre. The other two (nos 326, 327) have been divided into panels. The first (no.326) (Pl.7c), where the sherd is just large enough for the whole of the decoration to be restored, has three large panels of triangles and horizontal lines and three smaller panels containing dots and squiggles. The fourth sherd (no.327), of which half of the body is present, has two equal-sized panels, one of which has a floral design painted in reserve while the other triangular-shaped panel (distorted in the drawing) has degenerate half moons containing a dot in each angle with a cross between the top two. In the centre of this panel, there is again a pair of half moons surrounding a 'blob' while the background is covered in dots. Although the shape of the bowl (no.327), with its flat rim, is similar to the Raqqa forms, the fabric, glaze and lustre is the same as the other three. All four probably come from the same production centre. It is possible that the manganese glaze (no.302) is also of

the 'Tell Minis' variety; the fine detail scratched through the lustre is similar. A 'Tell Minis' bowl with manganese-purple glaze is known to have been produced (Poulsen 1970). It is interesting to note that the 'Tell Minis' sherd (no.324) was found in the same context as a Raqqa piece (no.335).

Of the other vessels over-painted with lustre, several pieces (nos 328, 335, 339 and 344) have a thick glaze with a green tinge characteristic of the Raqqa wares. Two of the sherds (nos 328 and 335) have a green lustre; one (no.335) also has a gold-coloured lustre line on the top of the rim. Two sherds (nos 340 and 341) have a distinctly yellowish white fabric; the all-over clear glaze was over-painted in green lustre. I have called the green decoration on some pieces (nos 328, 335, 340 and 341) a lustre although it does not really give a shiny effect. My reason for this usage is based on the suggestion that the green colour is probably achieved by the application of copper but for some reason the copper did not give a true lustre effect.

Lustre decoration was found on other colour glazes: blue (nos 329 and 334) and cobalt-blue (no.336). The only other over-painted piece was the jar (no.350) which had all-over white glaze with traces of red decoration on the exterior. The cobalt-blue lustre piece (no.336) may have been imported from Damascus (Lane 1962).

Monochrome Glaze

Monochrome glazes were found in several varieties: all-over cobalt-blue (nos 331 and 332), all-over white (nos 348 and 349) and (on the interior only) clear (no.343). Incised wares were present in cobalt-blue (nos 351 and 354) and white (nos 352, 353 and 355). One sherd (no.306) had an all-over white glaze with an all-over brown glaze on the interior and patches of a green glaze on the exterior. The fabric for this piece was orange in colour. Two sherds (nos 356 and 357) probably came from the same vessel; they have a clear glaze on the interior, manganese, white, cobalt-blue and copper to yellow glazes on the external segments. The green-tinged glaze on the divided dish (no.358) is similar to the Raqqa glazes.

Lamps

Lamps fitted into three categories: coarse rounded (nos 184–189), elongated (nos 190-192) some of which had a dark brown to black glaze in the interior and round (nos 193–196) with a bee-hive boss and with an all-over blue glaze. The latter category all came from the earlier half of the occupation period while the dark brown to black glazed elongated lamps only occurred in the later half of the period. The coarse rounded category were found throughout the occupation. The round lamps with a bee-hive boss were found at Hama but were unglazed (Poulsen 1957: 279) and at Aşvan (Mitchell 1980: 189).

The large vessel (no.198) and the pot stand (no.197) came from the bath-house (pp.37 and 38). The pithos illustrated (no.199) was the only complete or near complete example as was the barrel-shaped vessel (no.200).

'Grenades'

The 'grenades' (nos 201–203 [?]and 204) are found on most Medieval sites in this region. There is extensive literature about their possible use (Lane 1947; Seyrig 1959; Ettinghausen 1965; Rogers 1969) although the example found at Samarra (Iraq Government 1940: 3) does seem to end the argument—as wine containers. The interesting feature about no.203 is that it does not have a hole. I may have interpreted this sherd incorrectly: it could be a base. The angular sherd (no.204) has been included in this category since I do not know to what other category it could belong.

Wasters

The discovery of three 'wasters' at Tille (nos 275, 301 and 357) is perhaps a significant warning for future survey work. Although it is possible that there were kilns at Tille, some badly formed vessels were, we suggest, sold as 'seconds' (cheap rejects), even though the distance from production centre to market is large. Certainly the manganese glaze (no.301) is Syrian. One would imagine that the local distributive centre was Samsat, 50km. downstream. The pottery from Syria, if it came up the Euphrates route from Syria to Samsat, could have been distributed locally from there.

List of Abbreviations used in Catalogues

D	=	diameter	H	=	height
RD	=	rim diameter	L	=	length
BD	=	base diameter	W	=	width
De	=	depth	TH	=	thickness
avg.	=	average	max.	=	maximum
min.	=	minimum	est.	=	estimated

Pottery Catalogue

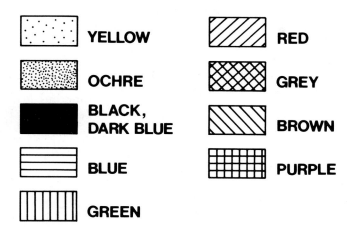

Colour scheme for pottery drawings

All drawings are at 1:4 unless otherwise stated. All measurements are in metres.

Colour conventions used in the drawings are as shown above. It should be noted that the drawings of glazed wares, and particularly those with lustre painting (Figs 51–53), occasionally depart from these conventions in order to ensure a clear representation of pattern.

Fig. 28

1. 7557/033/01/024. One-handled jar. Orange to brown fabric with large grit inclusions. Decoration: series of ridges on neck; incised, linear and curvilinear decoration on shoulder. Applied 'worm' motif on handle. RD 0.10. Level 3.1–3.2.

2. 7758/201/01/179. One-handled jug. Red to brown fabric, core brown, many large inclusions, hard. Decoration: ridge on upper neck; incised linear and curvilinear on lower neck. Small knob on top of handle. RD 0.065. Level 1.2a.

3. 7558/028/01/023. Two-handled jar. Mid-orange fabric, moderate amount of grit inclusions. Dark orange slip on exterior. Incised band on neck. RD 0.115, H 0.483. Level 3.4.

4. 7656/041/01/028. Two-handled jar. Orange fabric, moderate amount of grit inclusions. Traces of red paint on exterior. Decoration: incised linear and curvilinear decoration on neck below rim and below top of handles. RD 0.105. Level 2.1–2.2.

5. 7658/046/01/036. (?)-handled jar. Dark orange fabric, many inclusions; fine to very large; mica, grit, shell, water-worn pebbles. Combed decoration below rim and on lower neck. RD 0.12. Modern robber trench.

6. 7656/41/01/028. Two-handled jar. Pale orange fabric with occasional large grit. Orange to red paint on rim and handles. Thumb impression on lower handle. RD 0.09. Level 2.1–2.2.

Fig. 29

7. 7857/059/02/003. Two-handled jar. Buff fabric with moderate amounts of grit and micaceous inclusions. Decoration: incised lines on shoulder/neck angle and shoulder/body angle; ridge of top on neck; stripes of red paint on shoulder and body. RD 0.09. Level 2.1a.

8. 7757/009/01/010. One- or two- handled jar. Orange to grey fabric with many fine inclusions. Ridge on upper neck. RD 0.10. Level 3.1–3.2.

9. 7858/178/01/141. One-handled jug. Grey fabric with some grit inclusions. Traces of brown to red slip on exterior. Decoration: on shoulder two incised lines becoming three lines in places. Knob on top of handle. RD 0.063. Level 1.2.

10. 7757/009/01/010. One-handled, jug. Dull orange fabric, hard, with many mica and grit inclusions. Ridge on upper neck. RD 0.08. Level 3.1–3.2.

11. 7858/184/01/144. Jar. Inner and external fabric red to brown, core grey. Many grit inclusions of mixed size. Incised lines on top of shoulder. RD 0.16. Level 1.1.

12. 7858/184/01/144. One-handled jug. Buff fabric with moderate quantity of medium-sized grit inclusions, some mica. Red slip over exterior. On upper neck incised horizontal lines. RD 0.085. Level 1.1.

13. 7458/024/01/011. Two-handled jar. Light grey fabric with occasional inclusions. Orange slip on exterior. Incised lines below rim and two raised ridges on top of shoulder. Base found (not illustrated): flat. RD 0.085, BD 0.13. Level 2.2.

14. 7558/091/01/074. Two-handled jar. Orange fabric with occasional fine inclusions and grit. Combed decoration at top of neck and top of shoulder. Raised band round neck at level of top of handles. RD 0.105. Level 3.2.

Fig. 30

15. 7457/003/02/003. Two-handled jar. Red to orange fabric containing many coarse grit inclusions. (0.003 to 0.005). Decoration: two incised bands on shoulder; six incised lines at top of neck. Small applied knob on top of handles. All over red wash. RD 0.10, H 0.443. Level 2.1.

16. 7458/076/02/011. One-handled juglet. Pale red fabric. All-over green glaze on white slip. RD 0.025. H 0.075. Level 1.1.

17. 7558/045/02/006. One-handled jug. Brown and reddish brown fabric with numerous varied inclusions. Reddish brown wash. Decoration: horizontal row of pellets; on upper body, around neck where handle joins; vertical line of pellets down handle with one large pellet at top of handle. RD 0.0435, BD 0.072, H 0.24. Level 2.1b.

18. 7556/092/02/013. One-handled jug. Red to orange fabric with many grit inclusions, hard. Incised decoration on upper body, two faint lines on mid-body. BD 0.075. Level 1.2.

19. 7858/141/02/004. One-handled jug. Bright orange fabric with numerous grit inclusions, hard. Dark orange slip on exterior. Incised and impressed decoration. BD 0.11. Level 2.1a.

20. 7758/106/02/015. Handleless jar. Buff fabric with occasional grits, soft. Pale red slip on exterior. Incised decoration. Body built on base. BD 0.15. Level 2.2.

21. 7658/310/02/024. Two-handled jar. Pink to orange fabric with numerous inclusions, both fine and large. White slip on exterior. BD 0.052. Level 1.1.

22. 7756/093/02/006. Handleless jar. Internal and external fabric red, core black grey, with numerous grit, mica and chaff inclusions. Very brittle. Remnants of red slip on upper body. Impressed decoration around mid-body. BD 0.09. Level 1.2.

Fig. 31

23. 7759/053/02/005. One-handled jug. Yellowish orange to grey fabric with occasional fine grits. Red slip with occasional mica. Incised decoration. BD 0.09. Level 3.4.

24. 7558/060/01/085. One-handled jug. Buff fabric with numerous grits (small and medium sized) and mica. Incised and combed decoration. Level 3.1.

25. 7658/138/02/010. Jug. Trefoil mouth. Brown and red to brown fabric with numerous inclusions. Reddish brown wash. At top of handle a 'fin'. In each angle of trefoil: a pellet eye. RD 0.045, BD 0.06, H 0.162. Level 1.2.

26. 7757/038/02/005. Jug. Trefoil mouth. White fabric with numerous small grit inclusions. All-over, except for base, turquoise-blue glaze, unevenly fired, blotching to near-white. BD 0.045, H 0.09. Level 2.1–2.2.

27. 7557/095/02/011. Jug. Trefoil mouth. Dark brown fabric with numerous grit and mica inclusions. BD 0.078, H 0.159. Level 1.2.

28. 7658/310/02/022. Jug. Quatrefoil mouth. Red fabric with numerous inclusions, micaceous. All-over red wash, burnished. A single pellet in each fold of mouth. RD 0.105, BD 0.06, H 0.126. Level 1.1.

29. 7656/051/02/003. Jug. Quatrefoil mouth. Pale red and light brown fabric with numerous grits, mica and other inclusions. Knob on top of handle with impressed line running down handle. RD 0.115, BD 0.059, H 0.105. Level 1.2a.

30. 7656/041/01/028. One-handled jug. Fabric: internal and external orange, core light grey, with large grits and occasional mica. Incised line on upper body. Vertical stripes and patches of orange to red paint. RD 0.08. Level 2.1–2.2.

31. 7656/041/01/028. One-handled jug. Fabric: internal and external red, core grey with moderate amounts of grit inclusions. Applied (i.e. in relief) 'worm' motif on top of handle. RD 0.09. Level 2.1–2.2.

Fig. 32

32. 7556/030/02/004. One-handled jug. Brown and reddish brown fabric with numerous grits and varied inclusions. Reddish brown wash. Incised grooves on mid-body and mid-neck. RD 0.087, BD 0.0825, H 0.243. Level 2.2.

33. 7657/107/02/006. One-handled jug. Orange fabric with moderate amount of limestone, large quantity of ill-sorted grit and moderate amount of vegetable inclusions. RD 0.08. Level 2.1b.

34. 7557/033/02/006. One-handled jug. Fabric: grey core, reddish brown external, containing many grit inclusions of varying sizes. Red wash over external surface. Decoration: ridge at base of neck; below ridge a single, incised wavy-line. RD est.0.035, BD 0.075, H est.0.185. Level 3.1–3.2.

35. 7557/230/01/161. One-handled jug. Grey fabric with numerous grits. Dull red slip on external surface. Incised lines at base of neck. Level 1.2.

36. 7757/056/01/044. One-handled jug. Brown fabric with moderate amounts of grit and mica inclusions. 'Worm-like' motif on handle. RD 0.08. Level 1.2a.

37. 7757/132/02/012. One-handled jug. Black, brown and pale red fabric, micaceous, with numerous small inclusions. Coated with dark red wash. RD 0.045, BD 0.06, H 0.151. Level (?)1.1.

38. 7658/310/02/021. One-handled jug. Brown and red fabric, micaceous, with numerous small, fine inclusions. Surface: pale red, smoothed. Decoration: three bands of c.5 incised lines on upper body to base of neck; between lower two bands, a continuous wavy line pattern of 5 incised lines; between upper two bands, groups of 5 incised vertical lines in a panel-pattern; overall, from rim to base, broad bands of red paint. RD est.0.069, BD 0.08, H est.0.193. Level 1.1.

39. 7559/080/01/127. (?)Jug. Light grey fabric with moderate amounts of grit and occasional mica. RD 0.134. Level 1.2.

40. 7559/080/01/127. (?)Jug. Red to brown fabric with moderate amounts of grit and occasional mica. RD 0.09. Level 1.2.

41. 7759/024/02/001. One-handled jar. Brown and red to brown, gritty with numerous and varied inclusions. Surface: pale brown, red to brown, smoothed. RD 0.089, BD 0.093, H 0.17. From debris on side of mound.

42. 7557/231/02/020. One-handled jug. Red fabric, micaceous, with numerous inclusions. Smoothed, coated with red wash. Decoration: 3 registers of 3 excised wavy lines between 3 excised horizontal lines; 4 panels of vertical wavy lines excised over horizontal decoration. RD 0.06. Level 1.1.

43. 7557/091/02/009. One-handled jar. Pale brown fabric with numerous inclusions, micaceous. Smoothed. RD c.0.085, BD 0.073, H 0.0885. Level 2.1a.

44. 7758/235/01/272. One-handled jar. Buff fabric, core grey, with numerous lithic inclusions. Incised decoration along shoulder. RD 0.09, BD 0.07, H 0.095. Level 1.2.

45. 7557/091/02/009. One-handled jar. Brown and black fabric, gritty, micaceous, with numerous inclusions. Surface: smoothed. Incised line at base of neck; raised band at mid-body, diagonally incised. A crude and coarse miniature pot. RD 0.058, BD 0.04, H 0.066. Level 2.1a.

46. 7659/019/01/051. One-handled jar. Dark orange fabric, very brittle, few inclusions. Vertical ridges on handle, incisions on rim. RD 0.11. Level 2.1.

Fig. 33

47. 7757/122/02/009. One-handled jar. Dark brown and red fabric, gritty, micaceous, numerous inclusions. Smoothed. Diagonal incisions on a low band at narrowest part of neck. RD 0.10, BD 0.068, H 0.13. Level 1.1.

48. 7556/108/01/107. One-handled jar. Black to brown fabric with fine grit and quartz inclusions. Two applied buttons with two incised lines between. Two incised crosses on handle. RD 0.08. Level 1.2.

49. 7656/041/01/028. One-handled jar. Dark orange fabric with many grit inclusions. RD 0.22. Level 2.1.

50. 7858/174/01/131. One-handled jar. Orange fabric with occasional very fine grits. Incised decoration. Handle ridges. RD 0.06. Level 1.1.

51. 7756/072/02/005. One-handled jar. Dark brown and black fabric, gritty, micaceous with numerous inclusions. Smoothed. Decoration: one band of diagonal incisions at base of neck and on upper body; between bands of incisions, two continuously incised, wavy lines. RD 0.079, BD 0.055. Level 1.1.

52. 7758/201/02/010. One-handled jar. Dark red and dark brown fabric, gritty, micaceous, with numerous inclusions. Surface: dark red, dark brown, brown, black, in irregular patches; smoothed. Single vertical groove down handle. RD 0.109, BD 0.087, H 0.11. Level 1.2a.

53. 7857/082/02/004. One-handled jug. Pale red fabric, fairly fine clay, micaceous. Coated with red wash. Two horizontal grooves at base of neck; between grooves, a continuous band of diagonal slashes. RD 0.081, BD 0.058, H 0.11. From pit on edge of mound.

54. 7559/001/01/109. One-handled jar. Dark orange fabric with numerous grit inclusions. Raised decoration on shoulder, impressed decoration on neck and handle; incised 'snake' decoration on handle. RD 0.20. From topsoil.

55. 7858/107/01/081. One-handled jar. Orange to grey to black fabric, hard, with numerous grit inclusions. Incised lines on neck. RD 0.24. Level 2.1b.

56. 7858/028/01/014. One-handled jar. Orange fabric with numerous grit inclusions, micaceous. Incised decoration on neck, incised vertical groove on handle. RD 0.12. Level 3.3–3.4.

57. 7756/067/01/036. One-handled jar. Dark brown to black fabric with fine to medium grained inclusions and fine quartz grains. Incised lines on neck. RD 0.08, Level 1.2.

58. 7656/010/01/020. One-handled jar. Black fabric, very brittle, numerous grit and mica inclusions. Incised grooves on handle. RD 0.237. Level 2.1.

59. 7657/042/01/042. One-handled jar. Orange fabric with numerous grit inclusions. RD 0.15. Level 2.1a–2.2.

Fig. 34

60. 7559/001/01/109. Two-handled jar. Orange fabric with many grit inclusions. In-cised decoration on top part of handle, neck and shoulder. Rough grooves on handle. RD 0.33. Topsoil.

61. 7656/067/02/010. One-handled jar. Pale brown fabric with numerous grit inclusions of varying sizes, up to 5mm. Surface: smoothed. Incised decoration on neck and upper body 1) wavy line, 2) single line groove, 3) half moons, 4) wavy line. RD 0.078, BD 0.063, H 0.10. Level 1.2.

62. 7756/029/01/052. One-handled jar. Pinkish orange fabric with numerous fine inclusions. Burnished. Incised decoration on neck and handle. RD 0.081. Level 1.1–1.2.

63. 7557/095/02/012. One-handled jar. Red to brown fabric with numerous ill-sorted grit inclusions. Incised curvilinear decoration. BD 0.084. Level 2.1a–2.1b.

64. 7758/201/02/008. One-handled jar. Red fabric with numerous inclusions, micaceous. Red wash. Two incised grooves at base of neck. RD 0.075, BD 0.069, H 0.166. Level 1.2a.

65. 7758/118/02/002. One-handled jug. Red to black fabric with numerous grits. Four incised lines at junction of neck and body, with double line of wavy incised decoration above. RD 0.058, BD 0.087, H 0.135. Level 3.1.

66. 7759/045/02/003. Two-handled jar. Pale brown fabric with various inclusions. Smoothed. RD 0.074, BD 0.068, H 0.119. Level 3.4.

67. 7457/011/02/005. Jar. Pale red fabric with occasional inclusions. RD 0.057, BD 0.053, H 0.126. Level 2.2.

68. 7858/178/01/141. Jar. Red to orange fabric containing numerous medium sized grit inclusions. Incised decoration on rim and shoulder. RD 0.105. Level 1.2.

69. 7656/090/02/009. Jar. Buff fabric with numerous tiny inclusions, micaceous. Smoothed. RD 0.097, BD 0.065, H 0.14. Level 1.1–1.2.

70. 7656/059/01/046. Jar. Light orange fabric containing moderate amount of fine grit inclusions. Red slip. Raised bands, one on neck, one around maximum diameter; the latter incised with a wavy line. RD 0.10. Level 2.1.

71. 7656/051/02/002. Jar. Dark grey fabric with occasional fine inclusions. Incised and impressed decoration. RD 0.12, BD 0.12, H 0.257. Topsoil.

Fig. 35

72. 7858/167/01/130. Jar. External fabric

orange, internal buff, with numerous medium-sized grit inclusions, micaceous. RD 0.126, BD 0.118, H 0.254. Level 2.1b.

73. 7657/065/02/005. Jar. Black, grey, brown, and red fabric with numerous small inclusions, micaceous. Smoothed. (?)Slipped or washed. Single incised grooves at base of neck and mid-body; six panel patterns of single, vertical grooves, in-filled with horizontal dashes, in form of a ladder. BD 0.051. Level 2.1–2.1a.

74. 7858/174/02/009. Jar. Red to orange fabric containing numerous medium to small sized grit inclusions. Incised decoration. RD 0.064, BD 0.052, H 0.082. Level 1.1.

75. 7556/066/02/006. Jar. Orange fabric with numerous grit and occasional fine inclusions. Level 1.2.

76. 7557/153/01/126. Jar. Orange fabric. Incised decoration. RD 0.12. Level 1.1–1.2.

77. 7757/113/01/083. Jar. Light grey to brown fabric with medium to fine inclusions including limestone. Light incised wavy lines and heavily incised crosses. RD 0.12. Level 1.2.

78. 7556/068/01/065. Jar. Red to brown fabric with occasional inclusions. RD 0.16. Level 1.2.

79. 7556/068/01/065. Jar. Red to brown fabric with moderate amounts of grit and mica inclusions. RD 0.16. Level 1.2.

80. 7758/041/01/035. One-handled jar. Dark orange fabric, very brittle, with numerous, varied inclusions. Combed decoration on neck. Red paint of vertical stripes. RD 0.212. Topsoil.

81. 7559/011/01/072. Two-handled jar. Pinkish orange biscuit fabric with grit inclusions. Incised and impressed decoration. Red paint on neck, upper and mid-body and handle. RD 0.25, BD 0.147, H 0.358. Level 2.2–3.1.

Fig. 36

82. 7558/021/02/008. Two-handled jar. Brown to red fabric, gritty with numerous, varied inclusions. Surface: pale brown, smoothed. Two sets of double horizontal ridges, three of the ridges partly decorated with incised dots. Ridge on mid-body undecorated. Red, matt paint with triangular-shaped sets of vertical lines, between which are broad wavy lines and big dots. Broad

vertical paint lines on ridged handle. Inside of pot given all over decoration of spots or blobs. RD 0.30, BD 0.15, H 0.42. Level 3.2.

83. 7558/028/02/007. Two-handled jar. Pale brown and red fabric, gritty with various inclusions. Smoothed. At base of neck: a single scored wavy line between a ridge above and three scored rings below. On each handle: two close-set, incised, vertical lines. Upper part of body decorated with broad, vertical lines of orange to brown paint. RD 0.23, BD 0.134, H 0.235. Level 3.4.

84. 7557/010/01/045. Body sherd. Orange fabric with moderate quantity of fine grit inclusions. Incised decoration and red paint vertical lines. From a jar similar to 81 and 82. Example of different type of decoration. Level 2.1–2.5.

85. 7656/112/02/021. One-handled jar. Black and brown fabric, gritty, micaceous, with numerous inclusions. Surface: brown, smoothed. Single ridge at mid-body, on shoulder wavy-line ridge. In register formed by two ridges on neck: a hatched band of alternating diagonal lines. Applied 'worm' motif on top of handle. RD 0.10, BD 0.064, H 0.102. Level 1.1.

85a. 7857/092/02/007. One-handled jar. Brown to black fabric with numerous inclusions. Surface: red, smoothed. Ridge at carination and base of neck; wavy-line ridge between with slashed pellets at each curve. RD 0.13, BD 0.096, Ht 0.118. Level 1.1

Fig. 37

86. 7858/084/01/068. One-handled jar. Orange to red, very gritty fabric, hard. Incised slashes on rim. Applied 'worm' motif on top of handle. RD 0.208. Level 2.1a.

87. 7458/036/02/002. One-handled jar. Light grey to orange to red fabric with numerous varied, medium-sized inclusions. Rim notched on under-surface; ridge below neck has been excised to form a continuous series of deep holes; ridge below middle of body; between two ridges a continuous wavy line ridge with three notches at each apex. Applied 'worm' motif on top of handle with four shallow, vertical grooves down the handle. RD 0.21, H est.0.205. Level 2.1a.

88. 7657/215/01/184. One-handled jar. Orange to red fabric with numerous grit inclusions, micaceous. Raised decoration with impressed marks. Applied 'worm' motif, incised, on

top of handle. RD 0.172, BD 0.12, H 0.23. Level 1.1.

89. 7658/138/01/107. One-handled jar. Dark grey to red fabric with numerous grits. At junction of neck and body is a horizontal line of small stab marks. On body is a raised undulating line with three or four stab marks at top and bottom extremes. On face of handle, at top are four slightly raised bumps with an incised line running downwards from each. RD 0.177, BD 0.12, H 0.215. Level 1.2.

88a. 7857/092/02/009. One-handled jar. Brown to black fabric with numerous inclusions. Surface: red, smoothed. Two rows of diagonal slash marts between neck; two vertical slash marks at top of handle. RD 0.123, BD 0.099, H 0.143. Level 1.1.

Fig. 38

90. 7858/164/02/007. One-handled jar. Red and black fabric with numerous inclusions, micaceous. Surface: smoothed. Line of incised decoration at base of neck, groups of three or more diagonal slashes. Continuous wide, wavy line ridge on body with an horizontal ridge above and below. Two wide, shallow grooves down handle. RD 0.15, BD 0.102, H 0.186. Level 2.1.

91. 7658/298/02/019. Two-handled jar. Red to brown fabric with numerous small to medium grit, and mica inclusions. Notched lower edge of rim; ridge at base of neck and round middle of body, each running from handle to handle; between the two ridges, a wavy line ridge, notched at top and bottom, curves. Two diagonal slashes across handles, two knobs at bend, depression on lower part of handle. RD 0.138, BD 0.95, H 0.158. Level 1.1.

92. 7759/097/02/010. Two-handled jar. Orange to red fabric with numerous grit and fine sand inclusions. Three ridges on each handle. Incised decoration on neck, raised band on body. RD 0.235, BD 0.147, H 0.31. Level 1.2.

93. 7657/045/02/003. Two-handled jar. Red and black, gritty fabric. Raised line around widest part of body with, above it, six applied decorations of inverted 'V' shape. Above these is a horizontal line of stab marks. Handles have four incised vertical lines. RD 0.23, BD 14.0, H 0.29. Level 2.1a.

Fig. 39

94. 7658/237/02/012. One-handled jar. Orange fabric with occasional large inclusions including white calcite. Surface: smoothed. Rim notched on under surface. Ridge of base of neck and on carnation; between these two ridges a series of inverted 'V' ridges; double notches on ridge at base of neck. Deep grooves running vertically down the handle. RD 0.164, BD 0.109, H 0.189. Level 1.2.

95. 7756/029/01/052. One-handled jar. Red to orange fabric, very brittle, with numerous grit and fine inclusions. Rim is notched. Ridge on neck is incised. Decoration on upper body is impressed. Two vertical, incised lines on handle. RD 0.12. Level 1.2.

96. 7758/235/01/212. One-handled jar. Brown fabric with moderate amount of grit and mica inclusions. Internal surface has an additional layer of clay added to original pot wall. Incised decoration on mid-body and neck. Incised chevron decoration on shoulder-neck angle below line of impressed marks. RD 0.166. Level 1.2.

97. 7658/206/02/011. Eight-handled jar. Red and brown fabric with numerous grit and other inclusions. Reddish brown wash. Two pairs of opposed flat handles; between each large handle, are small squared handles. On each large handle: a single applied 'worm' motif. Presumably on each small handle (only one preserved) a stamped impression on a raised disc. Running from the top of large handle to the top of another, a single ridge. RD 0.26, BD 0.18, H 0.26. Level 1.2.

98. 7557/186/01/136. One-handled jar. Black and dark brown fabric with numerous grits and other inclusions, micaceous. Surface: red, brown, dark brown, black, smoothed. Raised ring between neck and body. Three broad, vertical grooves on handle. RD 0.138, BD 0.093, H 0.188. Level 1.2.

99. 7556/108/01/107. Two-handled jar. Grey core, red to orange external and internal fabric with moderate amount of grit inclusions. Impressed decoration on handle ridges. Impressed line of irregularly spaced dots on neck. Raised line on top of shoulder and raised decoration on body. RD 0.20. Level 1.2.

Fig. 40

100. 7758/098/02/001. One-handled jar. Dark

grey biscuit fabric with moderate amount of large and small inclusions. Surface: black. Incised decoration. RD 0.22, BD 0.145, H 0.30. Level 3.3.

101. 7559/011/01/016. Sherd. Stamped decoration on light brown, gritty fabric. Level 2.2–3.1.

102. 7758/068/01/060. Sherd. Impressed decoration on highly burnished surface. Buff fabric with fine grit inclusions. Level 3.3.

103. 7558/156/01/158. Sherd. Incised decoration on raised band. Interior red, exterior grey, gritty surface. Level 2.1a.

104. 7658/310/02/028. One-handled bowl. Red fabric with numerous fine inclusions. Orange to red slip on exterior. Three applied pellets on top of handle with incised lines between them.. Thin ridge at bottom of neck. RD 0.095, BD. 0.63, H 0.055. Level 1.1.

105. 7658/298/01/194. One-handled jar. Orange fabric with numerous grit and fine inclusions. Incised decoration on body and handle with applied pellets at peaks of body decoration. RD 0.08, H est.0.07. Level 1.1.

106. 7658/310/02/029. One-handled bowl. Pale brown fabric with occasional inclusions, micaceous. Surface: smoothed. Impressed decoration on neck between two incised lines. Incised wavy line on upper body, ridge on mid-body. Impressed decoration on top of handle. RD 0.145, BD 0.155, H 0.082. Level 1.1.

107. 7558/151/01/137. One-handled jar. Light orange fabric with moderate quantity of medium sized grit inclusions and numerous fine grits. Impressed row of dots on neck. Red painted decoration on handle and body. RD 0.14. Level 2.2.

108. 7556/108/01/107. One-handled jar. Red to brown fabric with moderate amount of medium sized grits. Thin ridge on top of shoulder, below which are irregularly spaced impressed dots. Ridge on lower shoulder. RD 0.20. Level 1.2.

109. 7656/063/01/080. One-handled bowl. Fabric: dark grey external, brown to red interior with large grit and limestone inclusions. Top of handle ribbed. RD 0.14. Level 1.1.

110. 7656/063/01/080. Bowl. Fabric: dark grey exterior, brick red interior, with quartz

inclusions. Incised decoration, those on body are faint. RD 0.20. Level 1.1.

111. 7558/133/01/132. Bowl. Fabric: grey core, exterior and interior brick red with moderate amount of coarse grit and occasional quartz inclusions. Incised decoration on rim. RD 0.20, H 0.07. Level 2.1b.

112. 7858/159/01/101. One-handled bowl. Dark orange fabric with numerous grit inclusions, micaceous. Incised decoration on neck and ridge on lower body. RD 0.14. Level 2.2.

113. 7657/006/01/004. One-handled bowl. Mid-grey to orange fabric with numerous grit inclusions. Incised decoration at handle ridges and on upper shoulder. Applied pellet on top of handle and above that a stamped cross. RD 0.21. Topsoil.

Fig. 41

114. 7557/122/01/111. (?)Two-handled bowl. Orange to brown fabric with numerous grit, and a moderate amount of large quartz inclusions. Applied 'worm' motif on handle. RD ? Level 1.2.

115. 7557/033/01/017. Two-handled bowl. Red to orange fabric with numerous grit inclusions. RD 0.12, BD 0.10, H 0.069. Level 3.1–3.2.

116. 7557/190/01/134. Two-handled bowl. Core light grey and red to brown, exterior and interior red to brown and black, gritty. Ridge on mid-body with incised line above; incised line at bottom of shoulder and impressed decoration on neck. RD 0.17. Level 1.2.

117. 7758/080/01/064. Bowl. Red to orange fabric with occasional inclusions. Two incised lines below rim. RD 0.18. Level 3.2.

118. 7658/138/01/144. Bowl. Black fabric with moderate amount of grits. Incised decoration. RD 0.24. Level 1.2.

119. 7658/027/01/021. Bowl. Yellow to orange fabric with numerous fine inclusions, micaceous. Dark orange to red slip on exterior and interior. RD 0.20. Level 3.1.

120. 7656/007/01/017. Bowl. Light orange fabric with occasional fine inclusions and occasional grits. Dark orange slip on interior and exterior surfaces. RD 0.16. Topsoil.

121. 7558/091/01/074. Bowl. Orange fabric with occasional grit inclusions. Surfaces: dark orange, burnished. RD 0.18. Level 3.2.

122. 7759/053/02/007. Bowl. Pale brown fabric

with numerous, varied inclusions. Surface: grey and brown, smoothed. RD 0.14, BD 0.082, H 0.058. Level 2.1–3.1.

123. 7557/002/01/003. Bowl. Red to orange fabric with numerous grit inclusions. Surfaces: burnished, except for underside of base. RD 0.27, H 0.038. Level 3.3–3.4.

124. 7658/310/02/027. Bowl. Red and brown fabric with occasional grit and other inclusions, micaceous. All over dark red wash. RD 0.113, BD 0.066, H 0.056. Level 1.1.

125. 7557/123/01/144. Bowl. Grey fabric with occasional grit inclusions. Brown slip on exterior. Incised lines on neck. RD 0.16. Level 2.1a.

126. 7759/078/01/082. Bowl. White fabric with few inclusions. RD 0.10. level 2.1a.

127. 7558/160/01/160. Jar neck. Red fabric with moderate amount of fine inclusions. Applied decoration. Level 2.1a.

128. 7457/015/01/011. Jar. Light grey with moderate amount of grit inclusions. Applied decoration. Level 1.2.

129. 7659/059/01/044. Flagon. Dull orange fabric with numerous fine grit inclusions, micaceous. Yellow to white slip on exterior. RD 0.031. From recent robber trench.

130. 7558/196/02/013. Jar. Off-white fabric, micaceous. Pale buff to cream slip. BD 0.036. Level 1.1.

131. 7656/002/01/007. Bowl. Yellow fabric with occasional inclusions. Surface: smoothed. BD 0.037. Topsoil.

132. 7758/094/01/122. Bowl. Cream fabric with occasional grit. Decoration: on upper body, stamped bird motifs with spirals; base and lower body incised and stamped decoration. BD 0.048. Level 3.2.

133. 7857/084/01/051. Jar. Cream fabric with occasional inclusions. Upper body has incised decoration; applied pellets below. RD 0.05. Level 1.2.

134. 7859/041/01/025. Bowl. Cream fabric with occasional inclusion. Decoration: on rim, finger-impressed; on body, applied. RD 0.30. Level 1.1.

135. 7859/041/01/025. Bowl. Cream fabric with occasional inclusions. Impressed decoration on rim. Internal surface: smoothed. RD 0.22. Level 1.1.

136. 7557/116/01/094. Bowl. Cream fabric with occasional mica inclusion. Impressed 'pie-crust' decoration on rim. Applied

decoration on body. Internal surface: smoothed. RD ? Level 2.1.

137. 7758/253/01/211. Jar. Fabric: internal, light grey; exterior, buff; micaceous. Incised linear and curvilinear decoration and impressed dots. Level 1.1.

Fig. 42

138. 7559/089/01/137. Bowl. Red to brown exterior and interior, core grey, with occasional grit and mica inclusions. Surface: burnished. Incised decoration. RD 0.26. Level 1.2.

139. 7756/034/01/014. Jar. Grey fabric with occasional gritty and mica inclusions. Impressed decoration on rim. RD 0.128. Medieval pit on edge of mound, level unknown.

140. 7758/235/01/212. Jar. Buff fabric with moderate amount of grit inclusions. Incised decoration on lower rim and body. RD ? Level 1.2.

141. 7758/234/01/204. Jar. Buff fabric with moderate amount of grit and mica inclusions. Incised line along shoulder. RD 0.12. Level 1.2.

142. 7559/081/01/129. Jar. Pink to orange fabric with numerous mica particles. RD 0.26. Level 1.2.

143. 7756/034/01/014. Bowl. Orange to brown fabric with moderate amount of grit inclusions. RD 0.10. Medieval pit on edge of mound, level unknown.

144. 7858/178/01/141. Bowl. Dark grey fabric with occasional grit inclusions. RD 0.16. Level 1.2.

145. 7858/178/01/141. Bowl. Cream fabric with moderate amount of grit and occasional mica inclusions. RD 0.26. Level 1.2.

146. 7858/072/01/058. Bowl. Orange to grey fabric with numerous grit inclusions. RD 0.29. Level 3.2.

147. 7559/039/01/112. Bowl. Orange fabric with occasional fine inclusions. Stamped decoration on shoulder; indented triangles with raised dot. Dark orange slip on exterior and interior. RD 0.22. Level 2.2.

148. 7559/080/01/127. Bowl. Pink to orange fabric with occasional very fine grits. RD 0.46. Level 1.2.

149. 7858/072/01/058. Bowl. Orange to grey fabric with numerous grit inclusions. RD 0.29. Level 3.2.

150. 7858/170/01/124. Bowl. Buff fabric with moderate amount of quartz and grit inclusions. Red to orange slip on interior and exterior. Incised curvilinear decoration on neck. Stamped decoration on shoulder; indented triangles with raised dots. RD 0.23. Level 2.1b.

151. 7558/051/01/042. Bowl. Orange fabric with occasional grit inclusions. Burnished. Raised bands with incised decoration. Incised wavy lines. RD ? Level 3.3.

Fig. 43

152. 7557/153/01/126. Bowl. Red fabric with numerous coarse inclusions. Two incised lines on body. RD 0.57, BD 0.452, H 0.066. Level 1.1–1.2.

153. 7557/153/01/126. Bowl. Brown to orange fabric with occasional fine grit inclusions. RD 0.38. Level 1.1–1.2.

154. 7557/153/01/126. Bowl. Pink to orange fabric with occasional fine grit inclusions. RD 0.44. Level 1.1–1.2.

155. 7556/086/01/071. Bowl. Light brown fabric with moderate amount of medium sized grit inclusions, micaceous. RD 0.34. Level 1.2.

156. 7556/086/01/071. Bowl. Brown fabric with numerous grit inclusions. RD 0.34, BD 0.22, H 0.10. Level 1.2.

157. 7759/024/01/034. Bowl. Cream to pale grey fabric with occasional grit inclusions. RD 0.30, BD 0.046, H 0.10. From recent robber pit.

158. 7656/010/01/020. Two-handled bowl. Orange fabric with numerous fine inclusions and occasional grit. Finger-impressed decoration on handle. RD 0.25. Level 2.1.

159. 7558/092/01/074. Bowl. Grey fabric with numerous grit inclusions. Incised decoration on rim. Lug handles. RD 0.29. Level 3.1.

160. 7757/015/01/031. Two-handled bowl. Orange fabric with numerous grit inclusions, micaceous. Surfaces: smoothed. RD 0.16. Level (?)3.3.

161. 7458/043/01/022. Two-handled bowl. Fabric: grey to black core; light grey exterior; red interior; with numerous grit inclusions. Handle broken. RD 0.34, BD 0.32, H 0.104. Level 2.1a.

Fig. 44

162. 7858/045/01/030. Lid. Buff fabric with numerous quartz inclusions and occasional grit inclusions. D 0.079, H 0.028. Level 2.1b–3.2.

163. 7656/007/02/006. Lid. Brown to grey fabric, micaceous, with numerous grit inclusions. D 0.09, H 0.065. Topsoil.

164. 7757/006/02/002. Lid. Pale brown fabric, micaceous, with moderate amount of inclusions. D 0.082. Topsoil.

165. 7656/119/02/013. Lid. Brown fabric, micaceous with numerous grit and other inclusions. Incised decoration. D 0.073, H 0.032. Level 1.1.

166. 7557/055/02/007. Lid. Pale brown fabric, micaceous with numerous inclusions. Surface: smoothed. Incised decoration. D. 0.0755. Level 2.2.

167. 7657/041/02/002. Lid. Red to orange fabric with numerous grit inclusions. D 0.214–0.220, H 0.057. Level 2.2.

168. 7758/094/01/122. Lid. Orange fabric with numerous grit and grog inclusions. D 0.227, H 0.086. Level 3.2.

169. 7756/044/02/004. Lid. Pale brown fabric with grit and straw inclusions, micaceous. Raised edge. D 0.092, H 0.056. Level 2.1.

170. 7758/018/02/005. Lid. Dark grey fabric with numerous grit inclusions. Five plain, raised rings and another that forms rim which has finger-pinched moulding. D 0.165. Level 3.3–3.5.

171. 7857/040/02/002. Lid. Buff fabric with numerous grit and quartz inclusions. Raised concentric rings and finger-moulded edge. 'Worm' motif on handle. D 0.235, H 0.069. Level 2.1b.

172. 7459/006/01/004. Lid. Buff fabric with numerous grit inclusions. Incised decoration. Level 1.1–1.2.

173. 7657/041/01/046. Lid. Black fabric with numerous grit inclusions. Incised decoration of edge. D 0.133. Level 2.2.

174. 7557/033/01/017. Lid. Reddish orange fabric with dark grey core; numerous grit inclusions. Raised decoration. D 0.20, H 0.018. Level 2.1–3.2.

Fig.45

175. 7558/028/01/023. Lid. Light orange fabric, light grey core, with numerous grit and moderate amount of vegetable inclusions. D 0.267. Level 3.4.

176. 7656/041/01/028. Lid. Dark grey fabric

with numerous large grit inclusions. D 0.23. Level 2.1–2.2.

177. 7556/064/01/049. Lid. Light orange fabric with moderate amount of small grit inclusions. Impressed decoration of edge; series of concentric ridges. Red paint. D 0.18. Level 2.1.

178. 7857/064/01/029. Lid. Buff fabric with numerous grits. Impressed decoration on edge. Applied decoration on handle. Red paint. D 0.20. Level 1.2.

179. 7658/044/01/113. Lid. Buff fabric with moderate amount fine grit inclusions. Central steam vent. D. 0.24. Level 2.2.

180. 7457/006/02/004. Lid. Black fabric with numerous inclusions, micaceous. Concentric ridges on upper surface; outer edge, finger-pinched. Central boss, pierced by five holes on top and four slits on sides. D. 0.235. Level 2.1b.

181. 7556/108/02/012. Lid. Black and dark brown fabric with medium sized inclusions, micaceous. Edge of disc finger-pinched. Incised decoration at base of boss. Boss has three vertical slits down sides. D 0.127. Level 1.2.

Fig.46

182. 7558/156/02/005. Crucible. Pale brown, grey, and black fabric with small-sized inclusions, micaceous. RD 0.062, BD 0.046, H 0.036. Level 2.1a.

183. 7558/222/03/007. Miniature pot. Buff fabric with occasional fine inclusions. Irregularly shaped. Contained white pigment. Level 1.2.

184. 7658/298/02/018. Lamp. Black fabric, micaceous. Surface: smoothed. RD 0.0725, H 0.075. Level 1.1.

185. 7556/030/02/003. Lamp. Pale brown fabric with numerous varied inclusions. Surface: smoothed. RD 0.088. Level 2.2.

186. 7458/041/02/003. Lamp. Pale brown fabric with numerous varied inclusions. Surface: smoothed. L 0.092, W 0.089. Level 2.1a. This shape also found with one applied pellet either side of spout (7656/060/02/004—not published).

187. 7658/298/02/026. Lamp. Pinkish buff fabric with numerous grit inclusions. L 0.072, W 0.06. Level 1.1.

188. 7658/310/02/023. Lamp. Pinkish orange fabric with numerous grit inclusions. L 0.084, W 0.066. Level 1.1.

189. 7657/028/02/001. Lamp. Pale brown fabric with numerous grit inclusions. L 0.066, W 0.060. Level 3.1.

190. 7659/106/02/001. Lamp. Fine red fabric with dark brown glaze on interior. L 0.094, W 0.092. Level 1.2.

191. 7759/053/02/006. Lamp. Dark grey fabric with grit inclusions. L 0.108, W 0.10. Level 3.4.

192. 7857/006/02/001. Lamp. Fine red fabric with dark brown glaze on interior and handle. L 0.092, W 0.090. Level 3.2–3.3.

193. 7657/219/02/016. Lamp. White fabric. Inside, all-over blue glaze; outside, all-over blue glaze, as far as lower body. Beehive shaped boss inside with curved round handle set on rim, bridging the gap over the edge of the funnel. Level 1.1.

194. 7757/096/02/007. Lamp. White fabric. All-over turquoise-blue glaze except for outside, under and just above base. Level 1.1.

195. 7658/289/02/015. Lamp. White fabric. All-over turquoise-blue glaze except for outside, under and just above base. Level 1.1.

196. 7557/121/02/013. Lamp. White fabric. All-over turquoise-blue glaze except for outside, under and just above base. Level 2.2–2.1a.

197. 7757/066/02/006. Pot-stand for 198. Orange fabric with numerous fine inclusions. D 0.21; H 0.017. Level 2.1.

198. 7757/012/02/004. Jar. Pale brown fabric with numerous small grit inclusions, micaceous. Surface: smoothed. Two shallow grooves at mid-point and again at three-quarter point. Pierced above base. RD 0.26; BD 0.145, H 0.452. Level 2.1, from room XLIII of bath-house (see above p.37).

Fig.47

199. 7556/048/02/005. Pithos. Reddish orange fabric with numerous fairly coarse grit inclusions. RD 0.304, BD 0.136, H 1.08. Level 2.1–2.1a. Scale 1:8.

200. 7559/087/02/005. Barrel. Light orange fabric with numerous grit inclusions. Linear red paint on body; spots of black paint on upper surface of handle. Incised decoration on maximum diameter of pot. Horizontal handle. Pot appeared to have been trimmed top and bottom and used as an oven. Level 2.1. Scale 1:8.

Fig.48

201. 7656/002/01/007, 7558/058/01/230. 'Grenade'. Olive-green stone ware; fine grit and small limestone inclusions. Stamped and raised decoration. White slip on interior. Level 3.2.

202. 7558/188/01/164. 'Grenade'. Pinkish orange exterior and interior, grey core. Hard. Burnished. Incised lines. Level 2.1a.

203. 7558/031/01/027. (?)'Grenade'. Orange to grey fabric with occasional fine inclusions. Dark orange exterior, grey brown interior. Impressed decoration. No hole at top. Level 3.4.

204. 7558/092/01/076. (?)'Grenade'. Orange to grey fabric with occasional fine inclusions. Decoration: applied vertical ridges; incised horizontal bands and curved pattern on upper shoulder. Level 3.1.

205. 7657/134/03/002. Drainpipe. Reddish orange fabric with moderate amount of medium sized grit inclusions. Male D 0.072; female D 0.155, L 0.29. Level 1.2.

206. 7657/134/03/003. Drainpipe. Orange fabric with numerous fine inclusions. Male D 0.08; female D 0.122, L. 0.294. Level 1.2.

207. 7458/001/02/001. Drainpipe. Light orange fabric with numerous inclusions, micaceous. Male D 0.064; female D 0.095, L 0.285. Topsoil.

208. 7458/001/02/001. Drainpipe. Pinkish orange fabric with numerous large inclusions. Male D 0.063; female D 0.096, L 0.281. Topsoil.

209. 7858/186/01/149. (?)Lid. Buff fabric with moderate amount small grit inclusions, micaceous. BD 0.05. Level 2.1.

210. 7558/095/01/138. Jug. Grey fabric with occasional large inclusions, micaceous. All-over rich brown glaze. Level 2.1b.

211. 7556/082/01/059. Jug. Interior and exterior fabric brown, core dark grey with numerous inclusions, micaceous. External surface: rich brown glaze. Two incised lines on neck. Level 1.2.

212. 7558/091/01/074. Bowl. Buff fabric with grit and sand inclusions. All-over rich brown glaze. RD 0.244. Level 3.2.

213. 7858/163/02/005. Jar. White fabric with numerous small inclusions. All-over turquoise-blue poor glaze except for base, peeling from clay body in places. RD 0.094, BD 0.06, H 0.226. Level 1.2a.

214. 7758/234/01/204. Jar. Buff fabric with moderate amount of grit inclusions. All-over poor glaze: interior, pale metallic turquoise with large patch of dark blue glaze; exterior, very thick turquoise- or aquamarine-blue, which has run at the base to form thick blobs. BD 0.065. Level 1.2.

215. 7658/298/01/194. Bowl. Orange pink fabric with occasional inclusions. Poor turquoise-blue glaze on interior and upper 0.05 of exterior. RD 0.16, BD 0.068, H 0.066. Level 1.1.

216. 7556/152/01/123. Bowl. Buff fabric with occasional inclusions. All-over poor turquoise glaze except for underneath of base and lower wall. BD 0.19. Level 1.1.

217. 7458/031/01/019. Jar. Yellow to white poorly fired. Exterior has turquoise poor glaze which is flaking off. BD 0.13. Level 3.1.

Fig.49

218. 7557/033/01/017. Handle. Buff fabric with moderate amount of fine grit inclusions. All-over turquoise, poor glaze flaking off. Level 3.3–3.2.

219. 7858/216/01/169. Bowl. Buff fabric with occasional grit and micaceous inclusions. All-over turquoise, poor glaze. RD 0.24. Level 1.1.

220. 7458/013/01/007. Cup. Pink to white fabric with occasional inclusions. All-over bright, light blue glaze. RD 0.094. Level 3.1.

221. 7858/174/02/008. Cup. Light reddish orange fabric with numerous fine grit inclusions. Turquoise glaze over all interior and most of exterior. RD 0.062, BD 0.032, H 0.033. Level 1.1.

222. 7657/150/02/010. Cup. Buff fabric with occasional grit inclusions. Turquoise glaze over interior and exterior rim. RD 0.07, BD 0.041, H 0.03. Level 2.1.

223. 7658/298/02/017. Cup. Buff fabric with occasional grit inclusion. Turquoise glaze over interior and most of exterior. RD 0.057, BD 0.035, H 0.025. Level 1.1.

224. 7557/141/02/010. Cup. Buff fabric with occasional grit and micaceous inclusions. Turquoise glaze over interior and most of exterior. RD 0.061, BD 0.04, H 0.0295. Level 1.2–2.1.

225. 7656/019/01/025. Cup. Yellow to white fabric with occasional grit and mica

inclusion. Greenish blue glaze over interior and most of exterior. RD 0.062. Level 2.1a.

226. 7659/002/01/024. Cup. White fabric with occasional inclusions. Light blue glaze on interior and most of exterior. RD 0.08. From recent pit.

227. 7857/081/01/046. Cup. Buff fabric with occasional inclusions. Dark blue glaze on interior, dark blue and white glaze on exterior. Impressed decoration on rim with alternate colours of glaze. RD 0.07, BD 0.042, H 0.02. Level 2.2.

228. 7758/208/01/186. Cup. Buff fabric with moderate amount of fine grit inclusions. All-over turquoise glaze with small spots of white paint on exterior. RD 0.10. Level 1.2.

229. 7657/147/01/145. Cup. Cream fabric with occasional mica inclusions. Pale blue to turquoise glaze over interior and most of exterior. RD 0.06. Level 1.2a.

230. 7556/082/02/007. Cup. Buff fabric with occasional grit inclusion. Green glaze on interior and most of exterior. RD 0.057, BD 0.05, H 0.027. Level 1.2.

231. 7758/235/02/011. Cup. Dark grey fabric with occasional inclusions. Clear glaze on interior and exterior rim. Impressed decoration on edge of rim. RD 0.061, BD 0.041, H 0.037. Level 1.2.

232. 7858/174/02/008. Cup. Creamish buff with occasional fine grit inclusions. Turquoise glaze on interior and top half of exterior. RD 0.063, BD 0.03, H 0.031. Level 1.1.

233. 7858/178/02/010. Cup. Creamish buff fabric with occasional small grit inclusions. Green glaze on interior and most of exterior. RD 0.063, BD 0.039, H 0.029. Level 1.2.

234. 7557/190/01/134. Cup. Very pale grey fabric with occasional fine grit inclusions. Thick turquoise-blue to dark blue glaze on interior and top part of exterior. RD 0.07. Level 1.2.

235. 7556/080/01/060. Cup. Buff fabric with occasional grit and mica inclusions. White glaze on interior, rim and part of shoulder. Patch of turquoise glaze on ridge below rim. RD 0.057, BD 0.07, H 0.022. Level 1.2.

236. 7858/091/01/079. Cup. Creamish white fabric. Turquoise glaze on interior and top of exterior. RD 0.108. Level 2.2.

237. 7657/105/02/007. Cup. White fabric. Black to brown poor quality glaze on interior and top of exterior. RD 0.062, BD 0.043, H 0.04. Level 2.1a–2.1b.

238. 7557/190/02/016. Cup. Cream fabric with occasional inclusions. Turquoise glaze on interior and exterior of rim. Impressed decoration on shoulder. RD 0.066, BD 0.044, H 0.039. Level 1.2.

239. 7556/152/01/125. Cup. Buff fabric with occasional sand inclusions. Turquoise glaze on interior and top half of exterior. RD 0.058, BD 0.05, H 0.048. Level 1.1.

240. 7556/152/01/125. Cup. Orange buff fabric with occasional inclusions. Turquoise glaze on interior and top half of exterior. RD 0.052, BD 0.048, H 0.046. Level 1.1.

241. 7759/099/02/011. Cup. Buff cream fabric with occasional inclusions. All-over patchy blue and white glaze except for part of foot and underneath of base. Decoration on rim, discs with central boss; on side: between each panel a disc with central boss; panels divided by triangular-sectioned ridge, top of ridge notched. RD 0.0875, BD 0.045, H 0.052. From pit on side of mound.

242. 7556/015/02/002. Cup. White fabric. Overall bright blue glaze except for base and underside of base. Decoration as 241. RD 0.088, BD 0.055, H 0.051. Level 3.1

243. 7558/122/01/134. Cup. White fabric. Overall bright blue glaze except for base. Decoration as 241. RD 0.088, Level 2.2. Also one example without notches on ridges— 7858/030/01/046, Level 3.3–3.5 (not illustrated).

244. 7558/131/01/119. Handle from (?)cup. Orange to white fabric with occasional fine inclusions. Bright blue glaze. Level 1.2.

245. 7758/121/01/120. Bowl. Orange fabric with moderate amount of mica inclusions. Brown glaze on interior and rim exterior. RD 0.20. Level 3.1.

246. 7858/001/01/004. Bowl. Light orange fabric. Black glaze on interior and rim exterior over white slip. RD 0.24. Topsoil.

247. 7656/044/01/030. Bowl. Buff fabric with moderate amount of grit inclusions. Metallic brown glaze on interior and top of exterior. Two incised lines on shoulder/neck angle. RD 0.22. Level 1.2.

248. 7558/050/02/001. Bowl. Yellow fabric. Dark brown to purple glaze on interior and rim exterior. Incised lines on rim. RD 0.207, BD 0.077, H 0.071. Level 3.3.

249. 7658/117/01/111. Bowl. Yellow fabric with numerous grit and mica inclusions. Possible light grey slip but very worn. RD 0.22. Level 2.2.

250. 7858/027/01/021. Bowl. Orange to grey fabric with occasional fine inclusions. RD 0.20. Level 3.5.

251. 7759/013/01/014. Bowl. Pale orange buff fabric with occasional grit inclusions. Reddish brown slip on interior and top of exterior. RD 0.23. Level 3.3.

252. 7759/053/01/067. Bowl. Orange to grey core; internal and external surfaces dark orange. Burnished on exterior. Numerous fine inclusions. Incised grooves on shoulder. RD 0.18. Level 2.2.

253. 7556/069/01/051. Bowl. Creamish orange fabric with numerous medium sized grit and mica inclusions. Red slip on exterior and rim interior. RD 0.20. Level 2.1.

Fig.50

254. 7656/044/01/030. Bowl. Grey fabric with moderate amount of large grit inclusions, micaceous. Surfaces: smoothed. All-over brown slip. RD 0.14. Level 1.2.

255. 7558/049/01/030. Bowl. Buff fabric with moderate amount grit inclusions and occasional mica inclusions. Metallic green glaze on interior and rim exterior. RD 0.17. Level 3.4.

256. 7858/001/01/004. Bowl. Light orange fabric with occasional inclusions. Turquoise-blue glaze on interior and rim exterior. RD 0.18. Topsoil.

257. 7757/019/02/003. Bowl. Red fabric with grit and mica inclusions. Dark blue or turquoise glaze on interior and rim exterior. Incised lines on rim. RD 0.23, BD 0.088, H 0.10. Level 2.1–2.2.

258. 7858/044/01/032. Bowl. Orange fabric with moderate amount fine inclusions. Brown glaze on interior and rim exterior. RD 0.24. Level 3.2.

259. 7759/045/01/047. Bowl. Light orange fabric with moderate amount fine grit inclusions. Turquoise glaze on interior and upper half of exterior. RD 0.28. Level 3.4.

260. 7759/045/01/047. Bowl. Light orange fabric with moderate amount fine grit inclusions. Brown glaze on interior and rim exterior. RD 0.21. Level 3.4.

261. 7558/051/01/042. Bowl. Buff fabric with moderate amount of very fine grit inclusions. Green glaze on interior and rim exterior. RD 0.16. Level 3.3.

262. 7759/053/01/067. Bowl. Orange fabric with occasional inclusions. Turquoise glaze on interior and rim exterior. RD 0.24, BD 0.12., H 0.10. Level 3.4.

263. 7759/002/01/003. Bowl. Pale orange buff fabric with occasional grit inclusion. Black glaze on interior. Incised line on shoulder/neck angle. RD 0.22. Topsoil.

264. 7559/011/01/059. Bowl. Light orange fabric with moderate amount fine inclusions. Green to blue glaze on interior and rim exterior. RD 0.24. Level 2.2–3.1.

265. 7658/010/01/006. Bowl. Pinkish orange fabric with occasional inclusions. Black glaze on interior and upper two-thirds of exterior. RD 0.20. Level 3.1.

266. 7858/037/01/024. Bowl. Orange fabric with moderate amount fine inclusions. Black glaze on interior and top of rim exterior. RD 0.28. Level 3.3.

267. 7857/066/01/027. Bowl. Cream fabric with occasional inclusions. Dark turquoise glaze on interior, lighter shade on exterior. RD 0.22. Level 2.1a.

268. 7558/055/01/100. Bowl. Orange fabric with moderate amount grit inclusions. Dark brown glaze on interior and exterior. RD 0.16. Level 2.1.

269. 7658/206/01/143. Bowl. Orange fabric, micaceous. Bright green glaze on interior and top of exterior. RD 0.20. Level 1.1.

270. 7658/138/01/136. Jar. Yellowish cream fabric with moderate amount of grit inclusions. All-over thick turquoise blue glaze. RD 0.10. Level 1.2.

271. 7758/081/01/125. Bowl. Orange fabric with moderate amount very fine grit inclusions. Emerald-green glaze on interior and exterior. RD 0.20. Level 3.2.

272. 7858/002/01/002. Bowl base. Orange fabric with occasional grit inclusions. Black glaze on interior. Potter's mark on bottom. BD 0.095. Topsoil.

273. 7557/060/01/063. Bowl. Buff orange fabric with moderate amount grit inclusions. Black brown glaze on interior. Potter's mark on bottom. BD 0.09. Level 2.2.

274. 7857/082/01/048. Base. Orange buff fabric with moderate amount grit and mica inclusions. Green, brown and yellow glaze on interior. BD 0.06. Pit on side of mound.

275. 7757/015/01/025. Base. Pale red to buff

fabric with chaff and grog tempering. Green glaze on interior. Second/Waster (see p.74). BD 0.08. Level 3.3.

276. 7759/048/01/063. Bowl. Pale orange red fabric with occasional inclusions. All-over greenish yellow glaze. RD 0.12. Level 2.1a–2.2.

277. 7757/015/01/035. Bowl. Reddish buff fabric. Black glaze on rim; dark green on interior; graduation from dark green at top to pale green on exterior. Level 3.3.

Fig.51

278. 7757/015/01/035. Bowl. Pale red to buff fabric with very fine grit inclusions. White slip. All-over yellow glaze with green on top on rim and in places on exterior. RD ? Level 3.3.

279. 7757/015/01/035. Bowl. Reddish buff fabric. Green glaze on interior and top of exterior on white slip. RD 0.22. Level 3.3.

280. 7757/015/01/035. Bowl. Reddish buff fabric with fine grit and chaff inclusions. Honey-yellow glaze over interior and top of exterior (illustrated) on white slip. RD ? Level 3.3.

281. 7757/015/01/035. Bowl. Reddish buff fabric with grog tempering. All-over olive-green glaze on white slip. RD ? Level 3.3.

282. 7757/015/01/035. Bowl. Buff fabric with small grit inclusions. Olive-green glaze over interior and rim exterior (illustrated) on white slip. Glaze appears brown in groove on inside of rim. RD ? Level 3.3.

283. 7757/015/01/035. (?)Bowl. Buff fabric with very fine grits. Emerald-green glaze on interior and part of exterior on white slip. Level 3.3.

284. 7757/015/01/035. Sherd. Buff fabric with very fine grits. Two incised lines on interior. Green glaze over interior on white slip. Level 3.3.

285. 7757/015/01/035. Rim sherd. Reddish buff fabric with very fine grit inclusions. Light green glaze on exterior and top of rim interior with very pale green glaze on interior. Brown to green broken line on exterior. All on white slip. RD ? Level 3.3.

286. 7757/015/01/035. Bowl. Reddish buff fabric. Green glaze on rim, light green glaze on interior, olive-green sgraffiato. RD ? Level 3.3.

287. 7757/015/01/035. Bowl. Reddish buff fabric. Pale green and olive-green glaze.

Dark sgraffiato. RD ? Level 3.3.

288. 7656/002/01/022. Bowl. Buff fabric with moderate quantity of fine grit inclusions. Green and very pale green glaze; olive-green sgraffiato. RD ? Topsoil.

289. 7659/002/01/011. Bowl. Buff fabric with moderate amount very fine grit inclusions. Green glaze on exterior and upper part of interior; olive-green sgraffiato. RD 0.20. Topsoil.

290. 7757/015/01/035. Sherd. Red fabric with very fine grit inclusions. Olive-green, green, pale green and brown glaze; dark sgraffiato. Level 3.3.

291. 7757/015/01/035. Sherd. Reddish buff fabric. Green, olive-green and brownish purple pattern; pale green background; dark sgraffiato. Deer head. Level 3.3.

292. 7757/015/01/035. Sherd. Reddish buff fabric. Pale green background; olive-green and brownish purple pattern; dark sgraffiato. Level 3.3.

293. 7757/015/01/035. Bowl. Buff fabric with occasional grit inclusions. Interior: pale green background; olive-green decoration; brownish purple sgraffiato. Exterior: olive-green. Top of rim: impressed circular marks. Level 3.3.

294. 7757/015/01/035. Bowl. Reddish buff fabric. Interior: pale green background; black decoration; dark green sgraffiato. Exterior: pale green. RD 0.24. Level 3.3.

295. 7757/015/01/035. Sherd. Reddish buff fabric. Interior: green, brownish purple and yellow; olive-green sgraffiato. Exterior: green. Level 3.3.

296. 7757/015/01/035. Bowl. Reddish buff fabric. Interior: brownish purple. green, olive-green; dark sgraffiato. Exterior: pale green. RD 0.18. Level 3.3.

297. 7757/015/01/035. Bowl. Reddish buff fabric with occasional white grit inclusions. Interior: green, brownish purple, ochre; brownish purple sgraffiato; pale green background. BD 0.058. Level 3.3.

298. 7757/015/01/035. Sherd. Reddish buff fabric. Exterior: olive-green and light brownish purple; pale green background. Level 3.3.

299. 7858/001/01/004. Bowl. Light orange fabric with occasional inclusions. Exterior: light green. Interior: bands of brown, light green and dark green. Dark sgraffiato. RD 0.16. Topsoil.

300. 7558/092/01/079. Bowl. White fabric. All-over blood-red glaze over-painted with copper lustre. RD 0.24. Level 3.1.

301. 7658/029/01/024. Bowl. White fabric. All-over blood-red glaze over-painted with copper lustre. Second/Waster (cross-hatched area) (see p.75). RD 0.32. Level 2.2.

302. 7658/138/01/136. Bowl. Off-white fabric with moderate amount fine grit inclusions. All-over blood-red glaze over-painted with copper lustre. Detail scratched through the lustre. RD 0.35. Level 1.2.

303. 7557/097/01/067. Bowl. Off-white fabric with occasional inclusions. All-over blood-red glaze except for lower exterior. RD 0.22. Level 2.1a.

304. 7657/041/01/037. Bowl. White fabric. All-over very pale turquoise glaze over-painted with copper lustre. RD ? Level 2.2.

305. 7858/044/01/032. Bowl. Off-white fabric with occasional mica inclusions. Double glaze. Dark blue, black, red to brown and green between clear glazes. RD 0.24. Level 3.2.

306. 7557/122/01/011. Base. Orange fabric with numerous grit inclusions; micaceous. Double glaze. All-over white glaze with brown glaze on top in interior and patches green glaze on top on exterior. BD 0.12. Level 1.2.

307. 7558/092/01/076, 7558/090/01/079. Base. White fabric with occasional very small white grit inclusions. All-over turquoise glaze over-painted with copper lustre decoration. (?)Dragon motif. BD 0.075. Level 3.1.

308. 7858/001/01/004. Bowl. Off-white fabric with occasional grit inclusions. Double glaze. All-over clear glaze, with black under partial blue glaze. RD 0.14. Topsoil.

309. 7858/001/01/004. Bowl. Off-white fabric with occasional inclusions. Double glaze. All-over clear glaze with, black under blue glaze. RD 0.13. Topsoil.

Fig.52

310. 7757/015/01/035. Bowl. White fabric. Double glaze. All-over clear glaze with, black under blue glaze. RD 0.22. Level 3.3.

311. 7757/015/01/035. Bowl. White fabric. Double glaze. All-over clear glaze with, black under blue glaze. RD ? Level 3.3.

312. 7757/015/01/035. Base. White fabric with grit inclusions. Double glaze. All-over clear glaze with, black under thick blue glaze. BD 0.07. Level 3.3.

313. 7757/015/01/035. Bowl. White fabric, micaceous. Double glaze. All-over clear glaze with, black under blue glaze. RD 0.24. Level 3.3.

314. 7858/001/01/004. Bowl. White fabric with occasional inclusions. Black under blue glaze. BD 0.05. Topsoil.

315. 7757/072/01/057. Sherd. Off-white fabric with occasional grit and mica inclusions. Double glaze. All-over clear glaze with, black under blue glaze. Level 2.1–2.2.

316. 7858/044/01/032. Bowl. Off-white fabric with occasional inclusions. Double glaze. All-over clear glaze with, black under blue glaze. RD 0.14. Level 3.2.

317. 7756/001/01/002. Bowl. White fabric. Double glaze. All-over clear glaze with, black under blue glaze. RD 0.16. Topsoil.

318. 7756/001/01/002. Bowl. White fabric. Black under blue glaze. Internal decoration obscured by glaze breaking up. BD 0.065. Topsoil.

319. 7756/001/01/001. Bowl. White fabric. Lustre under all-over clear glaze. RD 0.24. Topsoil.

320. 7658/018/01/074. Sherd. Off-white fabric with occasional inclusions. Two-tone green on interior under all-over clear glaze. Level 2.1.

321. 7757/124/01/095. Bowl. Cream fabric with occasional fine grit inclusions. Brown under all-over pale green to clear glaze. RD 0.33. Level 1.1.

322. 7558/122/01/135. Bowl. White fabric. Brown under all-over thick pale green to clear glaze. RD 0.28. Level 2.2.

323. 7658/310/01/200. Bowl. Off-white fabric. Green under all-over clear glaze with thin over-painted lines. RD 0.14. Level 1.1.

324. 7558/099/01/091. Bowl. White fabric. Clear glaze over-painted with copper lustre. Detail scratched through lustre. BD 0.07. Level 2.2. Pl.7a.

325. 7857/001/01/001. Bowl. White fabric. Clear glaze over-painted with copper lustre. Detail scratched through lustre. RD 0.20, BD 0.07, H 0.075. Topsoil. Pl.7b.

326. 7558/102/01/097. Bowl. White fabric. Clear glaze over-painted with copper lustre. RD 0.20. Level 2.2. Pl.7c.

327. 7558/092/01/081. Bowl. White fabric. Clear glaze over-painted with copper lustre. RD 0.30, BD 0.10, H 0.08. Level 3.1. Pl.7d.

328. 7657/041/01/037. Bowl. Off-white fabric with occasional inclusions. Turquoise glaze over-painted with green. RD 0.09. Level 2.2.

329. 7558/121/01/114. Bowl. Off-white fabric with moderate amount very fine grit inclusions. All-over pale blue glaze over-painted with golden brown. RD 0.22. Level 2.2.

330. 7558/054/01/037. Bowl. White fabric. Cobalt-blue under clear glaze, over-painted with copper lustre. RD ? Level 3.4.

331. 7659/002/01/018. Base. White fabric with occasional inclusions. All-over (except for base exterior) monochrome cobalt-blue glaze. BD 0.08. Topsoil.

332. 7558/188/01/166. Base. Pinkish white fabric. Pink slip. All-over (except for under-side of base) thick monochrome cobalt-blue glaze. BD 0.05. Level 2.1.

333. 7857/001/01/001. Bowl. White fabric. All-over monochrome cobalt-blue glaze. RD 0.24. Topsoil.

334. 7558/121/01/114. Bowl. Off-white fabric with moderate amount fine grit inclusions. All-over blue glaze over-painted with lustre. RD 0.18. Level 2.2.

335. 7558/099/01/102. Bowl. Off-white fabric with moderate amount very fine grit inclusions. All-over turquoise glaze over-painted with green on interior and gold line on rim. Level 2.2.

336. 7558/027/01/034. Sherd. Off-white fabric with moderate amount fine grit inclusions. All-over cobalt-blue over-painted with green on interior. Level 3.4.

Fig. 53

337. 7558/013/01/006. Bowl. Off-white fabric with moderate amount very fine grit inclusions. Cobalt-blue under clear glaze, with lustre over-painting: light golden brown along rim edge, golden brown on upper surface of rim. RD 0.30. From recent pit.

338. 7558/013/01/006. Bowl. Off-white fabric with moderate quantity of fine grit inclusions. Interior: golden brown lustre under clear glaze. Exterior: clear glaze on upper half. RD 0.07, BD 0.038, H 0.06. From recent pit.

339. 7558/054/01/037. Bowl. Off-white fabric with grit inclusions. All-over pale turquoise to clear glaze over-painted with copper lustre on rim upper surface and rim edge. RD 0.36. Level 3.4.

340. 7558/019/01/013. Base. Yellowish white fabric with occasional grit inclusions. All-over clear glaze over-painted with green on interior. BD 0.12. Level 3.3.

341. 7558/019/01/013. Bowl. Yellowish white fabric with occasional grit inclusions. All-over clear glaze over-painted with green bands. RD 0.12. Level 3.3.

342. 7858/078/01/063. Bowl. Off-white fabric. All-over clear glaze with cobalt-blue under-painting. BD 0.045. Level 3.3–3.4.

343. 7858/006/01/013. Base. Off-white fabric with occasional inclusions. Thick clear glaze on interior. BD 0.08. Level 3.5.

344. 7758/121/01/120. Bowl. Off-white fabric with grit inclusions. Thick turquoise to clear glaze on interior and top of exterior. Traces of copper lustre over-painting on exterior. RD 0.13. Level 3.1.

345. 7758/096/02/007. Bowl. White fabric. All-over clear glaze with blue tinge with under-glaze red to brown, pale blue and dark blue painting. Various brown to red patterns, in brown panels divided by single pale blue line. Inverted dark blue triangles at top between panels. RD 0.138, BD 0.056, H 0.056. Level 3.3. Pl.8a.

346. 7759/055/01/076. Bowl. White fabric. Double glaze; black, blue and red painting between clear glazes. RD 0.28. Level 3.2. Pl.8b.

347. 7756/013/01/005. Bowl. Off-white fabric with moderate amount very fine grit inclusions. Double glaze. All-over clear glaze with dark green under pale green glaze. RD 0.20. Level 2.1b.

348. 7557/045/01/022. Base. Off-white fabric with occasional fine grit inclusions. All-over white glaze. BD 0.08. Level 2.2.

349. 7557/035/01/035. Bowl. White fabric with moderate amount very fine grit inclusions. All-over white glaze. RD 0.21. Level 2.1.

350. 7556/152/01/123. Jar. Off-white fabric with occasional inclusions. All-over white glaze with traces of red over-painting on exterior. RD 0.09. Level 1.1.

351. 7557/002/01/005. Sherd. White fabric with moderate amount very fine grit inclusions. All-over monochrome cobalt-blue glaze.

Carved decoration on exterior. Level 3.3–3.4.

352. 7557/033/01/017. Bowl. White fabric with moderate amount fine grit inclusions. All-over white glaze. Carved decoration on interior. RD 0.12. Level 3.1–3.2.

353. 7557/033/01/017. Sherd. Off-white fabric with moderate amount very fine grit inclusions. All-over white glaze. Carved decoration on exterior. Level 3.1–3.2.

354. 7658/138/01/144. Sherd. Off-white fabric with moderate quantity of fine grit inclusions. All-over cobalt-blue glaze. Carved decoration on interior. Level 1.2.

355. 7656/025/01/019. Bowl. Off-white fabric with moderate amount fine grit inclusions. All-over thin white glaze. Carved decoration on interior. RD 0.18. From recent robber trench.

356. 7659/034/01/045. Body sherds. Off-white fabric with moderate amount of fine grit inclusions. Interior: clear glaze, exterior: segments of different colours, cobalt-blue and purplish brown. Level 2.2.

357. 7558/115/01/116. Base. Off-white fabric with moderate amount fine grit inclusions. 356 may belong to same vessel. Wall of vessel divided by ridges on exterior, which determine extent of different glaze colours: blood-red, white, cobalt-blue, and copper-yellow. Interior clear glaze. Second/Waster (see p.75). BD 0.12. Level 3.1.

358. 7757/133/01/103. Divided dish. White fabric. All-over clear glaze, shading into turquoise. Glaze collects thickly in incised cross-shaped decoration, in interior, and shows as pale green. Underside has relief decoration. RD 0.12., H 0.022. Level 1.1.

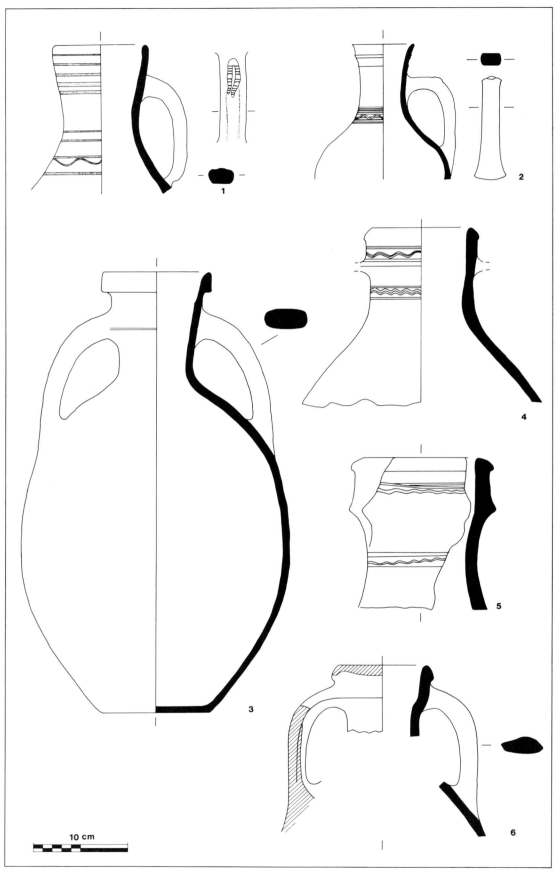

10 cm

Fig. 28.

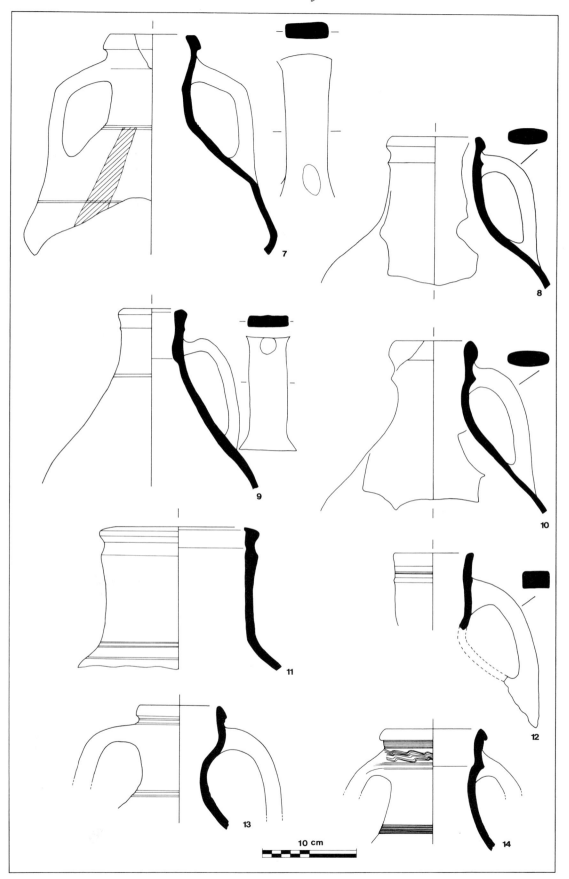

Fig. 29.

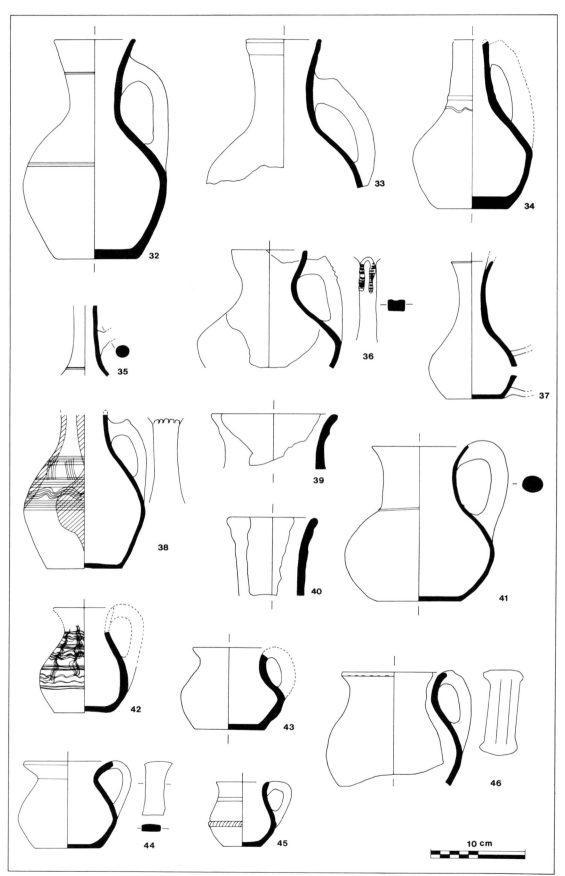

Fig. 32.

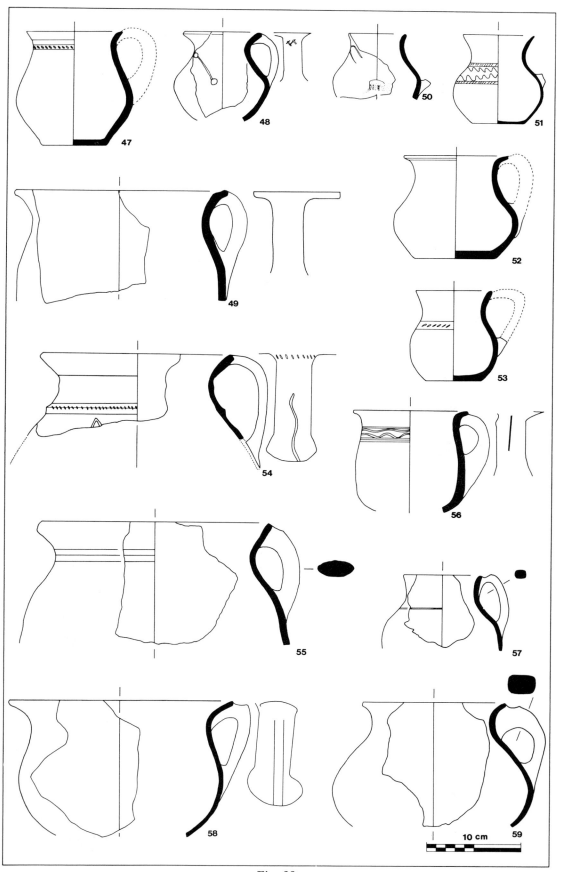

Fig. 33.

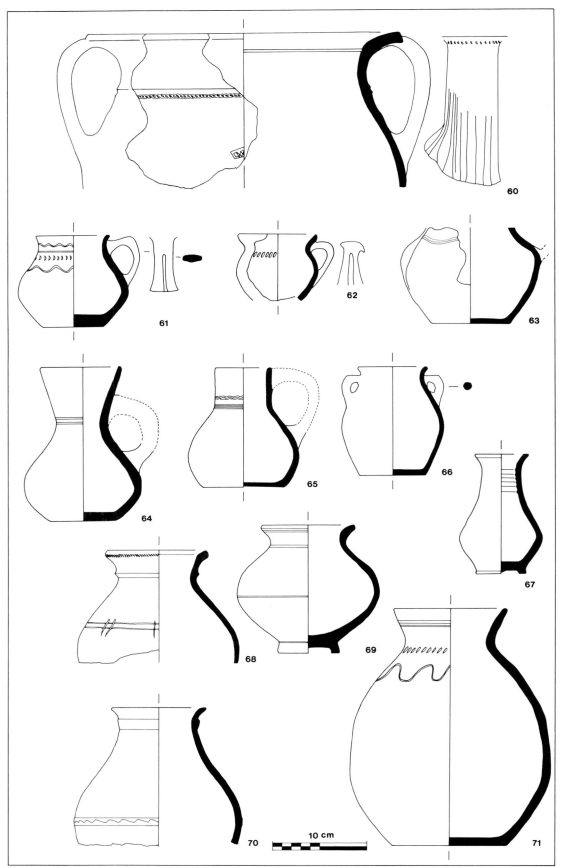

Fig. 34.

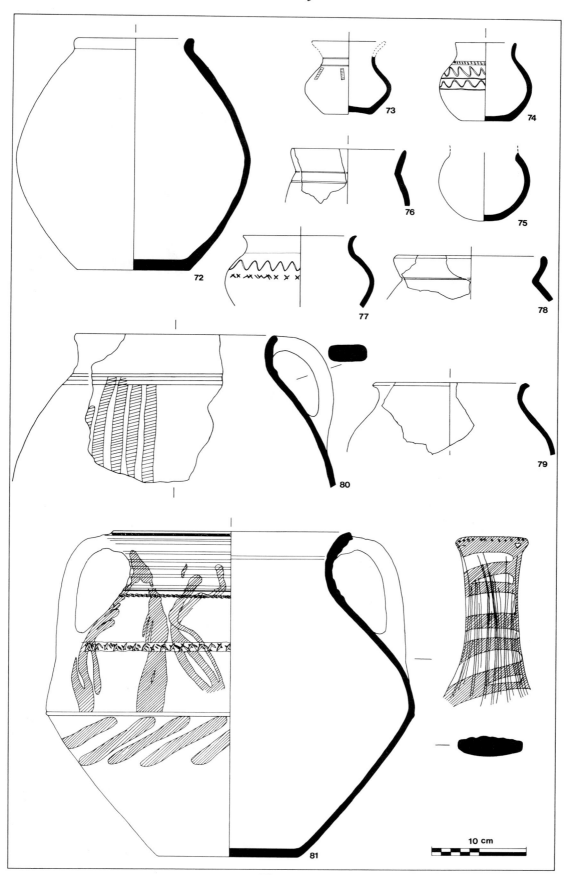

Fig. 35.

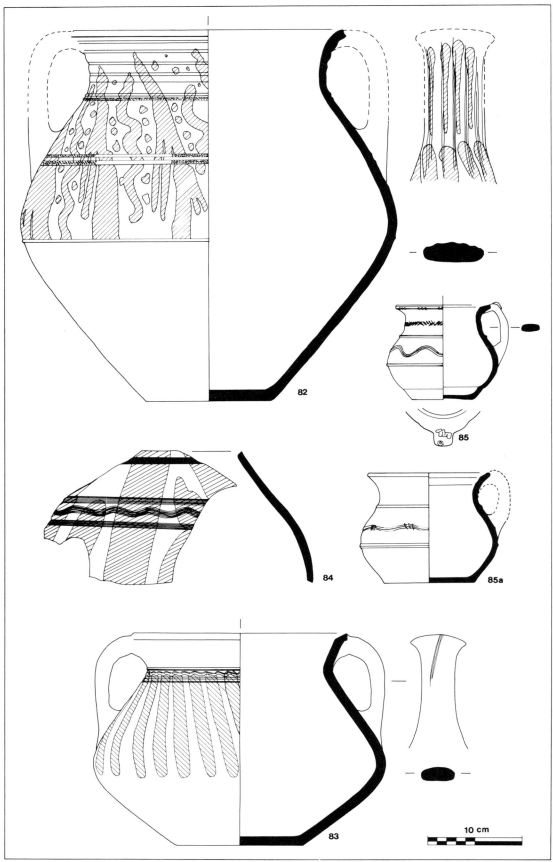

Fig. 36.

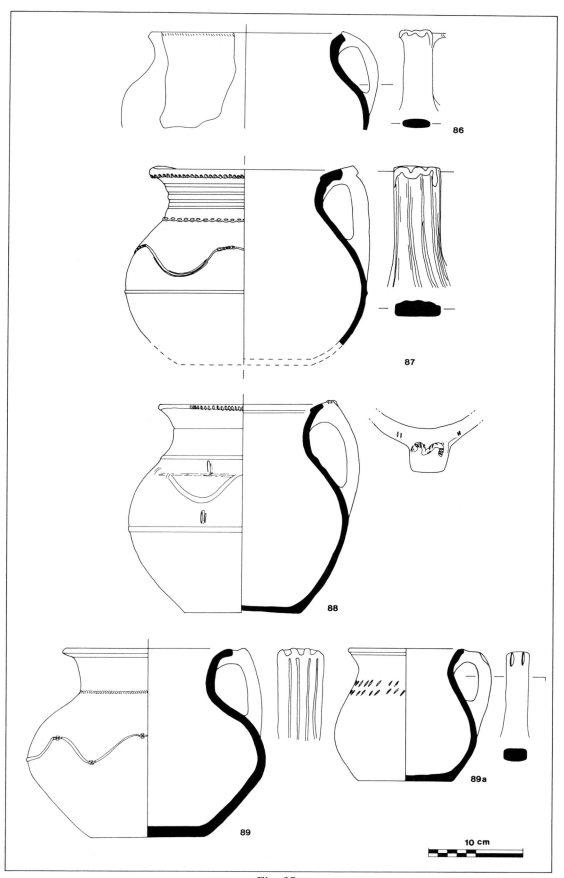

Fig. 37.

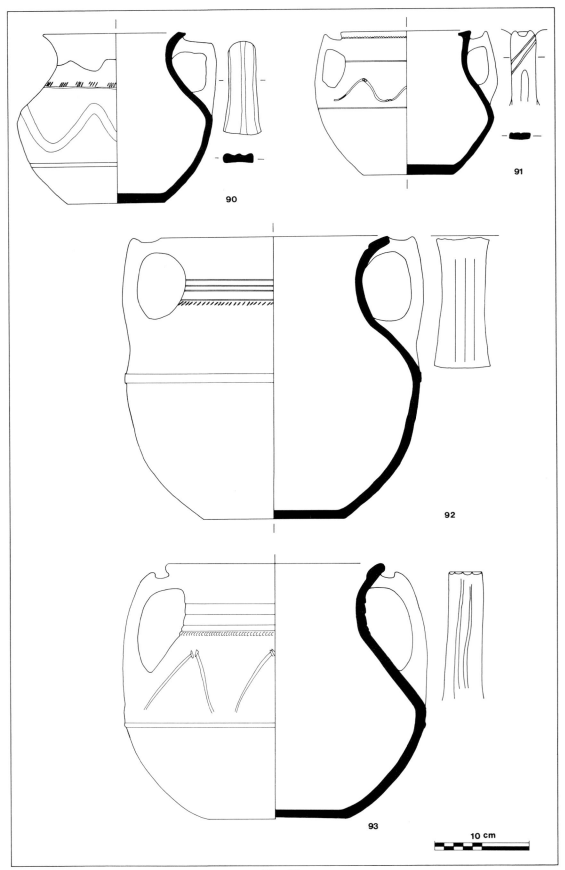

Fig. 38.

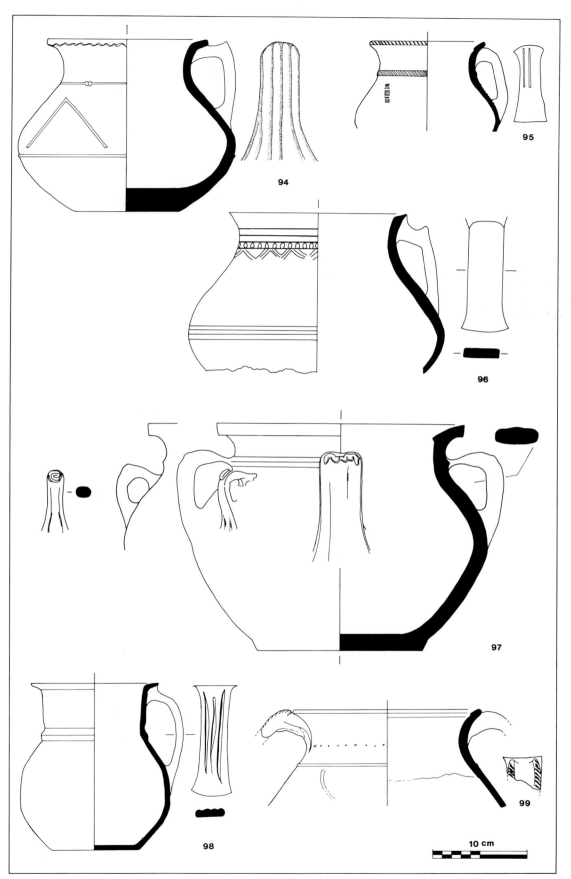

Fig. 39.

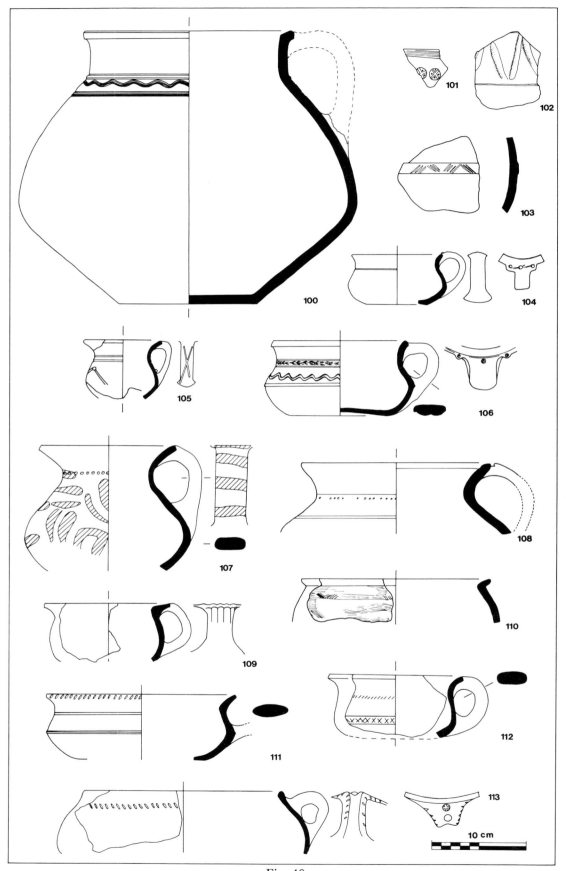

Fig. 40.

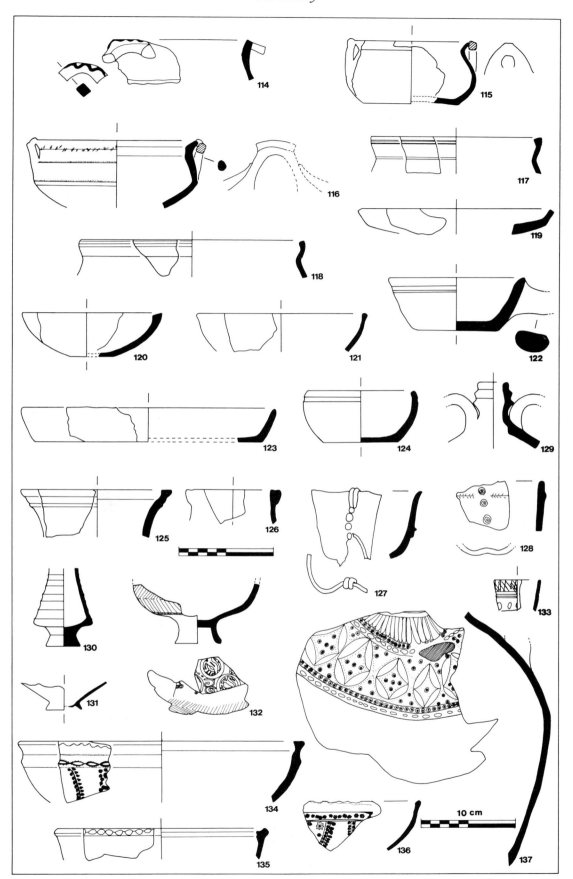

Fig. 41.

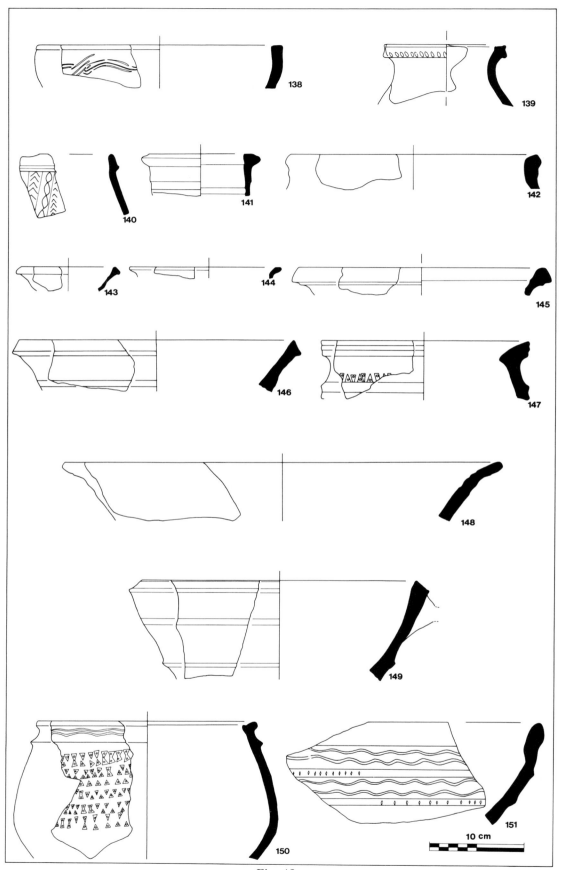

Fig. 42.

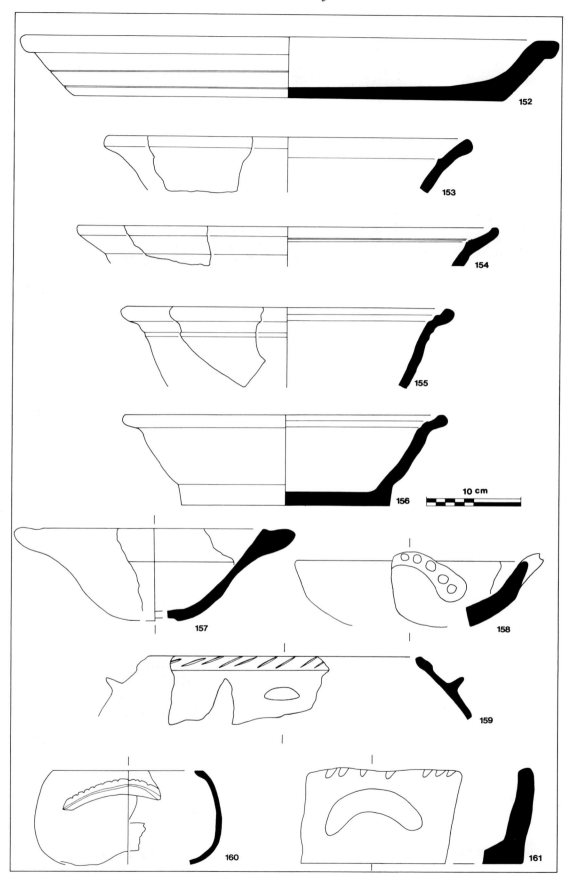

Fig. 43.

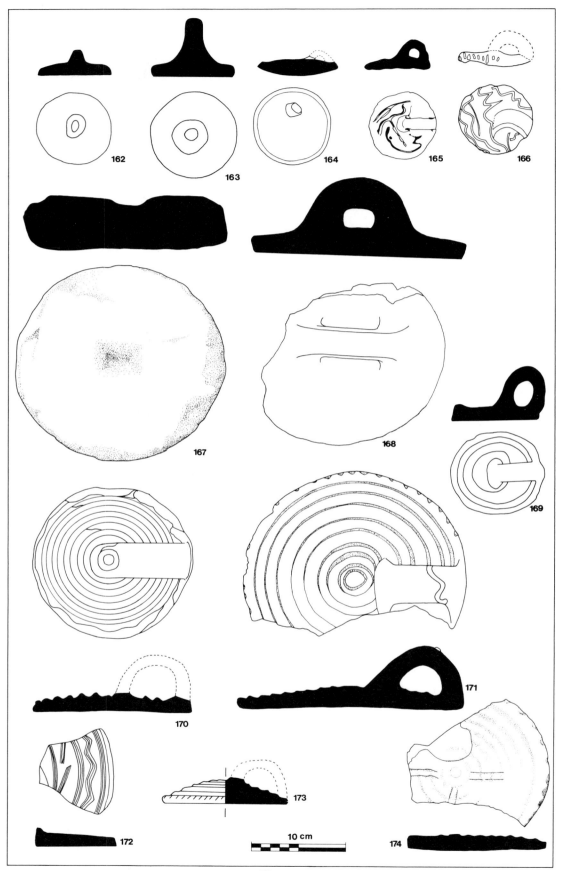

Fig. 44.

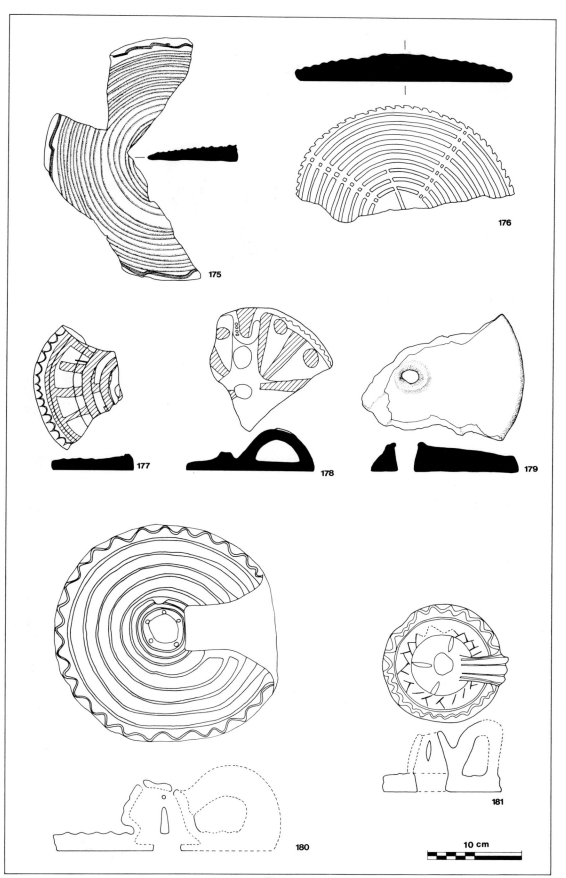

Fig. 45.

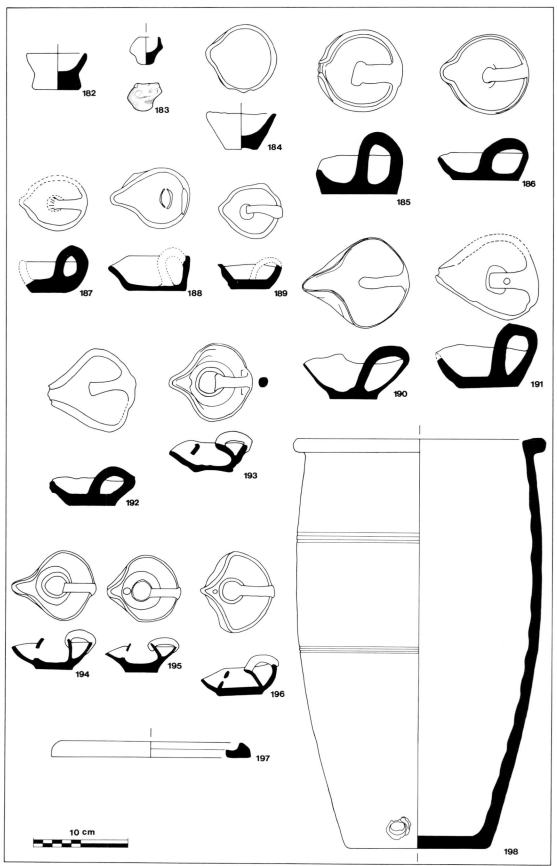

Fig. 46.

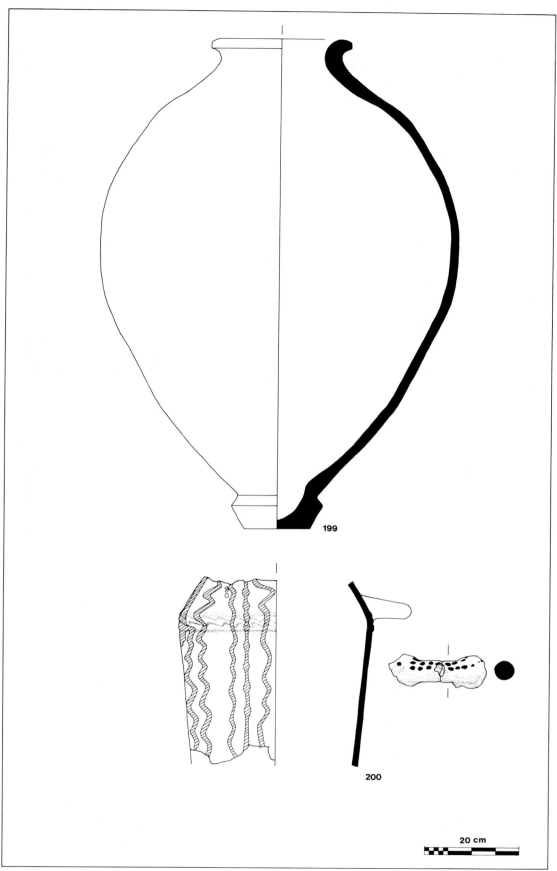

Fig. 47.

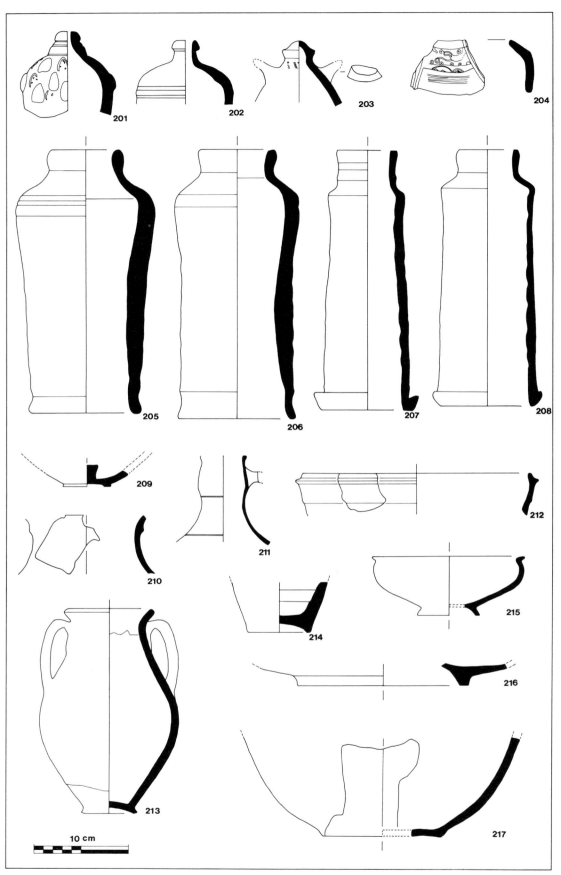

Fig. 48.

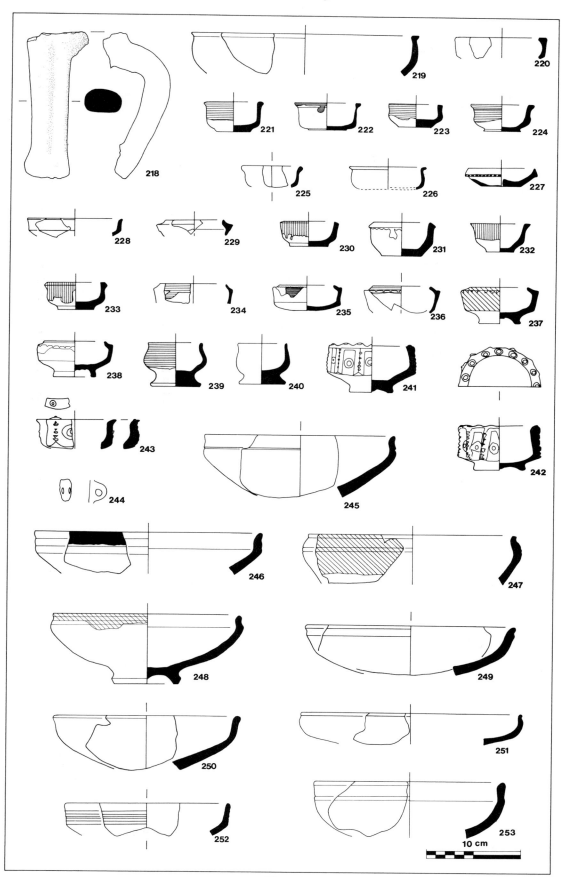

Fig. 49.

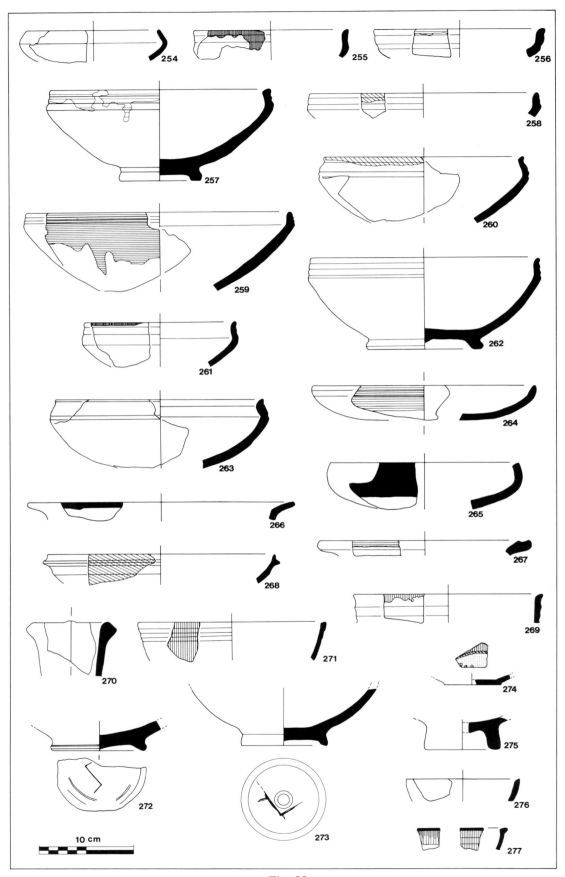

Fig. 50.

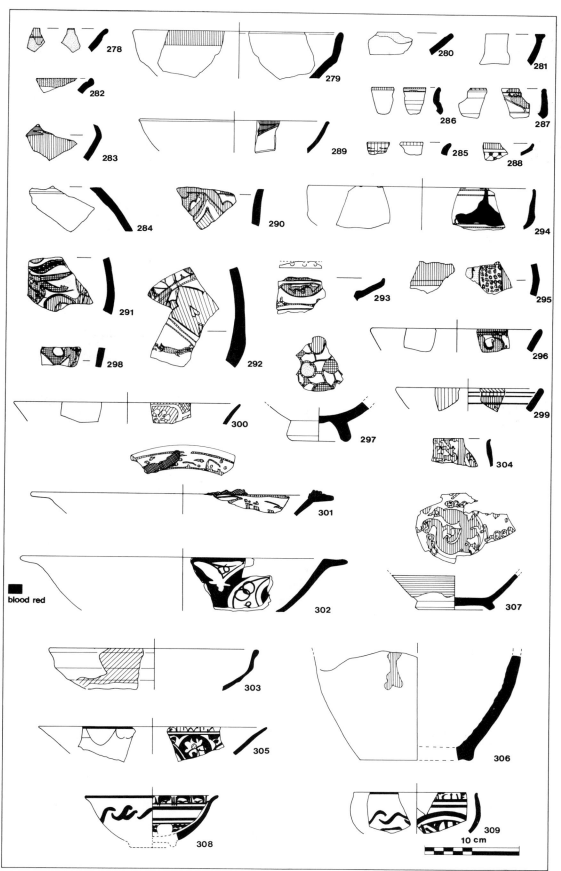

Fig. 51.

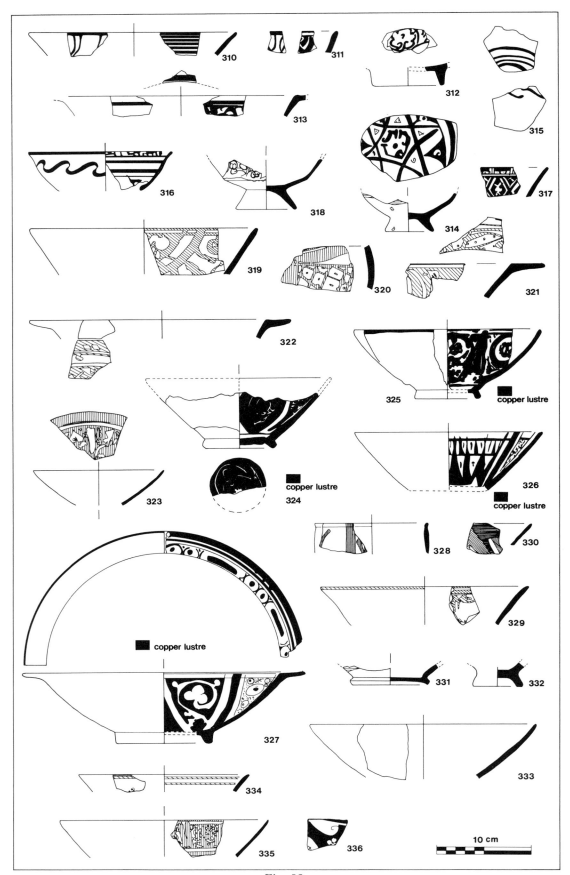

Fig. 52.

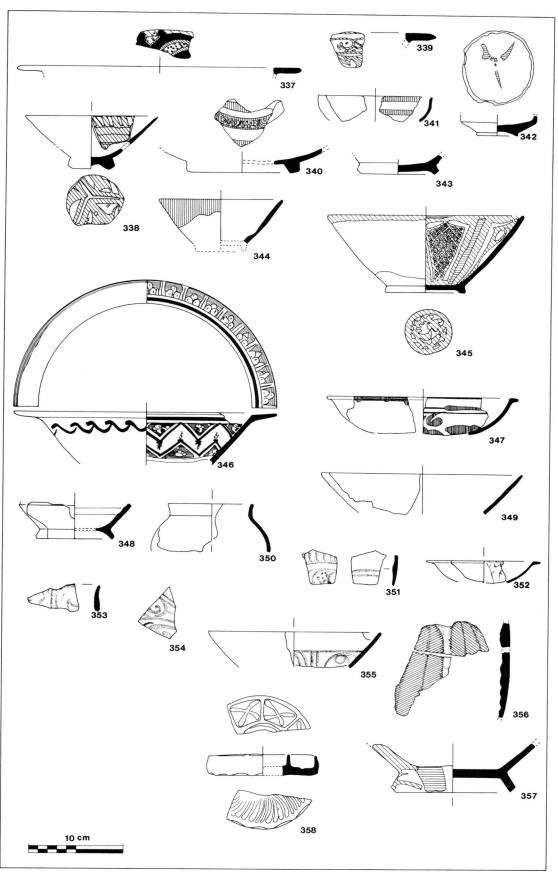

Fig.53.

CHAPTER 7

The Objects

The objects that are published here result from the policy of finds selection outlined above (pp.19, 20 and 71 on pottery). They are complete, or near complete, objects that show part of the everyday life of the inhabitants on the höyük during the Medieval period. These include ornaments, household objects, agricultural implements, tools, weapons and architectural fragments.

Metal

The filed decoration on the pins (nos 21 and 22) and on the spoons (nos 78 and 79) is the same as that on the make-up sticks and spatulae at Hama (Ploug and Oldenburg 1969: Fig.24 nos 7 and 10; Fig.26 no.7). The style of the handle on the copper alloy lamp (no.28) is similar to a handle illustrated from Hama (Ploug and Oldenburg 1969: Fig.19 no.9). The open iron lamp (no.86), although smaller, is of the same shape as one again from Hama (Ploug and Oldenburg 1969: Fig.16 no.8). The reliquary cross (no.73) although found on our spoil heap, is certainly contemporary with the Medieval settlement and is of a twelfth century style (British Museum 1921: Fig.16). The iron sickle (no.97) has parallels at Aşvan (Mitchell 1980: Fig.118 nos 32 and 33). The bell (no.87a), although smaller, is very similar in style to one found at Samarra (Iraq Government 1940: 9 and Pl.139). The style of decoration of incised concentric circles with or without a central dot is found on stone and bone objects at Tille. This decorative style again was common at Hama and Aşvan.

Bone

The decoration and shape of the Tille bone spindle whorls (nos 148–158) are similar to ones found at Hama (Oldenburg 1969: Figs 44–46) and Aşvan (Mitchell 1980: Fig. 123 no. 77).

Stone

Spindle whorls at Hama (Ploug 1969: fig. 39 nos 8, 10 and 11) match the shape of ones from Tille (nos 160–175).

Metal

The arrow heads illustrated (nos 101–103, 105–120) fall into five groups: (1) leaf-shaped (nos 113 and 115), (2) flat, rhomboid (nos 101, 102, 105, 112, 114, 116 and 117), (3) triangular in plan, square in section (nos 103 and 106–111), (4) rounded (nos 119 and 120), although these may originally have been diamond-shaped, now badly corroded, (5) barbed (no.118), the only example recovered. The nails can be divided into two groups (round-headed and square-headed) although, owing to corrosion, it can be difficult at times to identify the group to which examples belong.

Clay

The fireplace surround 142 finds a parallel in more complete examples found *in situ* at Gritille, downstream from Tille (Redford 1986: 110–111, Pl.Xb). The gaming board for 'Nine Men's Morris' (no.200) is found on a variety of sites (Johns 1935; Thalman 1978).

Glass

The glass vessels that are illustrated are a selection of rim and base types, with a few handles. They mostly cover the whole range of types present at Tille. The glass was very fragmentary and little attempt was made to restore profiles. No comment is offered here on the vessels since other sites in the area have not (at the time of writing) been published.

The purpose in examining the sample of glass bracelet fragments was to establish a type series, the range of colours, the thicknesses of the band and the diameters of the bracelets. The sample, in all 374 fragments, was selected haphazardly. Groups of batches from squares were either kept or discarded, according to mood, without reference to previous selections.

The different types are illustrated (Fig. 54). A brief description of each type is given below. After the description is given the range of thickness of the glass band.

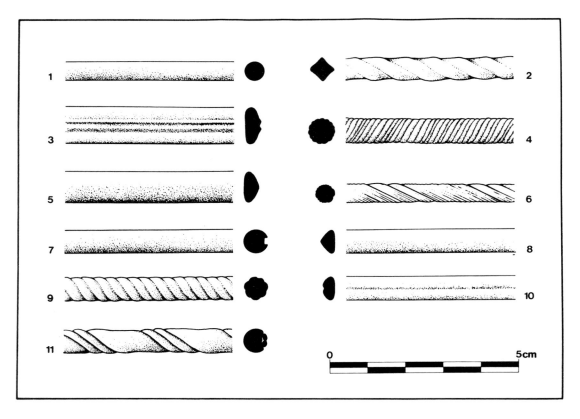

Fig. 54. Glass Bracelet Types

Type 1   is plain, round in section. 0.003 to 0.0095m.
Type 2   is loosely twisted. 0.004 to 0.0115m.
Type 3   outer face has a raised ridge with a groove running along it. 0.003 to 0.006m.
Type 4   is tightly twisted. 0.004 to 0.010m.
Type 5   is raised on the outside to form a flat triangle. 0.003 to 0.006m.
Type 6   is made from three pieces, one tightly twisted and the other two twisted loosely around the first piece. 0.005 to 0.007m.
Type 7   is similar to type 1 but has shallow groove on the inside face. 0.0065m.
Type 8   is raised on the outside to form an isosceles triangle. 0.003 to 0.007m.
Type 9   is twisted more tightly than type 2 but not as tightly as type 4. 0.004 to 0.008m.
Type 10   is flattened with a groove down the outer face. 0.003 to 0.008m.
Type 11   is made of three pieces; the two thinner rods are twisted around larger. 0.004 to 0.0065m.

The following tables give the colour range down the side and the bracelet diameters (in cm.) across the top, for each type.

Type 1

	4	5	6	7	8	10	?	TOTAL
pale green		2	6	1	6			15
pale blue		1	8		3			12
green		1	5	3	5			14
black	1	1	27	2	19	1		51
black to yellow			7	3	5			15
blue	3		21	4	6			34
clear	1				1			2
black with yellow strip				1				1
blue with red stripe							1	1
purple				1				1
yellow			3					3
TOTAL	5	5	77	15	45	1	1	149

Type 2

	6	7	8	TOTAL
pale green	1		1	2
pale blue	2		2	4
green	2			2
black	1	2	6	9
black to yellow	1			1
blue	3	1		4
pale green with red thread			1	1
purple			1	1
TOTAL	10	3	11	24

Type 3

	5	6	7	8	TOTAL
pale blue		2			2
green		2			2
black		2		3	5
black to yellow		1		1	2
blue	1	3		1	5
blood red		1			1
dark purple		1			1
yellow		2			2
TOTAL	1	14		5	20

Type 4

	4	5	6	7	8	?	TOTAL
pale green	2	1	2	1	1		7
pale blue			3				3
green			4		1		5
black	1	2	13		2		18
black to yellow		1	2		1		4
blue	1	2	6	2	2		13
blood red					1		1
pale blue with white thread	1						1
purple						1	1
dark blue with red thread				1	3		4
black with red thread					1		1
black with blue thread			1				1
yellow and green					1		1
green with white thread					1		1
TOTAL	5	6	31	4	14	1	61

Type 5

	4	5	6	7	8	?	TOTAL
pale green			2	1	1		4
pale blue			2				2
green	1		1		1		3
black to yellow			1			1	2
blue		1	2	1			4
purple					1		1
?black		1					1
TOTAL	1	2	8	2	3	1	17

Type 6

	6	7	8	TOTAL
green	1			1
black	1			1
blue	1		2	3
purple	1			1
black with pale blue thread	1			1
yellow			1	1
TOTAL	5		3	8

Type 7

	6	TOTAL
blue	1	1
TOTAL	1	1

Type 8

	4	5	6	7	8	10	TOTAL
pale green			3				3
pale blue		2	1				3
green			3				3
black	1		7				8
black to yellow			8	1	1	1	11
blue			3		1		4
TOTAL	1	2	25	1	2	1	32

Type 9

	5	6	7	8	TOTAL
pale green		4			4
pale blue		1		1	2
green	2	3	1	1	7
black	2	5		2	9
black to yellow	1	5	1	2	9
blue	1	6		1	8
dark green			1		1
dark blue with red strips				1	1
TOTAL	6	24	3	8	41

Type 10

	5	6	7	8	TOTAL
pale green	1	2			3
pale blue		2			2
green	1	2			3
black		2			2
black to yellow	1	1		1	3
blue		3			3
yellow		1			1
TOTAL	3	13		1	17

Type 11

	4	5	6	7	8	TOTAL
black	1		1		1	3
blue			1			1
TOTAL	1		2		1	4

The following table gives the number and percentage of fragments for each type.

Type	Bracelet Fragments	Percentage
1	149	39.8
2	24	6.4
3	20	5.3
4	61	16.3
5	17	4.5
6	8	2.1
7	1	0.3
8	32	8.6
9	41	11.0
10	17	4.5
11	4	1.1
TOTAL	374	99.9

The following gives the number of fragments for each colour.

Colour	Number of Fragments	Percentage
pale blue	30	8.0
blue	80	21.4
pale green	38	10.1
green	40	10.7
dark green	1	0.3
black	107	28.6
black to yellow	47	12.6
purple	6	1.6
yellow	7	1.9
blood red	2	0.5
clear	2	0.5
black with coloured thread	4	1.1
blue with coloured thread	7	1.9
green with coloured thread	3	0.8
TOTAL	374	100.0

The following gives the number and percentage for the diameter of bracelets to the nearest centimeter.

Diameter	Number of Fragments	Percentage
4	13	3.5
5	30	8.0
6	205	54.8
7	28	7.5
8	93	24.9
9	0	0.0
10	2	0.5
?	?	0.8
TOTAL	374	100.0

The tables show that type one is by far the most common type, being 39.8% of the total, while type four, the next most common, accounted for only 16.3%. Just over two-thirds (67.1%) belonged to the three most common types, 1, 4 and 9. Of the colours, black was the most common (28.6%) with blue (21.4%) next, followed by black to yellow (12.8%). When the basic colours are clustered, black accounts for 42.2%, blue for 31.3%, green for 21.9% and others for 4.5%. Over half (54.8%) of the fragments came from bracelets that had a diameter of 6cm. while 24.9% came from bracelets of diameter 8cm.

Catalogue of Objects

Fig. 55 Bracelets and Pendant

1. 7557/175/31/092. Iron bracelet. Simple band tapering to points. Span (max.) 0.062; (band) D 0.006. Level 1.2.

2. 7756/029/31/058. Iron bracelet. Hexagonal shaped band. Ends rounded. Span (max.) 0.06; (band) D (avg.) 0.007. Level 1.1–1.2.

3. 7457/021/31/011. Copper alloy bracelet. Made from two pieces of wire, each doubled back to form an end loop. Inside face of wire is flattened. End loop has filed lines for decoration. D c.0.055; (band) D 0.005; (wire strands) D 0.0023. Level 1.2.

4. 7858/178/31/075. Copper alloy bracelet. Simple band, slightly flattened on inside; ends of band pointed. Decoration: rope pattern on upper surface but very worn. Span (max.) 0.049; (band) D 0.004. Level 1.2.

5. 7457/021/31/012. Copper alloy bracelet. Simple band, flattened on inside. Filed lines on sides of bracelet. Ends flattened and stamped geometrical patterns. Span (max.) 0.056; (band) W 0.005, Th 0.0041. Level 1.2.

6. 7658/310/31/105. Copper alloy bracelet. Band flattened to an oval in cross-section. Finial shaped by hammering. Decoration: between finial and band, a spacer formed by rings (only on outer surface); finial is broad, flat, triangular in plan; decorated by drilled dots. (Band) W 0.0079, Th 0.0037. Level 1.1.

7. 7457/041/31/018. Copper alloy bracelet. Flattened band. On wider parts of band there are traces of solder. Span (max.) 0.049; (band) W 0.006 and 0.01, Th 0.001. Level 1.1.

8. 7557/231/31/115. Copper alloy bracelet. At end, a simple tapering point without finial decoration. Broken in middle; soldering visible around break ([?]for ornament or for repair). Span 0.05 to 0.07; (band) D (max.) 0.0055 . Level 1.1.

9. 7756/039/31/044. Copper alloy pendant. Simple shaft round which thin wire has been twisted. Ends of arms pointed. At centre: a ball made from two hemispherical cups. Span (max.) 0.047. Level 2.1.

N.B. The bracelet previously published as Medieval is Hellenistic (French, Moore and Russell 1982: fig. 10 no.3).

Fig. 56 Rings, Pins and Needles

10. 7556/091/31/073. Copper alloy ring. Single strand of wire; the two ends twisted together to form a knot. Span (max.) 0.0234; (wire) Th 0.002. Level 1.1.

11. 7657/083/31/056. Copper alloy ring. Band oval in cross-section. Flat bezel with incised inverted triangle. D 0.017, W 0.0033, Th 0.001. Level 1.1–1.2.

12. 7558/026/31/008. Copper alloy ring. Simple band with flattened ends. Span (max.) 0.018; (band) D 0.0023-0.0028. Level 3.4.

13. 7556/025/31/019. Copper alloy ring. Single strand of wire with thin strip of copper alloy twisted round band at one point. D 0.0185; (wire) Th 0.0011; (strip) W 0.0025, Th 0.0005. Level 2.1b.

14. 7557/175/31/095. Silver ring. Single strand of wire; ends flattened but not joined. D 0.0195; (wire) Th 0.0013. Level 1.2.

15. 7756/013/31/004. Copper alloy ring. Simple band; ends flattened and crossed over. D 0.0145; (band) Th 0.0017 to 0.002. Level 2.1b.

16. 7758/109/31/070. Copper alloy ring. Plain. D 0.034, Th 0.003 to 0.004. Level 2.2–3.1.

17. 7758/010/31/009. Copper alloy ring. Single strand of wire with ends flattened. D (max.) 0.017; (wire) Th 0.0014. Level 3.5.

18. 7558/106/31/040. Copper alloy ring. Single strand of wire with thin strip of copper alloy twisted round band at one point. Probable D 0.016; (wire) Th 0.00125. Level 2.2.

19. 7757/093/31/069. Copper alloy needle. Tapered shaft, round-sectioned at top, square-sectioned at bottom. Head flattened and turned over. D (max.) 0.0027, L 0.0617. Level 1.2.

20. 7758/252/31/129. Copper alloy needle. Round-sectioned tapering shaft. One end broken, other end bent over. Top flat. L 0.0478. Level 1.1a.

21. 7557/087/31/068. Copper alloy pin. Round-sectioned tapering shaft with square-sectioned head. Top of head broken off. Head decorated with incised lines on all four faces. Made of strip turned over. L 0.095; (shaft) D (max.) 0.004; (head) W 0.0048, Th 0.0016. Level 2.1a–2.2.

22. 7657/168/31/118. Copper alloy pin. Round, straight shaft with finial of three cubes, hammered square; the middle cube then hammered into a diamond lozenge on each face; above and below, the boxes have been hammered into hexagons with a groove cut horizontally across each face. L 0.066. Level 1.2.

23. 7858/184/31/076. Copper alloy needle. Simple shaft, slightly tapering. Top of shaft flattened and pierced. L 0.084. Level 1.1.

24. 7858/081/31/050. Copper alloy pin. Simple shaft. One end rounded, other pointed. Round in cross-section. L 0.118. Scale 1:2. Level 2.2.

25. 7556/103/31/069. Copper alloy needle. Round-sectioned tapering shaft. End flattened and bent over. L 0.073. Level 1.1a.

26. 7659/059/31/012. Copper alloy pin. Simple round-sectioned shaft. Rounded head with flat top. L c.0.085. Level 2.2.

27. 7656/105/31/063. Copper alloy needle. Shaft formed by a strip which has been bent over. Head flattened and turned over. Tip blunt. L 0.0485; W (top) 0.0058 by 0.0040, (top shaft) 0.0033 by 0.0028, (tip shaft) 0.0025 by 0.0023. Level 1.1.

Fig. 57 Copper alloy lamp

28. 7858/071/31/039. Copper alloy lamp consisting of two parts, (1) the base which consists of a shallow cylinder standing on three legs, twin spouts and an ornate handle soldered to the base, (2) the lid, or upper part, which fits onto the base and was secured in place by fitting tightly under the lower part of the handle. The lid is formed from a flat plate with a raised rim (0.008 high). Affixed to the plate are two perforated covers for the spouts. In the centre of the lid is a domed section, 0.058 in diameter, in the top of which is an opening, covered by a small hinged lid, presumably for filling the lamp. On the flat part of the lid are a number of small drill or punch holes in regular positions. Four lie on lines between the centre of the lamp and the middle of each spout, two on each line, one at the base of the domed part, the other by the rim. A further three, in triangular pattern, lie slightly to one side of the main axis of the lamp between the two spouts. A triangular tail secures the handle to the body of the lamp. It is a trefoil shape, surmounted by a spherical knob. The legs terminate in stud-shaped feet. (Body) H 0.03, (with lid) 0.04, H (total) (including legs and handle) 0.102; L (total) (including spout) 0.146. Level 2.2.

Fig. 58

29. 7656/060/31/040. Copper alloy lamp. Straight sides, flat back with two spouts close together on one side. Three feet on under side in shape of human foot. Lid a separate piece with two projections exactly fitting over the spouts of the main body but allowing abundant space for the wick. Bee-hive shaped boss on cover, with filler hole and (?)hinge for missing lid. Surface of cover pierced in an approximately geometric pattern. No evidence for a handle. H (total) 0.054, L (total) 0.12; (body) D 0.0825. Level 2.1–2.2.

30. 7556/092/31/068. Copper alloy lamp. Thin, hammered sheeting: made in two halves. Shape: conical, flat (?)base (now dented); a simple bee-hive centre with filler-hole; hole for wick at base of bee-hive; spout/nozzle not preserved. D 0.0835, H 0.086. Scale 1:2. Level 1.2.

Fig. 59 Sickle, Copper Alloy Hanger and Scale-pan

30a. 7759/130/31/038. Iron sickle. Short handle, long flat-curved blade. W c.0.44; L c.0.50; (blade) W c.0.031, Th 0.004. Scale 1:4. Level 1.1.

31. 7758/121/31/077. Copper alloy hanger. Made from lengths of wire joined by looping the ends. (Top piece) L 0.094, Th 0.0023; (middle three pieces) L c.0.125, Th 0.001; (bottom piece) L c.0.175, Th 0.001. Scale 1:2. Level 3.1.

32. 7656/067/31/044. Copper alloy scale-pan. Simple flat dish with raised rim. Pierced at three equidistant points. Inside: three groups of two concentric incised lines; in centre, inside innermost group of lines: a flower-pattern formed by semicircular, compass-drawn lines. A groove below rim outside. D 0.19, De 0.027. Scale 1:2. Level 1.2.

Fig. 60 Copper Alloy Objects

33. 7858/081/31/044. Copper alloy bell. Smooth, slightly bee-hive shaped profile. At the top are the remains of the cannon, a saddle shaped protrusion with roughened patches, where presumably the loop has

broken off. There are also two holes in the upper part of the bell, one of these, the upper one, may have held the clapper. RD 0.06, H 0.042, Th 0.002 to 0.0025. Level 2.1.

34. 7756/013/31/004. Copper alloy plate. Simple flat dish with raised rim. Ham-mered. D 0.055, Th 0.001 De 0.009. Level 2.1b.

35. 7556/117/31/074. Copper alloy scale-pan. Simple flat dish with raised rim. Pierced at three equidistant points; two broken. Hammered. D 0.056, Th 0.001, De 0.011. Level 1.1.

36. 7858/184/31/077. Copper alloy part of a (?)plate. Slightly curved. Decoration: a series of incised circles with central punched dot. Th 0.001. Level 1.1.

37. 7559/119/31/052. Copper alloy part of a disc. Flat, slightly rough surface. Incised line 0.0036 in from edge on one side. D 0.09, Th 0.00105. Level: not assigned.

38. 7656/059/31/037. Copper alloy disc. Simple slightly curved dish with raised rim. D 0.0546, Th 0.00115. Level 2.1.

Fig. 61 Buttons, Studs and Straps

39. 7659/064/31/023. Copper alloy capping. Cup-shaped with eight slits; slightly raised area either side of slits. Central part depressed with pierced hole in centre. D 0.018, H (max.) 0.0075. Level 2.1–2.2.

40. 7556/086/31/059. Copper alloy button. Circular; centre of top concave. Sides bent back. Hook soldered on to rest. Hook square in cross-section. D 0.0265. Level 1.2.

41. 7557/150/31/077. Copper alloy ornament. Simple disc, concave; inside: two broad, raised rings divided by one narrow, raised ring. At centre: a hole. On edge of disc: a tooth pattern, mostly lost. D 0.032, Th 0.001. Level 1.2–2.1.

42. 7858/178/31/078. Copper alloy (?)capping. Simple cup shape. Centre pierced. D 0.0141, H 0.0075, Th 0.0007. Level 1.2.

43. 7757/113/31/082. Copper alloy part of a (?)pendant. Two half spheres, with hole punched through from outside. Applied pellet on one half near join. D 0.018, H 0.017; (metal) Th 0.001. Level 1.2.

44. 7556/087/31/064. Copper alloy stud. Simple cup shape. Pin soldered to inside. D 0.012; (head) H 0.005; (pin) L 0.008. Level 1.1a.

45. 7557/219/31/107. Copper alloy capping. Cup-shaped. Pierced hole in centre. Pin head in hole. H 0.0115, W 0.017 to 0.021. Level 1.1.

46. 7556/086/31/061. Copper alloy stud. Simple cup shape. Pin soldered to inside. D 0.022; (head) H 0.008; (pin) L 0.006 (broken). Level 1.2.

47. 7859/018/31/006. Copper alloy tie. Rounded shank with two curved, round discs as heads. (Heads) D 0.0155, Th 0.001 to 0.004; (shaft) D c.0.005, H 0.01; H (total) 0.017. Level 2.1b.

48. 7559/122/31/061. Copper alloy part of a (?)pendant. Two half spheres, held to-gether by iron rivet. Rivet shaft section square; rivet ends flattened. H (total) 0.013, W 0.0135-0.0145. Level: not assigned.

49. 7557/195/31/101. Copper alloy button. Simple, shallow cup-shaped object shank soldered onto button at both ends. Shank square in section. D 0.022, H 0.0065; (head) Th 0.0008; (hook) Th 0.0025. Level 1.2a.

50. 7657/208/31/149. Copper alloy button. Circular; convex. Hook soldered on to button at both ends; section round. D 0.0224 to 0.0235; (top) Th 0.0018; H (total) 0.0065. Level 1.1.

51. 7556/080/31/050. Copper alloy strip, (?)part of bracelet. Strip of copper alloy slightly curved. One end broken. Other end taper-ing to curved end; decorated with two in-cised lines parallel to length. W 0.0078, Th 0.0011, L 0.0782. Level 1.2.

52. 7556/080/31/051. Copper alloy strip, (?)part of bracelet. Thin strip, decorated where two ends joined. Decoration in form of twist of copper alloy around strip. W 0.0025, Th 0.0008, L 0.0825. Level 1.2.

53. 7558/068/31/029. Copper alloy strip. Strip of copper alloy, perhaps segment of a necklace; cable pattern on upper, rounded face. The terminals consist of a slightly flattened area (0.006 by 0.005) with a hole bored through them. The upper, decorated face bears traces of gilding. The lower is flat and ungilded. W 0.004 to 0.005, Th up to 0.0025, L 0.127. Level 3.2.

Fig. 62 Copper Alloy and Iron Fittings

54. 7758/122/31/099. Copper alloy fitting. Back hollow as if to fit around a rounded object. Front of shaft rounded; bottom broken. Between shaft and finial there is a rounded spacer. Front of finial is flat and decorated with incision. L 0.021. Level 1.2–3.1.

55. 7759/039/31/021. Copper alloy binding. Thin strip widening out around pierced hole. W 0.006 to 0.014 (around hole), Th c.0.005, L (total) c.0.185. Found with 56. Debris on side of mound.

56. 7759/039/31/020. Copper alloy fitting. Broken sheet of copper alloy held to strip by two copper alloy rivets. Strip bent over top of sheet and the object onto which it is fitted. Drawn showing back view. (Sheet) Th 0.001 to 0.0015; (strip) Th 0.0005 to 0.001. Debris on side of mound.

57. 7557/071/31/062. Copper alloy (?)harness fitting. End of fitting broken from rest of object. Shaped at end into a stylized head with open mouth and two eyes. On top of fitting is an animal lying with head turned to side; mouth is shown; at its feet is another animal facing the opposite direction. H 0.039. Level 2.1a–2.1b.

58. 7758/109/31/065. Copper alloy and iron fitting. Strip of copper alloy bent over; on the left hand side there are two copper alloy rivets attaching small piece of iron (on inner side). Two more rivets through other side of object. H 0.0427. Level 2.2–3.1.

59. 7858/102/31/063. Copper alloy (?)harness fitting. Trefoil shaped. Protrusion in centre on one side. H 0.039 by 0.046, Th 0.004. Level 2.1b.

60. 7758/261/31/136. Iron fitting. Shaped as a crucifix. Made from one piece of rect-angular-sectioned iron and shaped into a crucifix by folding; at the top, bottom and sides the folds are loose. The hole in the bottom limb is formed by a loop folded right-angles to the other three limbs of the crucifix. H 0.0794; (arms) W 0.0393, Th 0.0076 to 0.0089 except for bottom loop—0.0111. Level 1.1.

61. 7556/030/31/024. Iron (?)harness fitting. Quatrefoil shape made from one piece of iron; rounded and rectangular in section. Each arm forms a loop with a hole central to the arms. H 0.055 by 0.052, Th 0.0025 to 0.003. Level 2.2.

62. 7758/234/31/127. Copper alloy fitting, (?)part of hinge. Trefoil-shaped finial with top lobe forming three points. Stalk which is curved backwards is broken. Two thin lines incised on stalk. H 0.0425, Th 0.001. Level 1.2.

Fig. 63 Copper Alloy and Iron Objects

63. 7757/040/31/037. Copper alloy handle. Now bent. Middle part oval in section, lower part flattened. Near top is pierced hole; slightly lower are two incised lines on top face with two nicks between them. The back of the area of the hole and the decorated part are flat. The front is round. Splayed, bottom end probably welded to vessel; wire through hole to suspend vessel. W 0.0047–0.0072, L 0.0915. Level 2.1.

64. 7656/002/31/007. Copper alloy handle. Both ends have holes for attaching the handle to the vessel; broken at bottom. Inside face flat. W 0.005 to 0.006, Th 0.002 to 0.003 (thicker at top). Topsoil.

65. 7858/184/31/079. Copper alloy handle. Loop of copper alloy with ends turned over to form loops. H 0.028, Th 0.0016 to 0.0018, Span (between loops) 0.02. Level 1.1.

66. 7557/147/31/086. Copper alloy handle. Circular in section with ends hammered flat and pierced. Part of iron 'pin' in one hole. Th 0.004 to 0.005 near ends, Span (between loops) 0.02. Level 1.2–2.1.

67. 7556/038/31/026. Iron ferrule. For 0.03 at the top the section is round while the remainder is rectangular. The bottom end is rounded. Formed from a sheet which has been bent round. H 0.104; (top) D 0.008 to 0.009; (iron) Th 0.001 to 0.002. Level 2.1a–2.1b.

68. 7556/057/31/030. Copper alloy (?)stopper. A series of rings above a slightly tapering circular (?)stopper. Top ring has loop; part of a copper alloy passes ring through the loop. H 0.04. Level 1.1.

69. 7858/081/31/051. Copper alloy sheath. Sheet bent round to form a cylinder; well overlapped. Top splayed out to form a shoulder or rim, protruding 0.0005 out from cylinder. Tapers slightly to open bottom. H 0.061; (top) D 0.012 by 0.014; (bottom) D 0.006 by 0.007, Th 0.0005 to 0.001. Level 2.2.

70. 7757/028/31/015. Copper alloy buckle. Only two sides survive. Top side is a simple, bar circular in cross-section. Other side is a heptagonal figure tapering from the middle to the two ends. At middle is indentation to hold the tongue. At the corner, the buckle increases in thickness. Level 2.1–2.2.

71. 7756/093/31/072. Copper alloy buckle. Simple, near-rectangular shape; two opposing sides convex, others slightly concave. Bent. W 0.0253, L 0.03; (bands) W 0.0033, Th 0.0024. Level 1.2.

72. 7656/128/31/081. Copper alloy buckle. Main part rounded; round in section; ends of arms pierced to take an iron pivot pin. Level 1.2.

Fig. 64 Copper Alloy and Silver Objects

73. TH 81/surface/31/002. Front plate of copper alloy reliquary cross. Mother and Christ (standing in front of Mary) on central hub of cross. Above Mary (MH ± OX). At top: two hinges; at base, two clasps. Surface.

74. 7656/121/31/071. Silver crucifix on iron chain. Cross with slightly splaying arms. Top of cross has loop through which iron chain passed. Links of chain badly corroded. The links were drawn when partially cleaned; originally, therefore, they were smaller than illustrated. H 0.055, W 0.036. Level 1.1.

75. 7457/026/31/013. Bronze cup. Gilded. Hollow base. RD 0.0515, BD 0.0315, H 0.031. Level 1.2.

76. 7557/091/31/056. Copper alloy spatula. Simple, straight shaft round in cross-section, slightly bulbous at top end; at bottom the shaft has been hammered into a flat, broad blade (now bent over). L 0.125. Level 2.1a.

77. 7756/043/31/034. Copper alloy miniature spoon. Simple shaft; tiny bowl to spoon; eye and ring at top end. Decoration: rope pattern between box-shaped end and centre spacers; between two boxes of centre spacer there is a lozenge. L 0.0635. Level 1.1.

78. 7559/089/31/034. Copper alloy seal. Eye at top with ring through it; below the eye, a bulbous part with incised lines on it above a heptagonal figure. On bottom is incised (?)deer. Level 1.2.

79. 7857/012/31/013. Bronze spoon. Shank is 0.034 long, with a broken end; circular in cross-section. Joined to bowl by a block, square in cross-section and decorated with a number of transverse incisions and nicks taken out of the edge. Bowl is roughly elliptical in shape. Spoon was cast, design filed in and the bronze tinned. Level 2.2.

80. 7660/002/31/001. Bronze spoon. Similar to no.79. The broken shank is 0.031 long. Bowl is more rounded than no.79. Topsoil.

81. 7756/091/31/060. Copper alloy fitting for a purse. Sheet shaped and bent over. Fastened together by four staples (one missing). H (max.) 0.0239, L 0.0774; (end) H 0.0146; (sheet) Th 0.0007, (across open button) W 0.0070 to 0.0087; (staples) W 0.0019, Th c.0.001. Level (?)1.

Fig. 65 Iron Objects

82. 7558/102/31/038. Iron hook. Top is square in cross-section; the end is broken; the rest was flattened. L 0.022; (top) Th 0.005; (hook) dimensions 0.003 by 0.004. Level 2.2.

83. 7758/132/31/092. Length of iron chain. Ten links, average size 0.04 by 0.02 with a hook for suspension fastened at one end; 'figure of eight' shape. L 0.38. Level 2.1–2.2.

84. 7758/081/31/088. Iron pricking spur. Prick domed to a point. Shanks broken. L (total) 0.071; (heel end) W 0.066; (spur) L 0.022. Level 3.2.

85. 7858/017/31/010. Iron loop from a split spike. Flat top. (Top side) Th 0.004, L 0.05, De 0.014; (loop) W 0.036. Level 3.5.

Fig. 66

86. 7858/081/31/045. Iron open lamp. One side broken. Rectangular object with straight sides. Corners pinched out, the object has the appearance of an ash-tray. H 0.017, W 0.058, Th 0.002 to 0.0025. Level 2.2.

87. 7558/025/31/004. Iron key. Loop and simple bit. L 0.051. Level 3.4.

87a.7756/138/31/080. Iron bell. Straight-sides; rounded top in shape of protruding cap. Cannon round in section. Clapper in form of simple rod; broken. Loop for hanging clapper broken. RD 0.0575, H 0.082, Th 0.005 to 0.0085. Pit on edge of mound.

88. 7557/012/31/011. Iron perforated disc. Simple, almost circular iron sheet; hole punched through it. D 0.021 to 0.0233, Th 0.0011. Level 3.4.

89. 7758/118/31/063. Iron knife blade. Tang broken off. Width tapers from 0.016 at tang to rounded tip. Rivet (at tang end): head 0.007 by 0.005, standing 0.005 out from blade; end 0.0035 by 0.003; standing 0.007 out from blade. Level 3.1.

Fig. 67 Iron Tools

90. 7559/039/31/023. Iron knife blade. Blade width decreases from 0.0125 to 0.0092 before tapering to point; width of top edge 0.0015 at point to 0.0045 at junction of blade and tang. At junction of blade and tang is a

bulbous part on cutting edge. (Blade) L 0.066; (tang) L 0.0125. Level 2.2.

91. 7556/080/31/052. Iron knife blade. Tang broken off. Blade curves slightly downwards. Two rivets at tang end of blade: (rear rivet) L 0.0116, D 0.0052; (other rivet) L 0.0106, D 0.0060. Traces of wood on rivets. (Blade) L 0.08, W (max.) 0.016. Level 1.2.

92. 7457/007/31/003. Iron knife blade. Blade width decreases from 0.019 to 0.0145 before tapering to a point. Tang width tapers from 0.0125 to point. Traces of wood on tang. (Blade) L 0.08; (tang) L 0.035. Modern robber trench.

93. 7657/034/31/016. Iron knife blade. Cutting edge starts 0.036 from junction of blade and tang. (Blade) W (at junction with tang) 0.014, Th (along non-cutting edge) 0.003, L 0.067; (tang) L 0.035. Level 2.2.

94. 7858/017/31/009. Small iron sickle. Outside edge slightly turned over in order to hold blade to wooden handle. Space left by two right angle turns is 0.03 (handle therefore, is 0.03 thick at this edge). (Blade) L 0.077; (handle) L 0.08, Th 0.004. Scale 1:2. Level 3.5.

95. 7656/071/31/046. Small iron (?)sickle or hoe. Similar to no.82. Two rivet holes. Thickest part at point. (Blade) L 0.07; (handle) L 0.053 (end broken). Scale 1:2. Level 2.2.

96. 7558/109/31/045. Part of small iron (?)sickle. ([?]Handle end) Th 0.004 varying to 0.002. Scale 1:2. Level 2.2.

97. 7858/066/31/066. Iron (?)sickle. Thin club-shaped blade attached to rectangular-sectioned shaft which tapers to a point. (Blade) W 0.024, Th 0.004 to 0.007, L 0.056; (shaft) Th 0.005 by 0.007, L 0.24. Scale 1:2. Level 2.2.

Fig. 68 Spearheads

98. 7556/108/31/080. Iron spearhead. Socket formed from a sheet, turned over; along join is copper alloy weld. Traces of wood in socket. (Socket) W (at bottom) 0.0235 by 0.0253 narrowing to 0.020 by 0.0205; top slightly flattened. Tip of blade is broken off; (blade) W narrowing from 0.0316 at junction with socket to 0.0261 at break, Th 0.0072. Bottom of blade flat; top slightly rounded. (Blade) L 0.055; (socket) L 0.095. Level 1.2.

99. 7758/253/31/132. Iron spearhead. Narrow blade, tapering to a point (broken off); blade oval in section. Socket for shaft round, slightly tapering. L 0.28; (blade) W 0.035 (at base); (socket) D c.0.027 (at end). Scale 1:2. Level 1.1.

Fig. 69 Adze and Arrowheads

100. 7556/108/31/078. Iron adze. Blade broad, splaying, flat. Shaft-hole at top. Hammer end blunted and flattened. L 0.148; (blade) W c.0.0571. Level 1.2.

101. 7858/001/31/005. Iron arrowhead. Tang round. Boss at shoulder. (Blade) W 0.017, Th 0.005, L 0.026; (tang) D (top) 0.004, L 0.0281; (boss) (at shoulder) W 0.007, Th 0.0025, L 0.005. L (total) 0.0591. Topsoil.

102. 7758/032/31/011. Iron arrowhead. Tang round. Boss at shoulder. Square at bottom (0.005 by 0.005); thicker in middle; tapering to sides and point. (Blade) W 0.012, L 0.029; (tang) D (top) 0.003, L 0.022; (boss) (at shoulder) W 0.007, Th 0.002. L (total) 0.051. Level 3.5.

103. 7758/040/31/019. Iron arrowhead. Blade rectangular at base (0.007 by 0.0065); tapers towards a point. Tang rectangular at top (0.003 by 0.004); broken. (Blade) L 0.032; (tang) L 0.016. L (total) 0.048. Level 3.5.

Fig.70

104. 7757/071/31/049. Iron adze. Blade narrow, straight, flat. Shaft-hole at top; near triangular. Hammer end blunted and flattened. L 0.13; (blade) W c.0.02. Level 1.2a.

105. 7857/001/31/002. Iron arrowhead. Tang and shoulder round. (Blade) W (max.) 0.023, Th (bottom) 0.003, (top) 0.001, L 0.056; (shoulder) D 0.01; (tang) D (top) c.0.006, L 0.042; (boss) L 0.005. L (total) 0.103. Topsoil.

106. 7658/008/31/008. Iron arrowhead. Tang rectangular (0.005 by 0.003 at top). Blade rectangular in section (0.009 by 0.008 at bottom). (Blade) L 0.046; (tang) L 0.039. L (total) 0.085. Level 3.2.

107. 7756/028/31/017. Iron arrowhead. Blade square in section (0.008 at bottom). Tang square (0.0042 at top). (Blade) L 0.0375; (tang) L 0.053. L (total) 0.0905. Level 2.1a.

108. 7658/001/31/001. Iron arrowhead. Blade rectangular in section (0.005 by 0.007 at bottom). Tang square (0.003 at top).

(Blade) L 0.035; (tang) L 0.014. L (total) 0.049. Topsoil.

109. 7658/065/31/049. Iron arrowhead. Blade square in section (0.007 at bottom). Tang rectangular (0.0045 by 0.004 at top). (Blade) L 0.032; (tang) L 0.023. L (total) 0.055. Modern robber trench.

110. 7657/036/31/021. Iron arrowhead. Blade rectangular in section (0.008 by 0.0065 at bottom); tip broken. Tang square in section (0.005 at top). (Blade) L 0.027 (tip broken); (tang) L 0.04. L (total) 0.067. Level 2.2.

111. 7657/071/31/051. Iron arrowhead. Blade rectangular in section (0.00725 by 0.006 at bottom). Tang square (0.005 at top). (Blade) L 0.02; (tang) L 0.019. L (total) 0.039. Level 2.2.

112. 7858/068/31/054. Iron arrowhead. Blade diamond-shaped in section (0.005 by 0.01 at widest point). Tang round (0.003 at top). Shoulder round (D 0.006). (Blade) L 0.04; (tang) L 0.022; (boss) L 0.008. L (total) 0.07. Level 3.1.

Fig. 71 Arrowheads and Nails

113. 7558/109/31/044. Iron arrowhead. Blade thin; tapers from a (max.) width of 0.021 to point. Tang round. (Blade) L 0.056; (tang) D 0.06, L 0.013. L (total) 0.069. Level 2.2.

114. 7657/028/31/018. Iron arrowhead. Shoulder round (D 0.01). Tang round (0.0065 at top). (Blade) L 0.042, W (max.) 0.02, Th (at bottom) 0.004; (tang) L 0.025; (boss) L 0.018. L (total) 0.085. Level 3.1.

115. 7758/056/31/025. Iron arrowhead. In blade two rectangular holes, longtitudinally positioned. Tang square (0.005 at top). (Blade) W (max.) 0.017, Th (max.) 0.003, L 0.041; (tang) L 0.025; (boss) L 0.019. L (total) 0.085. Level 3.5.

116. 7657/070/31/037. Iron arrowhead. Blade, tip broken; Shoulder rounded top and bottom; flat sides. Tang 0.005 by 0.006 at break. (Blade) W (max.) 0.032, L 0.048. Level 2.1a–2.1b.

117. 7556/108/31/086. Iron arrowhead. Tang broken; round. (Blade) W (max.) 0.029; Th (max.) 0.0045, L 0.04. (tang) L 0.02. L (total) 0.06. Level 1.2.

118. 7759/002/31/001. Iron barbed arrowhead. Tang made from two pieces of metal twisted together. (Blade) L 0.02, (plus barbs) 0.03; (tang) L 0.04. L (total) 0.065. Topsoil.

119. 7758/045/31/034. Iron arrowhead. Blade rounded; top drawn out into point. Tang rectangular in section (0.0025 by 0.005); rounded point. (Blade) W (max.) 0.017, Th 0.00325 to 0.004, L 0.028; (tang) L 0.04. L (total) 0.068. Level 3.4.

120. 7858/017/31/013. Iron arrowhead. Blade rounded. Tang in two parts: top rounded (0.005 thickening to 0.006 long); bottom squared (0.003). (Blade) W (max.) 0.018, L 0.0245; (tang) L (top) 0.015, (bottom) 0.009. L (total) 0.0485. Level 3.5.

121. 7858/017/31/015. Copper alloy nail. Head rounded. Shafthas a rounded point. (Head) D 0.006, H 0.005; (shaft) D (top) 0.003, L 0.024. L (total) 0.029. Level 3.5.

122. 7758/118/31/063. Iron nail. Head rounded. Shaft bent and broken. (Head) D 0.022, H 0.008 to 0.009; (shaft) D (top) 0.0075. L (total) 0.04. Level 3.1.

123. 7758/121/31/046. Iron nail. Flat head. Tapers from head to point. L 0.112; (head) D 0.013. Level 3.1.

Fig. 72 Nails

124. 7759/107/31/036. Iron nail. Head circular; slightly rounded. Shaft rectangular (0.009 by 0.012 at top). L 0.205; (head) D 0.047, Th 0.0055. Level 1.1–1.2.

125. 7758/080/31/073. Iron nail. Head circular. Shaft rectangular (0.05 by 0.07 at top); end broken. L 0.0565; (shaft) L (end broken) 0.05; (head) D 0.029 to 0.032, Th 0.025 to 0.035. Level 3.2.

126. 7758/080/31/042. Iron nail. Head rectangular (0.012 by 0.015). Shaft rectangular (0.005 by 0.007 at top); set to one side of head. L 0.0431; (head) Th c.0.005. Level 3.2.

127. 7758/080/31/045. Iron nail. Head circular; Shaft square (0.005); rounded tip. L 0.0451; (head) D 0.014 to 0.015, Th 0.002 to 0.004. Level 3.2.

128. 7759/037/31/027. Iron nail. Small circular head. Shaft rectangular (0.0035 by 0.005 at top). L 0.04; (head) D 0.009, Th 0.0022. Level 2.1.

129. 7559/028/31/014. Iron nail. Head round; bent slightly over. Shaft rectangular (0.01 by 0.007 at top); tip broken. L 0.059; (head) D 0.031 to 0.036, Th 0.0055 to 0.007. Level 2.2.

130. 7657/071/31/042. Iron nail. Head square

(0.017). Shaft square (0.007 at top); tip broken; set to one side of head. L 0.049; (head) Th 0.002 to 0.003. Level 2.2.

131. 7657/071/31/048. Iron nail. Head rectangular (0.018 by 0.014). Shaft; near rectangular (0.004 by 0.004 at top); tip broken; shaft set to one side of head. L 0.0383; (head) Th 0.005. Level 2.2.

132. 7758/080/31/037. Iron nail. Head squared. Shaft rectangular (0.004 by 0.005 at top). L 0.0365; (head) W (max.) 0.017, Th 0.02 to 0.04. Level 3.2.

133. 7857/035/31/022. Iron nail. Head rect-=angular (0.012 by 0.015). Shaft square (0.004 at top); set to one side of head. L 0.0375; (head) Th 0.003 by 0.004. Level 3.2.

134. 7857/015/31/012. Iron nail. Head rectangular (0.013 by 0.015). Shaft square (0.005 at top); tip broken; shaft set to one side of head. L 0.046; (head) Th 0.0025 to 0.003. Level 3.1.

Fig. 73 Ceramic Objects

135. 7758/174/03/014. Ceramic plaque. Fabric: white clay. Surface: overall coat of white glaze with cobalt-blue colouring in some areas (horizontal lines on drawing). Shape: flat; on under side, four (?)feet (broken-stippled in drawing). Decoration: on upper side, (?)elaborate floral motif; on under side, (?)floral motif; on all four sides, cross-hatch pattern. Complete except for feet. Scale 1:2. Level 2.1a.

136. 7857/082/03/001. Figure-protome. Fabric: fairly fine, pale-red. Surface: smooth; all over red wash; not burnished. Head, upper-body and arms of a man, right hand clutching beard, left hand laid on head; hunch-back; holes for eyes, mouth and navel; long, high nose; no ears shown; fingers differentiated by slits. Left arm missing. Scale 1:2. Level 2.

137. 7557/001/03/001. Pierced cylinder. D (ends) 0.025, (middle) 0.023, (hole) 0.0065, L 0.042. Topsoil.

138. 7658/238/03/009. Spindle whorl. D 0.023, H 0.017; (hole) D 0.005. Level 1.1.

139. 7556/124/03/002. (?)Toy. Clay: coarse, granular, poorly fired. (?)Intended to represent an animal face. L 0.0717. Level 1.1.

140. 7557/023/03/002. Gaming counter. Roughly circular. On one side very rough circle scratched. Each side is depression c.0.005

deep. D c.0.024, Th 0.0055 to 0.007. Level 2.2.

141. 7657/083/03/001. Bird head. (?)Eagle. Protruding nose and eye. One eye broken. Head broken off from rest. Poorly fired. H 0.029. Level 2.1a.

Fig. 74 Ceramic Objects

142. 7558/043/03/004. Surround for a fireplace. Rows of impressed decoration and triangular shaped hollows. Back, top and one side broken. H 0.322, W 0.154, De 0.003. Scale 1:2. Level 3.4.

143. 7857/082/80/002. Object. Shell of baked clay with flat bottom and slightly domed top. Coarse clay; many large grits. Inside there are scraps of copper alloy sheets. D 0.06, H 0.055. Two found together in pit, perhaps from side of pit, not from pit itself. Scale 1:2. Level 2.

Fig. 75 Ceramic Object and Bone Objects

144. 7458/041/03/001. Coarse ceramic pierced cylinder. Buff. Hole slightly off centre. On top is a (?)pouring lip. Bottom did not appear to be broken. The object is not, therefore, a container. D 0.031, H 0.04; (hole) D 0.01 to 0.0115. Level 2.1a.

145. 7558/196/15/004. Bone pin or needle. Both ends broken. For half of its length the shaft is round in cross-section while the remaining half has two flattened sides. L 0.14. Level 1.1–1.2.

146. 7556/094/15/001. Bone (?)bracelet part. Incised line c.0.002 inside each edge on outer face. One end thinner; c.0.003. D (outside) c.0.05, (inside) c.0.04, W 0.018, Th (max.) 0.01; (semi-circular holes) D 0.009. Level 1.1.

147. 7558/050/15/001. Bone spindle whorl. Flat top and bottom. Decoration, same on both sides: three incised rings c.0.001 wide, 0.001 deep; around edge two incised rings c.0.001 wide, 0.0005 deep. Edge damaged by nicks. D 0.039, Th 0.01; (hole) D 0.0045. Level 3.3.

148. 7858/056/14/001. Bone spindle whorl. Flat bottom. The top for 0.001 around hole is flat, then rounded to narrow ledge. Incised double ledge above base. D 0.0205, H 0.007; (hole) D 0.0055. Level 3.1–3.2.

149. 7557/167/15/002. Bone spindle whorl. Flat

bottom. Incised circle near top. Incised ledge above base. D 0.021, H 0.011; (hole) D 0.005. Level 1.1.

150. 7758/219/15/002. Bone spindle whorl. Flat bottom. Raised circle around hole. Incised ledge above base. D 0.018, H 0.007; (hole) D 0.005. Level 2.1.

151. Surface/15/001. Bone spindle whorl. Flat bottom. Incised circle around hole; another incised circle near top. Incised ledge above base. D 0.0196, H 0.0075; (hole) D 0.006. Surface.

152. 7657/177/15/001. Bone spindle whorl. Around central hole there is an incised circle, then an incised ledge. Incised ledge just above base. D 0.018, H 0.0075; (hole) D 0.0055. Level 1.2a.

153. 7658/077/14/001. Bone spindle whorl. Flat bottom. Top, series of concentric rings and ledges. D 0.025, H 0.0076; (hole) D 0.006. Level 3.1.

Fig. 76 Bone and Stone Spindle Whorls

154. 7557/002/15/001. Bone spindle whorl. Flat bottom. Incised ring near top; finely incised double inverted-V's between ring and bottom. D 0.027, H 0.0045; (hole) D 0.005. Level 3.3–3.4.

155. 7756/029/15/001. Bone spindle whorl. Flat bottom. Incised circle around central hole; two incised ledges near top. Two incised circles just above base. Between the latter and the higher ledges are four groups of incised lines. D 0.022, H 0.006; (hole) D 0.006. Level 1.2.

156. 7857/082/15/001. Bone spindle whorl. Flat bottom. Incised ledge near top and one above base. Between the two are incised lines forming four double inverted-V's. D 0.0195, H 0.007; (hole) D 0.005. Level 2.

157. 7659/081/14/001. Bone spindle whorl. Flat bottom. Top well rounded. There is a ledge below the raised ring around hole. Above base incised ledge (0.005 deep). Four pairs (one above other) of holes (0.001 in diameter) around each hole. Pairs not symmetrical around button. D 0.015, H 0.007; (hole) D 0.005. Level 2.1a.

157a. 7759/196/15/002. Bone spindle whorl. Decoration: incised line near top, incised lines radiating from centre. Above base an incised ledge. D 0.018, H 0.007; (hole) D 0.005. Level 1.1.

158. 7458/041/13/001. Bone spindle whorl. Flat bottom. Incised ledge near hole. Decorated with six segments, each with hole surrounded by an incised ring (0.0025 in diameter). separated from each other by two vertical lines. An incised line branches off at 45 from left hand line. D 0.0145, H 0.0095; (hole) D 0.0045. Level 2.1a.

159. 7858/123/42/002. Stone spindle whorl. Top: decorated (see drawing); dots 0.0015 deep, lines 0.0005 deep. Back: series of lines radiating out from centre, crudely executed. Incised line round edge. D 0.053, H 0.0095; (hole) D 00.035. Level 2.1.

160. 7557/069/42/004. Stone spindle whorl. Flat bottom. Near top, incised line. D 0.0265, H 0.08; (hole) D 0.0035. Level 2.1.

161. 7859/009/42/001. Stone spindle whorl. Slightly rounded bottom. Just above base, incised line. Rough top. D 0.023, H 0.0095; (hole) D 0.004. Level 3.1.

162. 7558/218/42/014. Stone spindle whorl. Plain. Rough top. Rounded at base/side break of angle. Slightly concave bottom. D 0.028, H 0.009; (hole) D 0.005. Level 1.1.

163. 7557/193/42/012. Stone spindle whorl. Plain. Rounded braks of angle. Flat bottom. D 0.0245, H 0.009; (hole) D 0.0035. Level 1.2.

164. 7557/230/42/014. Stone spindle whorl. Two grooves on upper edge of base. D 0.022, H 0.012; (hole) D 0.0049. Level 1.1.

165. 7557/219/42/013. Stone spindle whorl. One groove below hole at top. Slightly concave bottom. D 0.020, H 0.007; (hole) D 0.0034. Level 1.1.

Fig. 77 Stone Spindle Whorls and Beads

166. 7458/052/42/001. Stone spindle whorl. Two-thirds up the side there is an incised line around object. Convex bottom. D 0.02, H 0.0092; (hole) D 0.0039. Level 2.1.

167. 7759/011/42/003. Stone spindle whorl. Two incised lines on lower surface. Bottom very slightly convex. D 0.024, H 0.007; (hole) D 0.0045. Level 3.3–3.5.

168. 7858/162/42/008. Stone spindle whorl. Half way down the side there are two incised lines. There is a possible incised line on bottom, 0.001 in from edge but very worn. Flat bottom. D 0.024, H 0.0055; (hole) D 0.004. Level 1.2–2.1.

169. 7658/235/42/023. Stone spindle whorl. Half way up the side there are two incised lines.

Concave bottom. D 0.028, H 0.007; (hole) D 0.0075. Level 1.2.

170. 7556/010/42/001. Stone spindle whorl. Slight depression around hole. Slightly concave bottom. D 0.027, H 0.008; (hole) D 0.0045. Level 3.2.

171. 7559/070/42/003. Stone spindle whorl. Plain. Flat bottom. D 0.0245, H 0.006; (hole) D 0.003. Level 2.1a.

172. 7756/039/42/006. Stone spindle whorl. Plain. Slightly concave bottom. Slight depression around hole. D 0.0235, H 0.008; (hole) D 0.0047. Level 2.1.

173. 7557/071/42/003. Stone spindle whorl. Plain. Slight depression around hole. Flat bottom. D 0.028, H 0.0105; (hole) D 0.006. Level 2.1a–2.1b.

174. 7758/126/42/011. Stone spindle whorl. Plain. Slight depression around hole. Flat bottom. D 0.021, H 0.0085; (hole) D 0.0045. Level 3.1.

175. 7656/007/42/001. Stone spindle whorl. Top flat with two incised lines near top, around it. At bottom four incised circles: 0.0055 in diameter with depression 0.002 in diameter, 0.001 deep. Bottom concave. D (max.) 0.0268, 0.022 (at bottom), H 0.013; (hole) D 0.0065. Topsoil.

176. 7657/064/41/006. Onyx bead. W (middle) 0.0105, (ends) 0.008 to 0.0085; L 0.032; (hole) D 0.0022. Hole bored from both ends. Level 2.1b.

177. 7756/019/42/001. Carnelian bead. Almost round. D 0.0092, W (hole to hole) 0.009; (hole) D 0.002. Level 2.1b.

178. 7556/040/42/004. Carnelian bead. Ends flat, rest round. D 0.0057, W 0.0035; (hole) D 0.0019. Level 2.1a.

179. 7656/010/42/003. Carnelian bead. Almost round. D 0.0092, W 0.009; (hole) D 0.002. Level 2.1.

180. 7558/218/42/017. Carnelian bead. Eight facets running lengthways. Facets are not even in width. Hole bored from both ends. W 0.009, L 0.0165; (hole) D 0.002. Level 1.1.

181. Vacat

182. 7558/134/42/008. Carnelian bead. Hole bored from both ends. Many facets. W 0.009, Th 0.007, L 0.01; (hole) D 0.002. Level 2.1b.

Fig.78 Stone objects

183. 7457/015/42/001. Stone box. Soft limestone. One side broken. Very crude. On each of the three surviving sides: cross cut with shaft from top to bottom of sides and arms along majority of side. Crude incisions along rim. External: 0.0525 by probably 0.0525; H 0.0375. Internal: (top) 0.038 by (?)0.038; (bottom) 0.023 by (?)0.023; H 0.025. Level 1.2.

184. 7557/019/42/001. Pestle. Basalt. D (top) 0.0605 to 0.068, (middle) 0.0485 to 0.052, (bottom) 0.066 to 0.071; H 0.088. Scale 1:2. Level 3.1.

185. 7857/028/42/004. Whetstone. L 0.155; bottom 0.027 by 0.0235, rounded; tapers to 0.023 by 0.019, before bulge to one side 0.0315 by 0.018. Scale 1:2. Level 3.1.

186. 7558/093/42/003. Whetstone. Rectangular shape. At one end there is a hole. D 0.0045, W 0.036, Th 0.01 (ends), 0.007 (middle), L 0.088. Level 3.1.

187. 7657/083/42/009. Small roller. Limestone. On each end there is a hole, D c.0.012, De 0.014. Rough finish. D 0.067 to 0.073, L 0.109. Scale 1:2. Level 2.1a.

Fig. 79

188. 7558/092/42/002. Rubber. Basalt. Triangular in cross-section. L 0.27 (broken). The end which is complete curves inward for last 0.02. H (max.) 0.085, 0.065 (end). Scale 1:4. Level 3.1.

189. 7758/222/42/016. Rubber. Basalt. L 0.20 (broken). Flat base: W 0.11 (at break). H (max.) 0.045. End slopes down. Rounded top. Scale 1:4. Level 1.2.

190. 7759/116/40/002. Inscribed piece of limestone. Broken. Sign of cross. W 0.11, L 0.13, De 0.0065. Scale 1:2 Level 1.1.

Fig. 80 Quernstones

191. 7558/173/42/011, 7657/076/42/003. Rotary quernstone, top half. Basalt. Found in two halves in different locations. D 0.43; Th 0.06 (middle), 0.033 to 0.055 (side). Central hole: D 0.08 (top), 0.05 to 0.055 (bottom); filling slot to one side of hole. Key slot on bottom: W 0.035, L 0.14, De 0.012 to 0.015. Handle hole: D 0.05 (top), 0.035 (bottom); set 0.04 in from edge. Around central hole, on top, is ridge 0.155 to 0.16 in diameter, up to 0.012 high. Scale 1:4. Level 2.1–2.1a.

Fig. 81

191. contd. Sections. Scale 1:4.

192. 7858/179/42/010. Rotary quernstone, top half. Basalt. Broken and worn on one side. D 0.35 to 0.36, Th 0.055 (middle), 0.03 (side). Central hole: D 0.08 at top narrowing to 0.045. Key slot: L 0.09, W 0.02, De 0.0095 to 0.015. Handle hole: D 0.04 (top), 0.027 (bottom), De 0.039; set 0.03 in from edge. Scale 1:4. Level 1.2.

193. 7556/116/42/009. Rotary quernstone, top half. Basalt. Sections. Scale 1:4.

Fig. 82

193. contd. D 0.39; Th 0.05 tapering to 0.03 at sides. Central hole 0.074 at top tapering to 0.04. Key slot: W c.0.025, L 0.12, De 0.009. Handle hole: D 0.05 (top), 0.03 (bottom); set 0.055 in from edge. Level 1.2.

194. 7557/078/42/002. Rotary quernstone, top half. Basalt. D 0.38, Th 0.04 (in middle), 0.032 on one side to 0.02 on another, Th (max.) 0.05. Central hole: D 0.06; straight sided. Key slot: W c.0.025, L 0.14, De 0.0115. Handle hole: D 0.035; straight side; set 0.04 in from edge. Scale 1:4. Level 2.1.

Fig. 83

195. 7657/187/42/014. Rotary quernstone. Upper element of a rotary mill. Basalt. D 0.45 to 0.53, Th 0.12 to 0.13. Central hole: D 0.12 at top narrowing to 0.052. Key slot: L 0.282, W 0.05 to 0.06, De 0.014 to 0.025. Handle hole: D 0.053 to 0.058, De 0.045; set 0.04 in from edge. Scale 1:4. Level 1.1.

Fig. 84

195. cont. Sections. Scale 1:4.

196. 7558/095/42/009. Socket stone for the swivel of a door post. Basalt. Dressed stone, rounded in shape. D (max.) 0.32; H 0.22. Flat base. Top D 0.25. Central depression; D 0.095; De 0.043; sides at 45 angle; rounded bottom; wear marks on side and bottom. Scale 1:4. Level 2.1b-3.1.

Fig. 85

197. 7657/071/42/007. Rotary quernstone, base. Basalt. D 0.40 to 0.42 (top), 0.30 (bottom). Sloping sides. Th 0.09 to 0.11. Turning

hole: D 0.047 (top), 0.03 (bottom), De 0.06; not central to stone. Scale 1:4. Level 2.2.

198. 7559/030. Stone mortar. Limestone. D (top-external) 0.648, (top-internal) 0.54, (bottom-external) 0.45, (bottom-internal) 0.06; H 0.525; De (internal) 0.36. Scale 1:6. Level 2.2.

Fig. 86 Lid

199. 7858/030/42/003. Stone lid. Limestone. Broken. D c.0.36. Th 0.02 (edge), 0.035 (middle). At a point 0.035 in from edge there is a row of double circles with central hole, touching each other. In front of handle is steam vent: D c.0.06 (bottom), c.0.02 (top). On side and top of handle are six double circles with central hole, touching each other. Around central vent are double circles with central hole, spaced from each other by 0.005. On base, at a point 0.09 in from edge, is a row of double circles, 0.06 distant from each other. Level 3.3–3.5.

The other stone lids found were simple, flat, round stones; some naturally shaped, others slightly modified.

Fig. 87 Gaming board

200. 7657/071/41/008. Gaming board on stone. Limestone block. At one end is a game scratched into block. Called 'Merels' or 'Nine Men's Morris' in Europe, 'Üç Taş' in Turkey. Still played today. L 0.55, H 0.14, W 0.18. Level 2.2.

Fig. 88 Chimney

201. 7757/015/40/003, 004. Chimney reconstruction. Two of the three and a half basalt sections recovered fitted together. Chimney had nine sections. On two of protruding parts were found female figure (no.202) and a phallus (no.203) in relief. The top of each sections had a groove, 0.04 in from inner edge. Depth of groove was 0.01 to 0.02. The groove may have been cut for an iron band intended to hold the sections together. Top, inside face and outside face well smoothed. On bottom: traces of white mortar. Inside face and outside faces vertical. (Sections) H 0.45; (chimney) D 0.70. Scale. 1:10. Level 2.

202. 7757/015/40/005. Relief. Pregnant women.

Shown frontally with abdomen to right in order to emphasize her condition. Very simply executed, in outline only. (Figure) H 0.19. Scale 1:4. Level 2.

203. 7757/015/40/004. Relief. Phallus. Stylized. H 0.145. Scale 1:4. Level 2.

Fig. 89

204. 7757/114/40/006. Column base. Limestone. Square base with double torus moulding above. Base c.0.40 square. H 0.34. Scale 1:4. Level 1.2.

Fig. 90 Glass

205. 7558/160/50/093. Glass bead. Clear. D (max.) 0.016, H 0.012; (top) D 0.0085; (hole) D 0.0062. Level 2.1a.

206. 7656/011/50/020. Glass bead. Light blue. D (max.) 0.014, H 0.01; (top) D 0.009; (hole) D 0.0075. Level 1.2.

207. 7556/071/50/041. Glass bead. Black. Round. D (max.) 0.0162; (hole) D 0.0045. Level (?)2.2.

208. 7658/044/50/165. Faience bead. Pale green. H 0.006, W (max.) 0.009; (hole) D 0.002. Level 2.2.

209. 7457/039/50/014. Glass bead. Clear. Barrel shaped. D (max.) 0.0048, H 0.0045; (hole) D 0.001. Level 2.1–2.1b.

210. 7458/043/50/014. Glass bead. Clear. Small indentions with yellow surround. H 0.006, W 0.0022, L 0.0085. Level 2.1a.

211. 7458/043/50/014. Glass beads. Selection of barrel shaped glass beads from double strand of beads. There are 211 beads in all, including white, blue transparent, blue opaque, yellow opaque, green transparent, green opaque, light blue opaque, clear, red opaque, purple, brown transparent, blue and white decorate, yellowish brown transparent, blue and yellow and white (all glass); light green translucent, red opaque, grey, faience, coral, lapis (all stone); gold foil and glass; silver foil; 'applied' gold foil. Level 2.1a.

212. 7758/160/50/117. Faience. Decorative object. Broken. Level (?)2.1b.

213. 7556/087/51/001. Glass dish. D 0.064. Level 1.1a.

214. 7558/178/50/081. Bottom of glass phial. Dark blue with matt red paint. Level 2.1a.

215. 7758/217/50/134. Bottom of glass phial. Black. Level 1.2.

216. 7756/029/50/012. Brownish yellow. RD 0.02. Level 1.2.

217. 7658/053/50/071. Clear. RD 0.10. Modern robber trench.

218. 7757/015/50/023. Clear. Base of vessel Level 3.3.

219. 7857/052/50/023. Clear. Level 2.1b.

220. 7658/044/50/084. Black. RD 0.03. Level 2.2.

221. 7758/206/50/133. Blue. RD 0.10. Level 2.1.

222. 7658/310/50/161. Pale green. Level 1.1.

223. 7657/154/50/078. Clear. RD 0.08. Level 1.2a.

224. 7558/091/50/041. Clear. RD 0.22. Scale 1:1. Level 3.2.

Fig. 91

225. 7558/026/50/011. Clear with pale blue rim. RD 0.08. Level 3.4.

226. 7857/072/50/030. Pale blue. BD 0.035. Level 2.1.

227. 7556/068/50/049. Clear. RD 0.08. Level 1.2.

228. 7557/001/50/001. Clear. BD 0.04. Topsoil.

229. 7658/010/50/038. Clear. RD 0.10. Level 3.1.

230. 7658/008/50/010. Clear. RD 0.06. Level 3.2.

231. 7559/011/50/015. Pale green. RD 0.06. Level 2.2–3.1.

232. 7557/050/50/022. Clear. RD 0.08. Level 2.2.

233. 7557/114/50/049. Clear. RD 0.04. Level 2.1.

234. 7557/013/50/023. Clear. RD 0.06. Level 2.1.

235. 7658/093/50/101. Pale green. RD 0.06. Level 2.1b.

236. 7758/077/50/055. Clear. Handle. Level 3.3.

237. 7757/015/50/027. Clear. Handle. Level 3.3.

238. 7758/096/50/056. Clear. handle. Level 3.3.

Fig. 92

239. 7458/044/50/015. Clear. Handle. Level 2.1a.

240. 7757/009/50/008. Clear. RD 0.031. Level 3.1–3.2.

241. 7458/068/50/024. Pale green. RD 0.030. Modern robber trench.

242. 7557/092/50/035. Clear. BD 0.032. Level 2.1a.

243. 7758/096/50/056. Clear. RD 0.095. Level 3.3.

Fig. 93

244. 7859/028/50/017. Rod. Green. D 0.004. Level 2.1a.

245. 7758/139/50/099. Rod. Clear. D 0.005. Level 2.1–3.1.

246. 7757/015/50/024. Rod. Clear. D 0.004. Level 3.3.

247. 7759/115/50/034. Rod. Clear. D 0.004. Level 1.2.

248. 7658/010/50/021. Turquoise glass with white paint. Level 3.1.

249. 7658/244/50/139. Pale green. RD 0.12. Scale 1:2. Level 1.2.

250. 7758/080/50/050, 7758/075/50/046. Pale green. BD 0.07. Scale 1:2. Level 2.1a.

251. 7656/012/50/024. Clear. RD 0.12. H 0.164. Scale 1:2. Level 2.1.

252. 7758/179/50/124. Clear. Applied decoration. Scale 1:2. Level 2.1a.

253. 7658/310/50/160. Turquoise. Stem of goblet. Scale 1:2. Level 1.1.

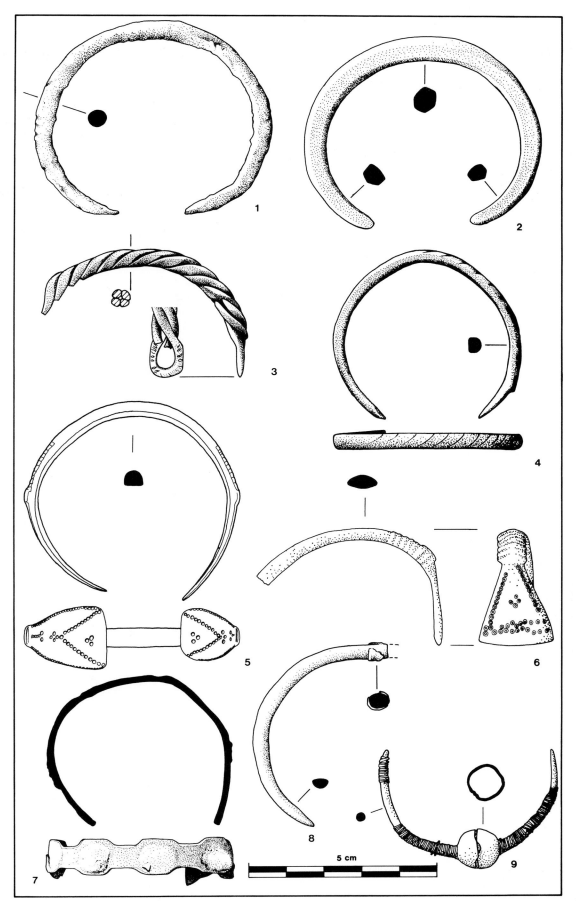

Fig. 55. Bracelets and Pendant

139

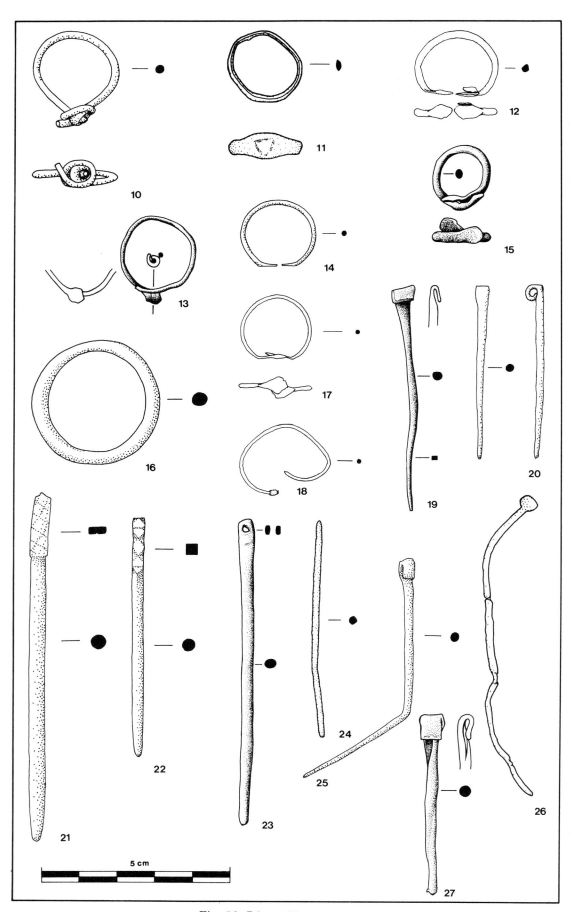

Fig. 56. Rings, Pins and Needles

140

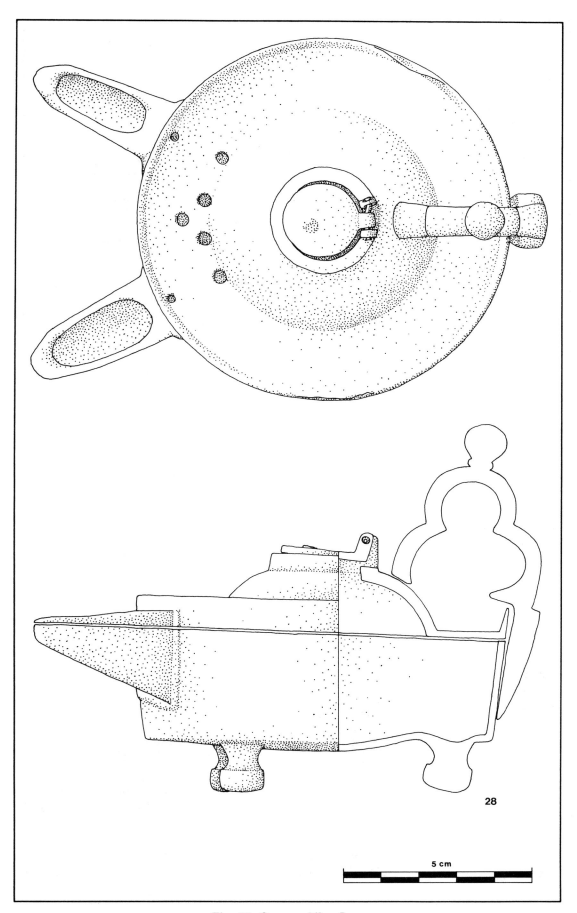

Fig. 57. Copper Alloy Lamp

141

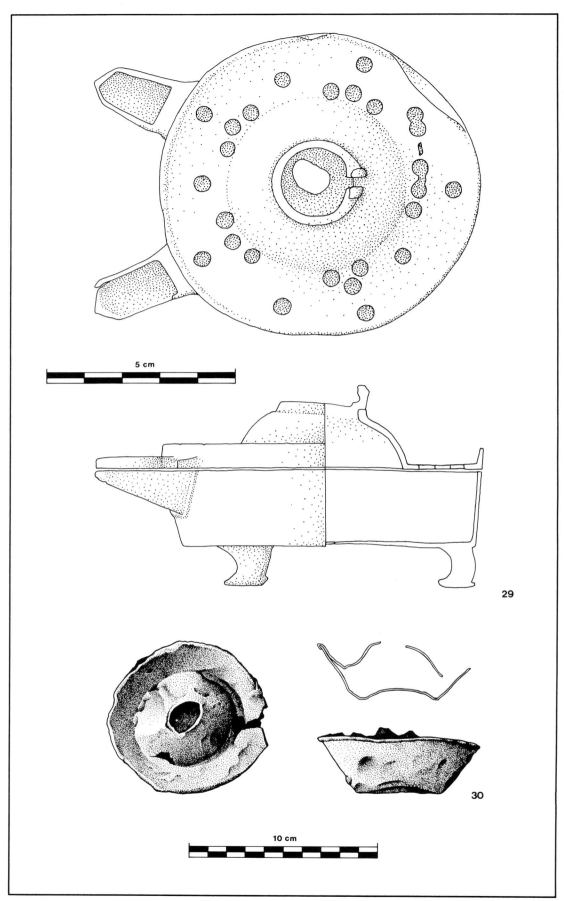

5 cm

29

10 cm

30

Fig. 58.

142

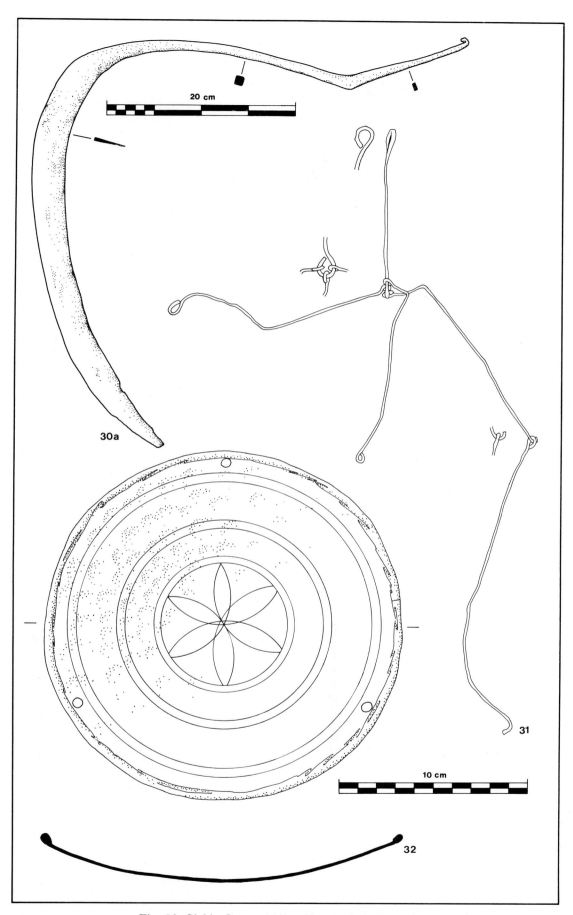

20 cm

30a

31

10 cm

32

Fig. 59. Sickle Copper Alloy Hanger and Scale-pan

143

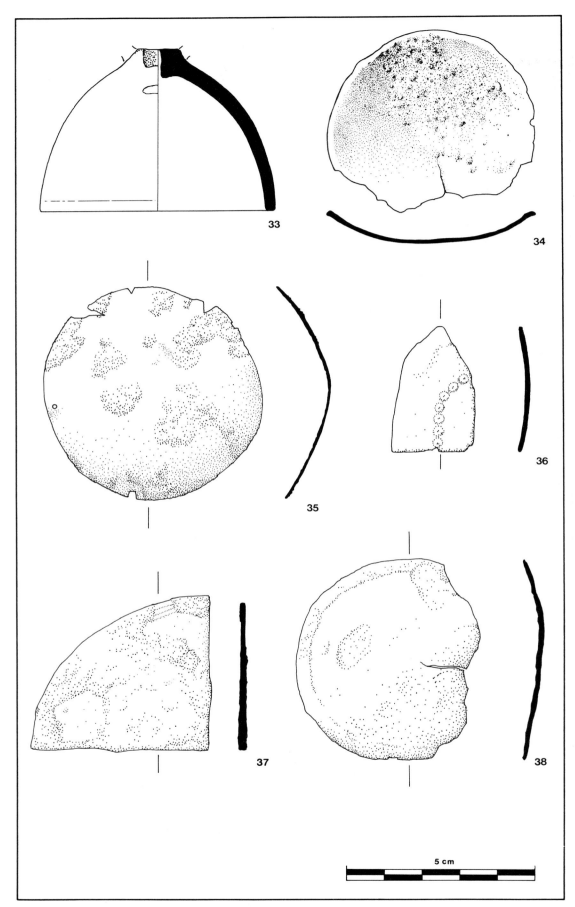

Fig. 60. Copper Alloy Objects

144

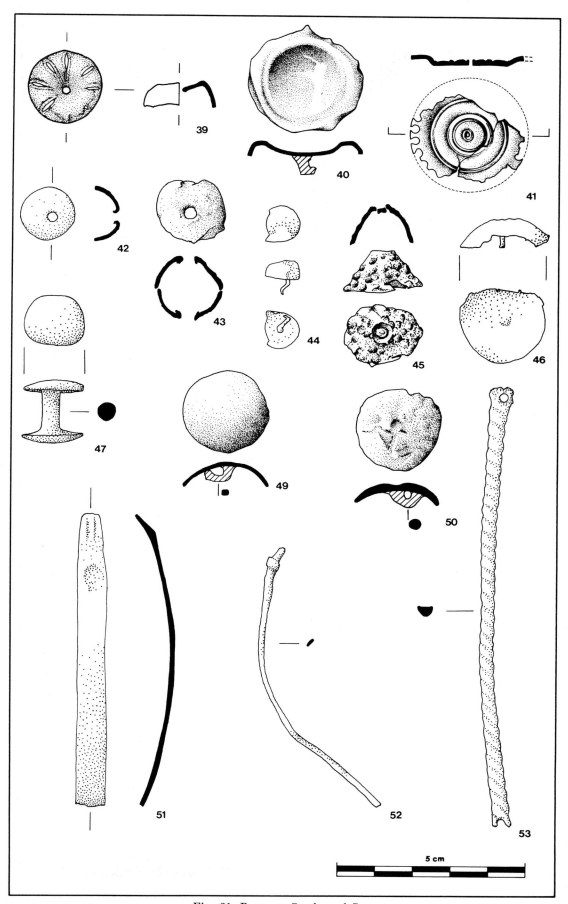

Fig. 61. Buttons, Studs and Straps

145

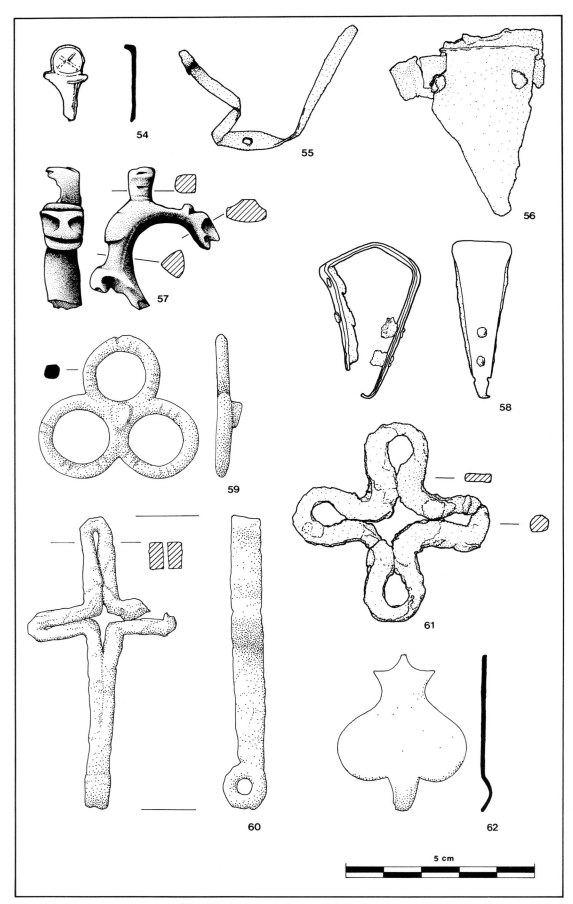

Fig. 62. Copper Alloy and Iron Fittings

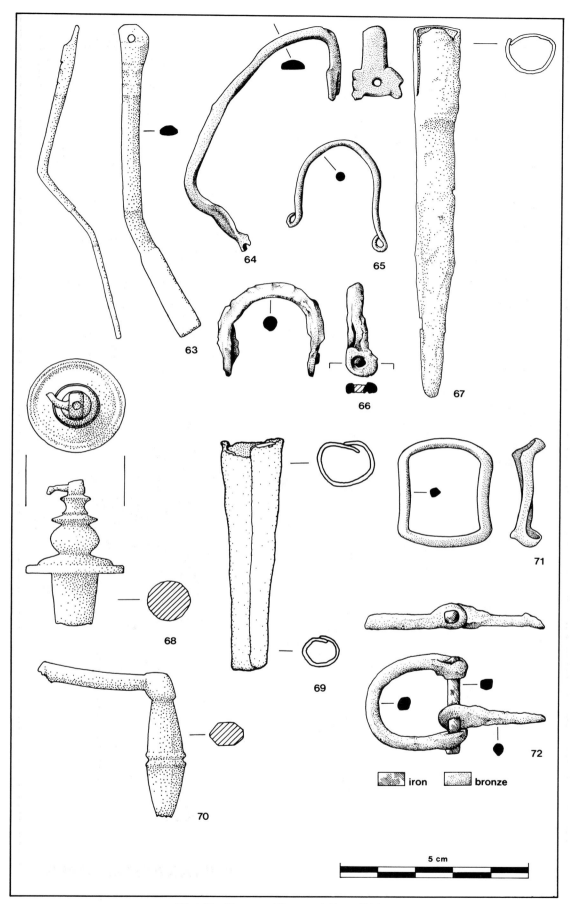

Fig. 63. Copper Alloy and Iron Objects

147

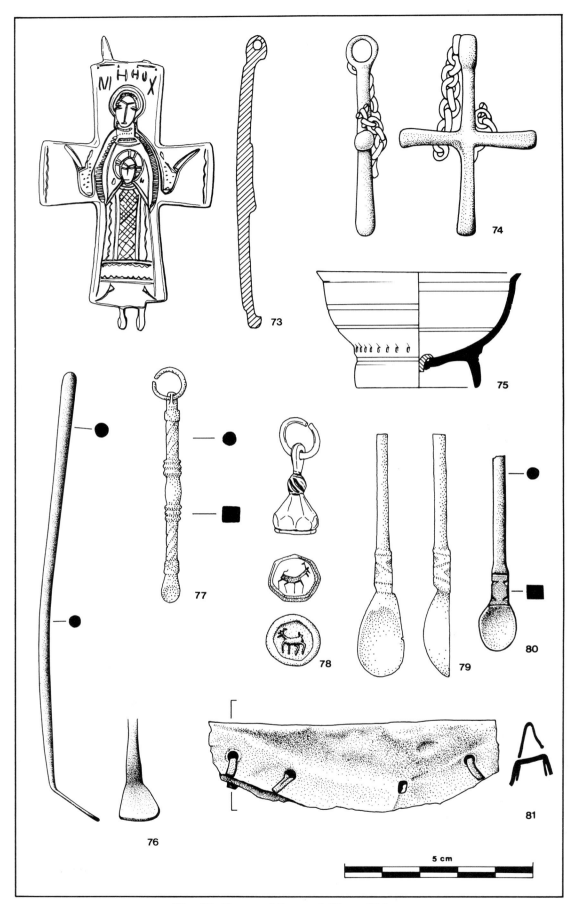

Fig. 64. Copper Alloy and Silver Objects

148

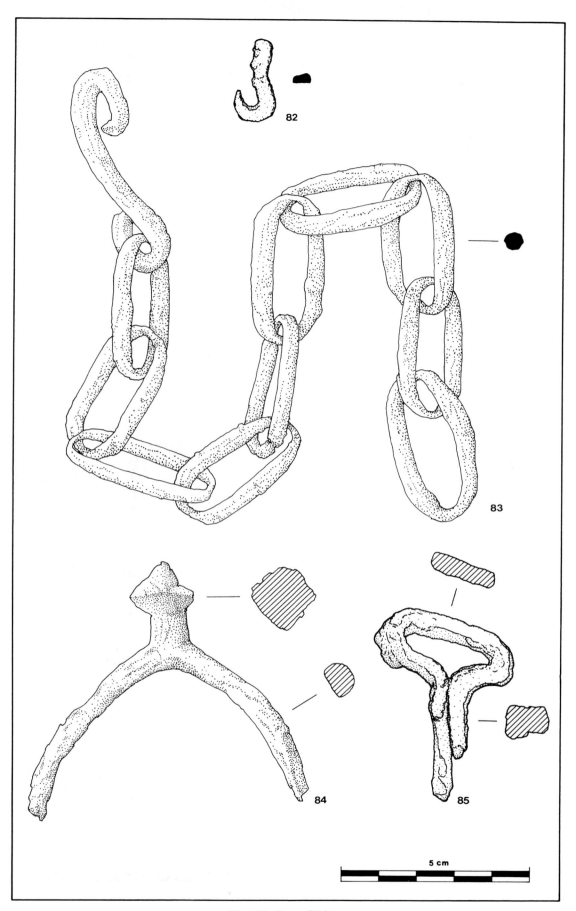

Fig. 65. Iron Objects

149

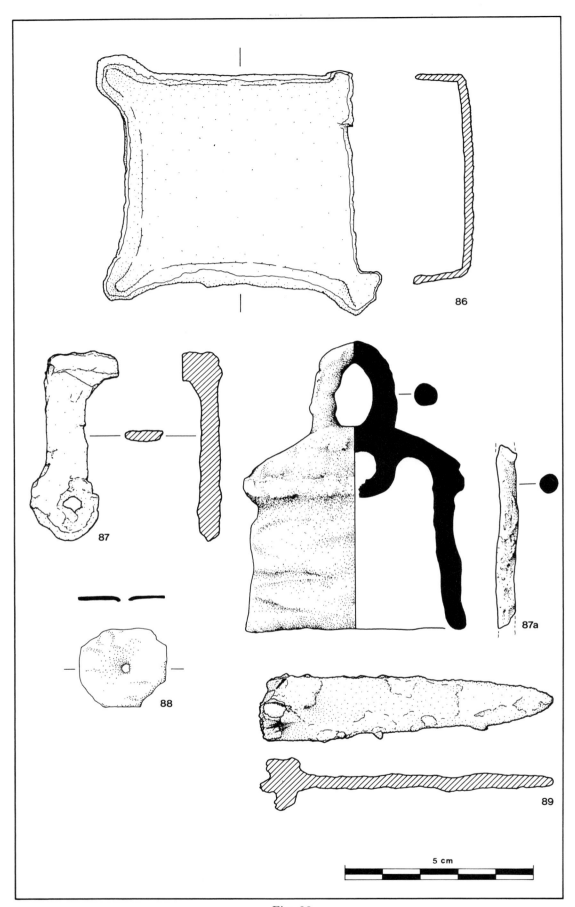

Fig. 66.

150

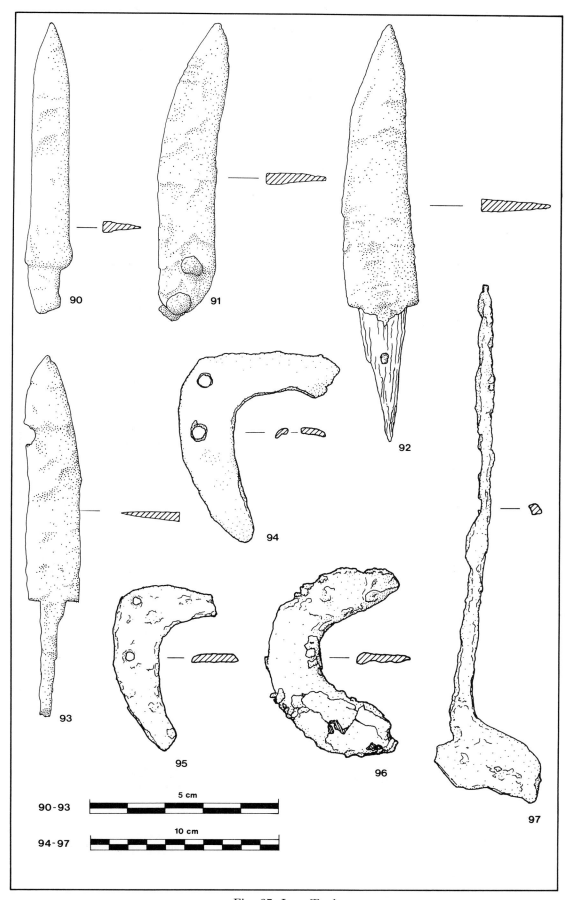

90

91

92

93

94

95

96

97

90-93   5 cm

94-97   10 cm

Fig. 67. Iron Tools

151

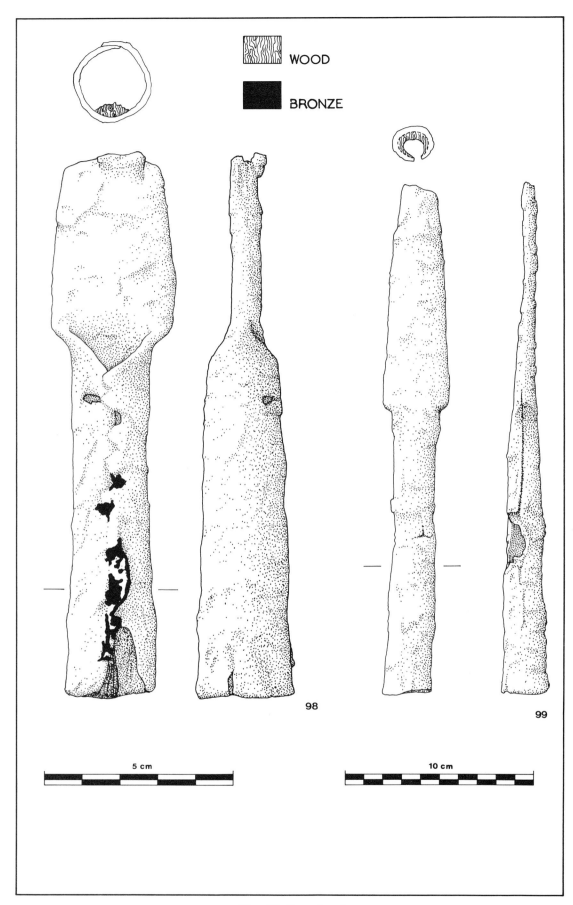

WOOD

BRONZE

98

99

5 cm

10 cm

Fig. 68. Spearheads

152

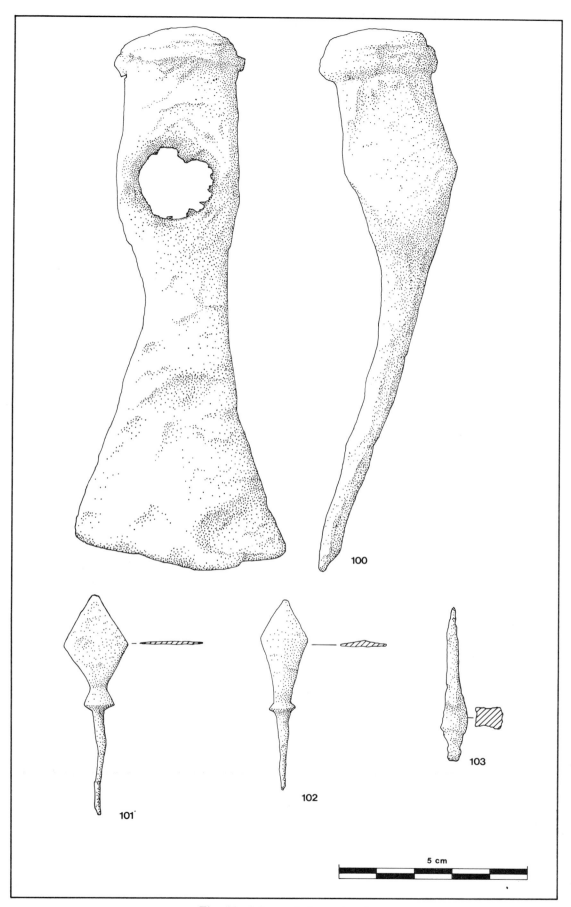

Fig. 69. Adze and Arrowheads

153

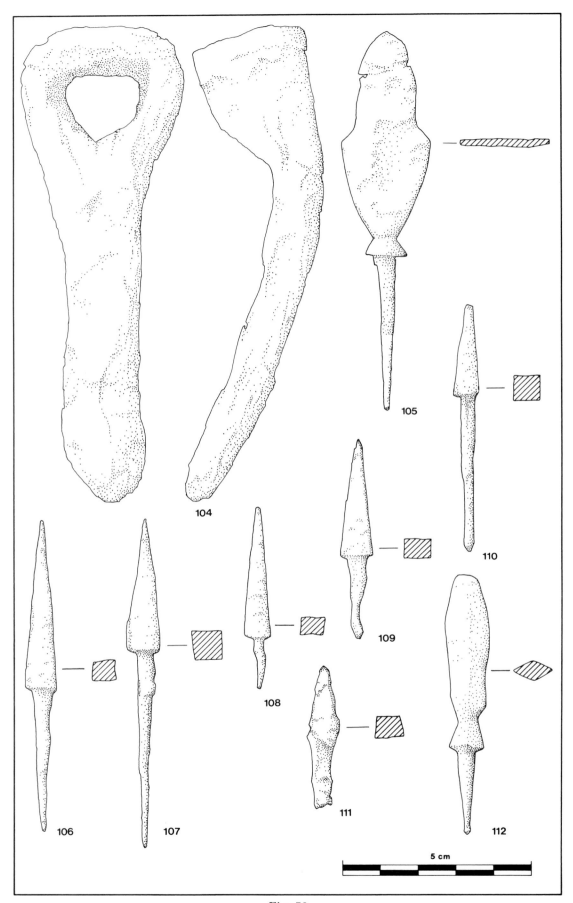

104

105

106   107   108   109

110

111   112

5 cm

Fig. 70.

154

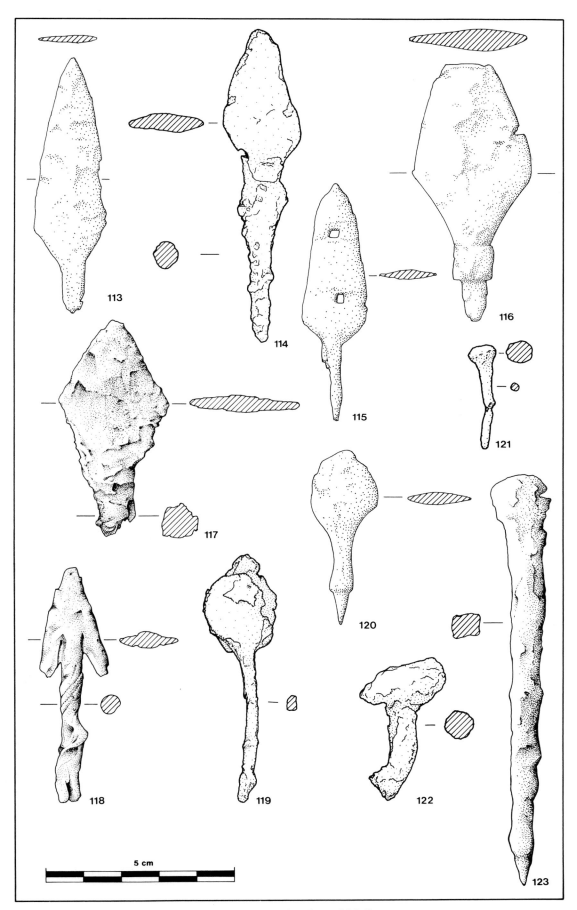

Fig. 71. Arrowheads and Nails

155

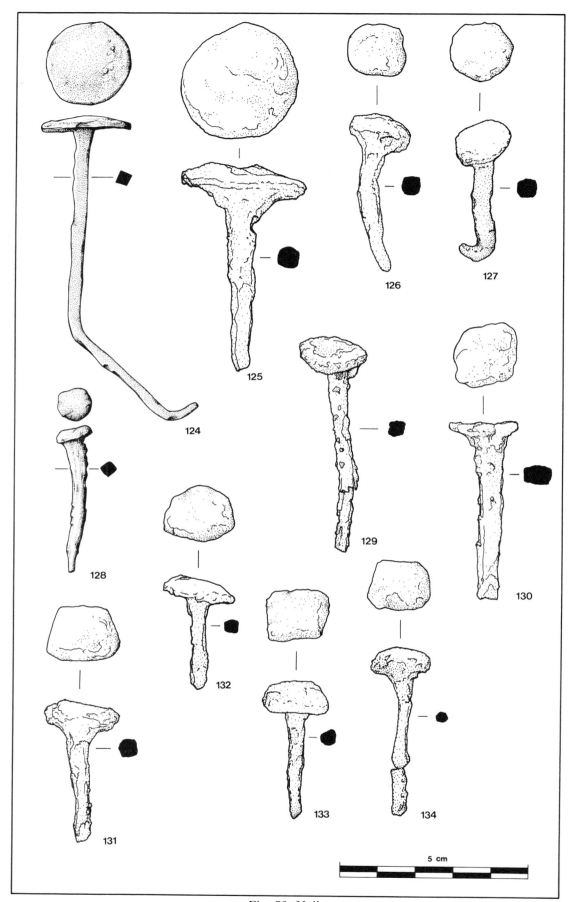

Fig. 72. Nails

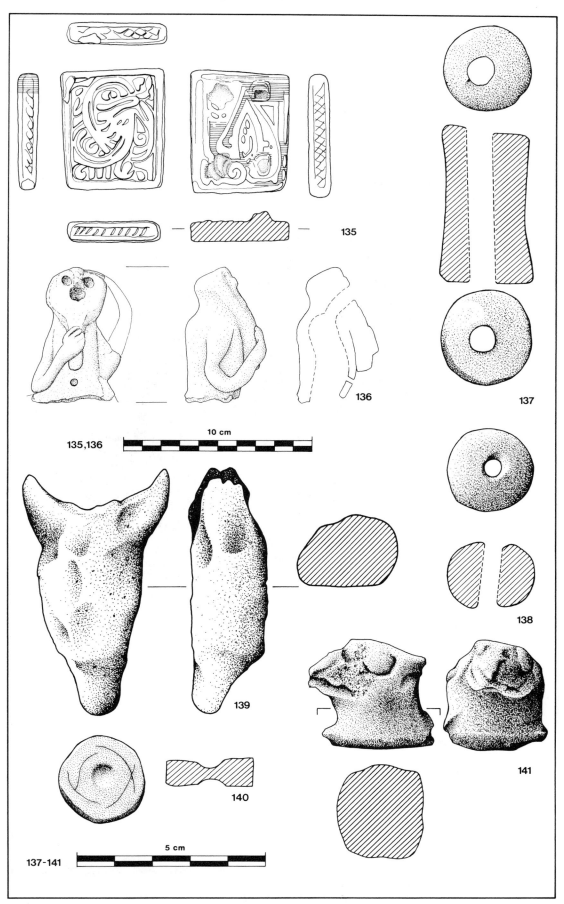

135

136

135,136

10 cm

137

138

139

140

141

137-141

5 cm

Fig. 73. Ceramic Objects

157

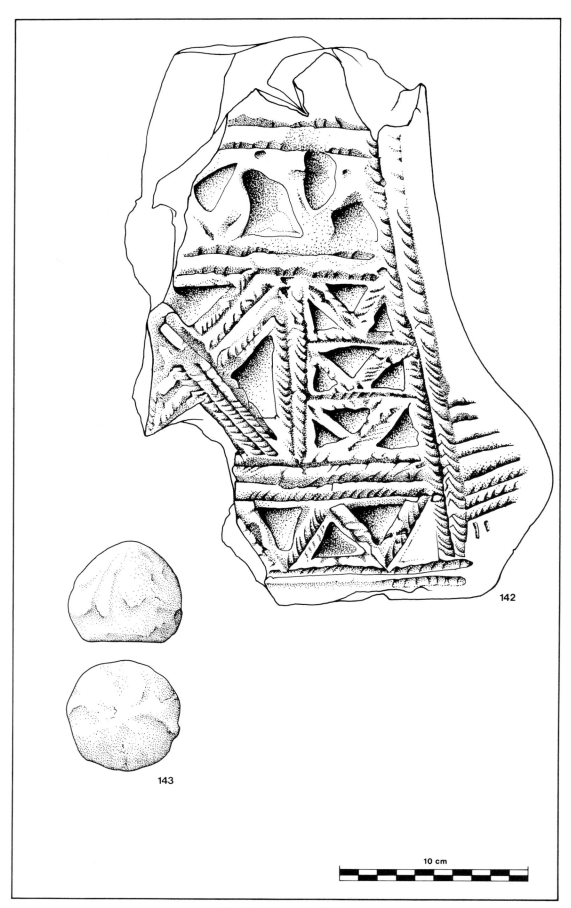

Fig. 74. Ceramic Objects

158

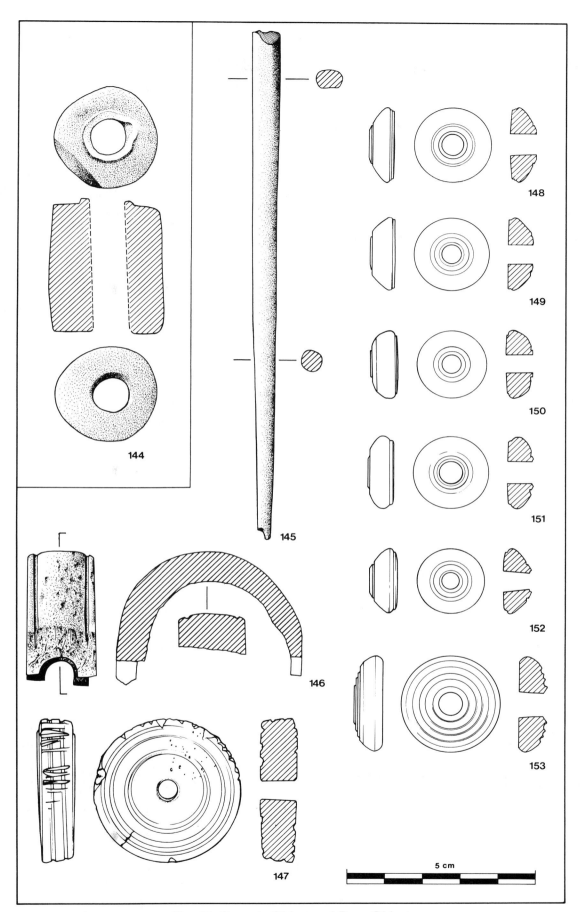

Fig. 75. Ceramic Object and Bone Objects

159

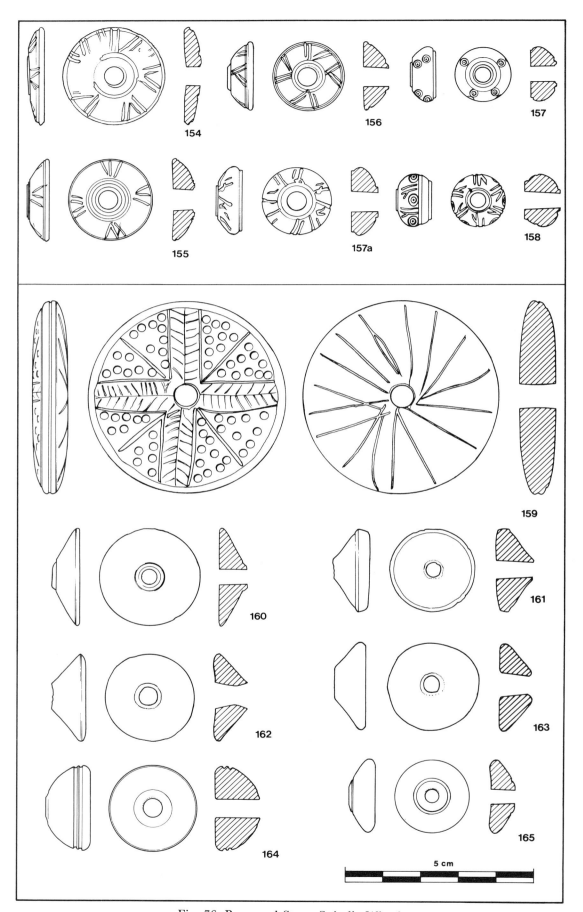

Fig. 76. Bone and Stone Spindle Whorls

160

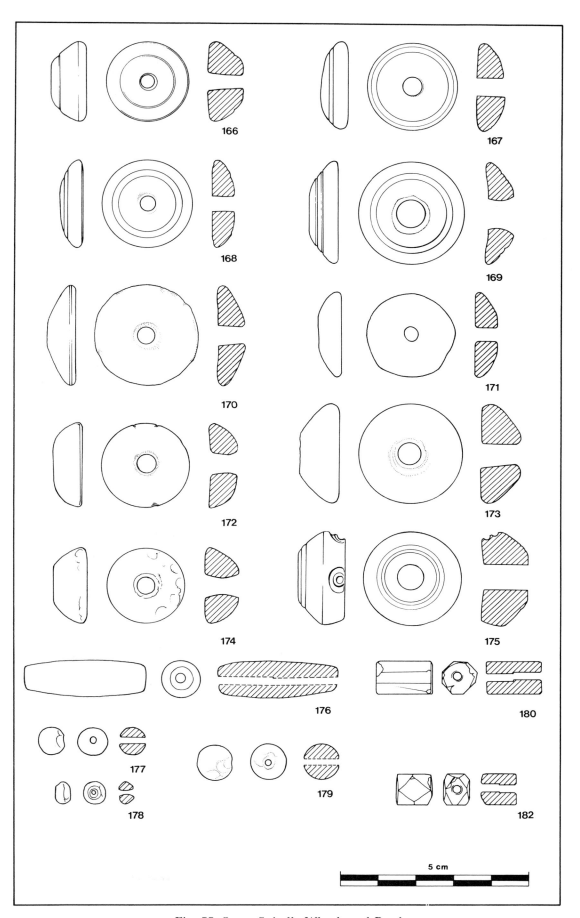

Fig. 77. Stone Spindle Whorls and Beads

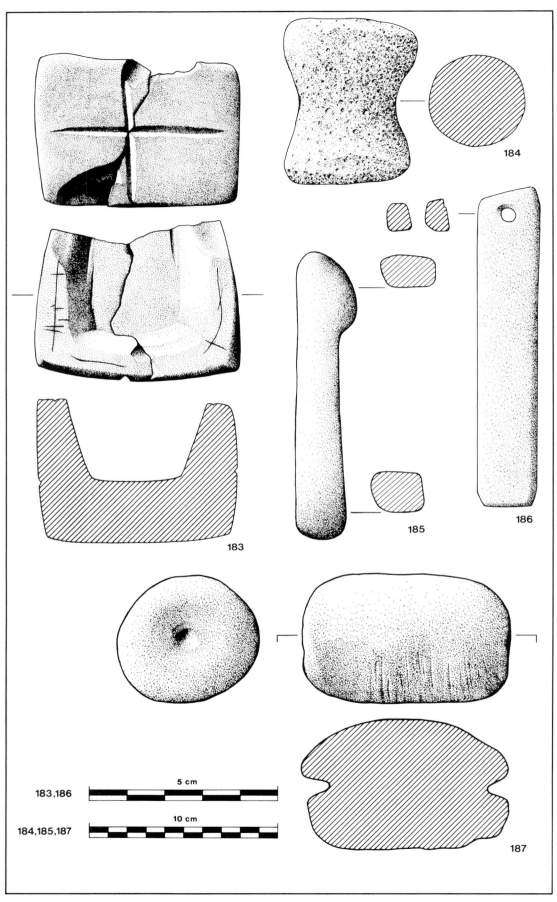

183,186

5 cm

184,185,187

10 cm

Fig. 78.

162

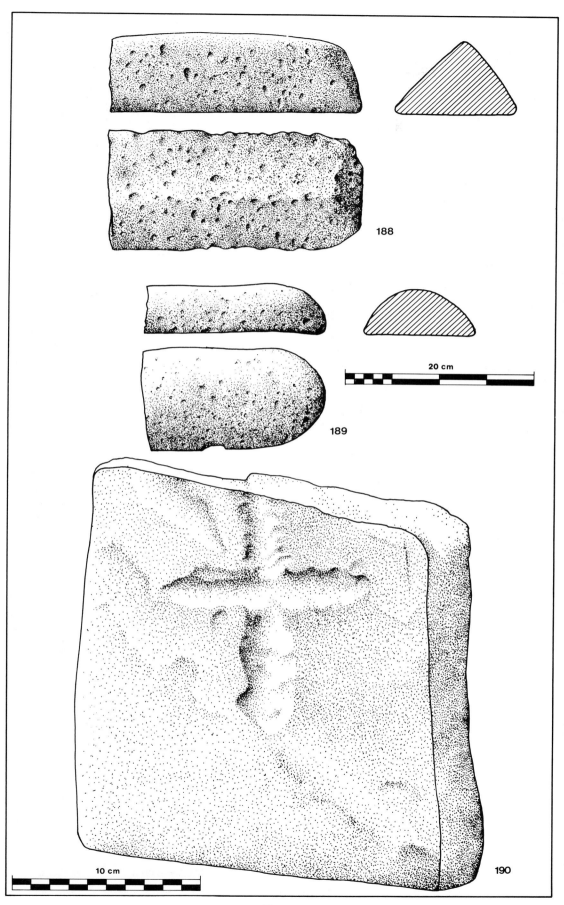

188

189

20 cm

10 cm

190

Fig. 79.

163

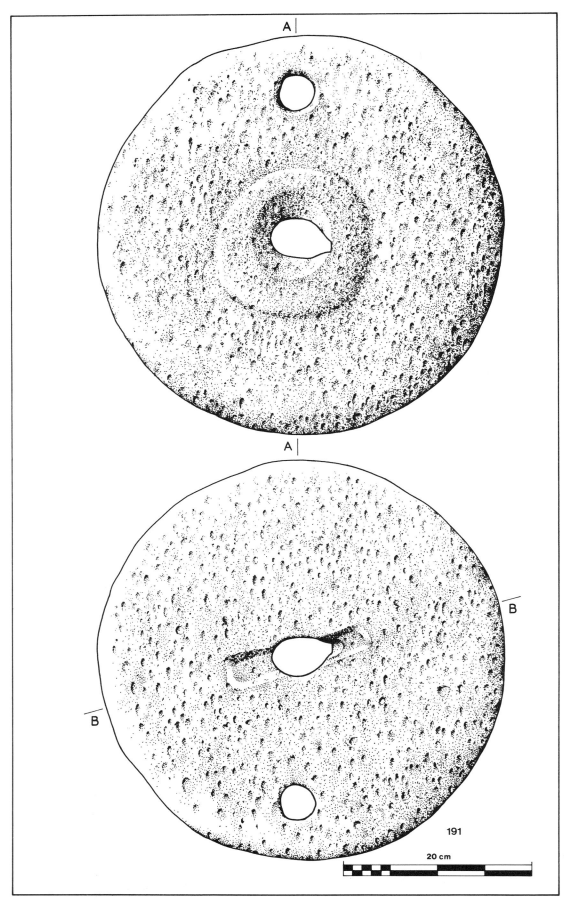

Fig. 80. Quernstones

164

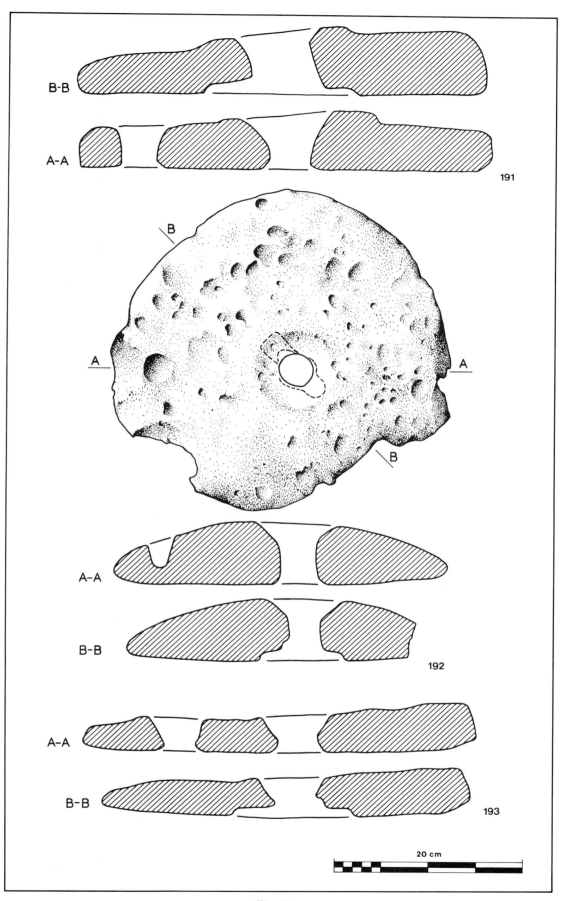

Fig. 81.

165

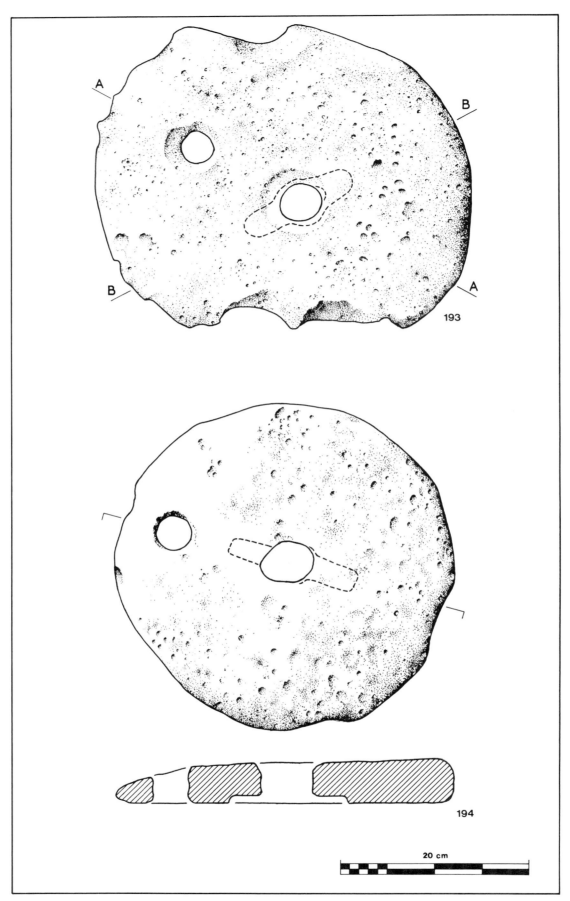

Fig. 82.

166

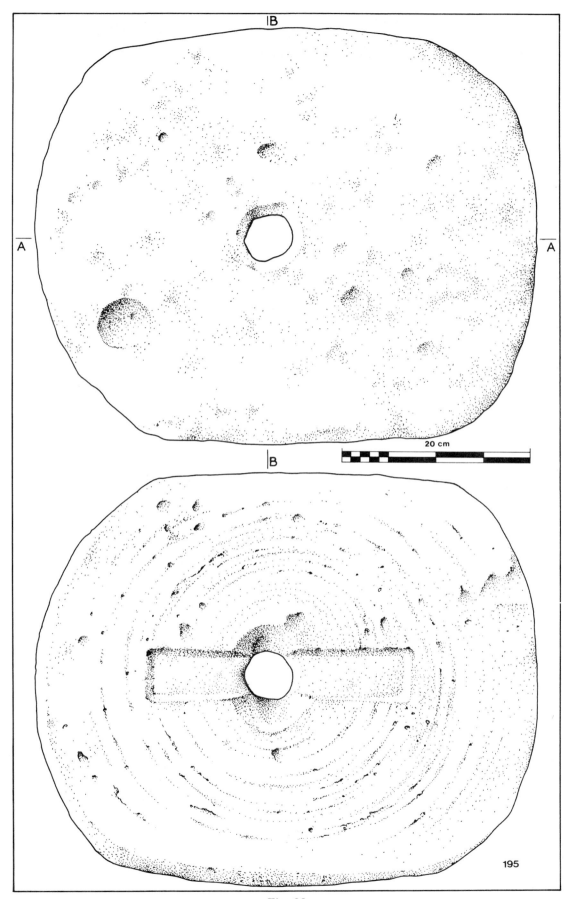

Fig. 83.

167

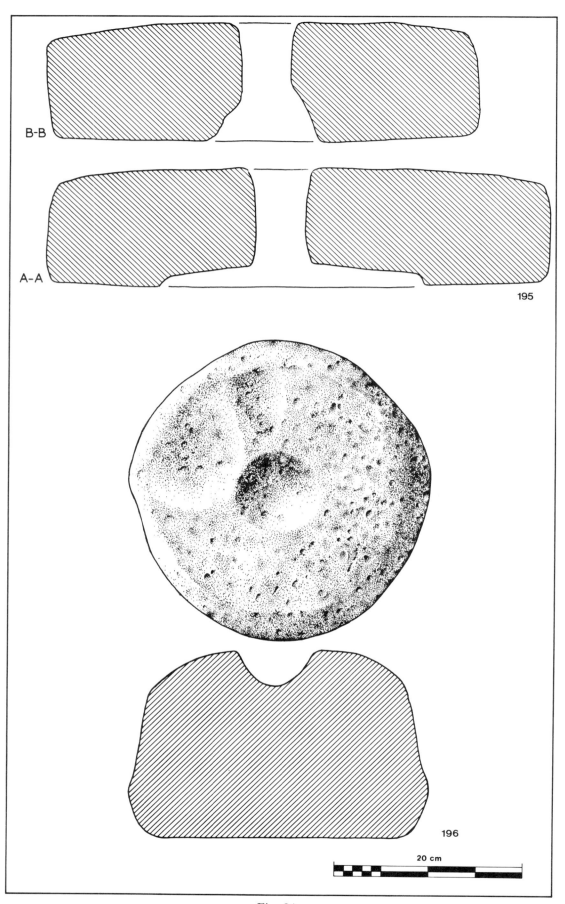

B-B

A-A

195

196

20 cm

Fig. 84.

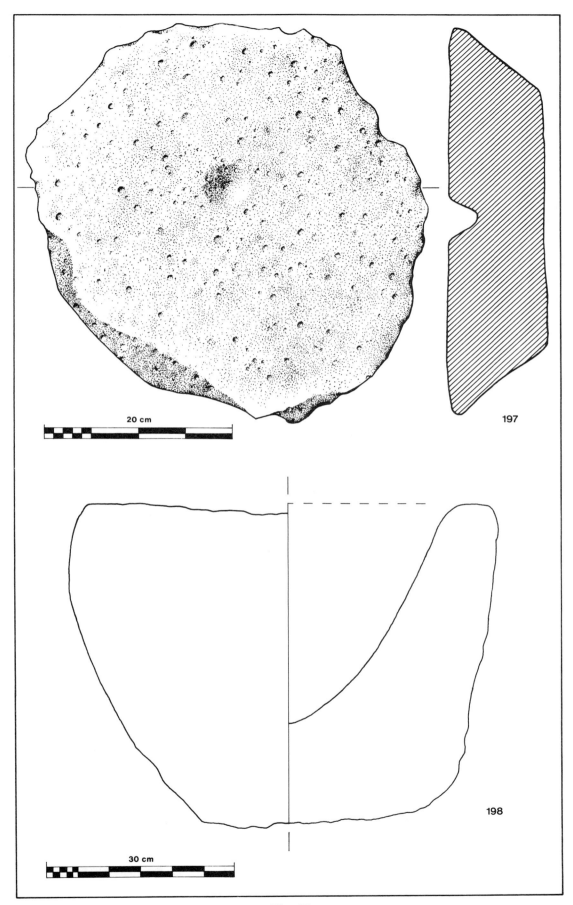

20 cm

197

30 cm

198

Fig. 85.

169

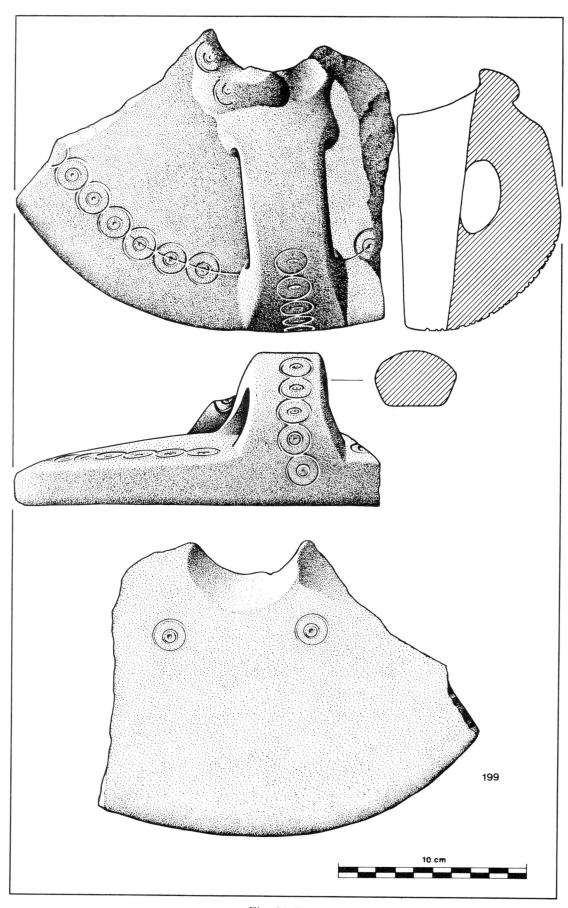

199

10 cm

Fig. 86. Lid

200

10 cm

Fig. 87. Gaming Board

171

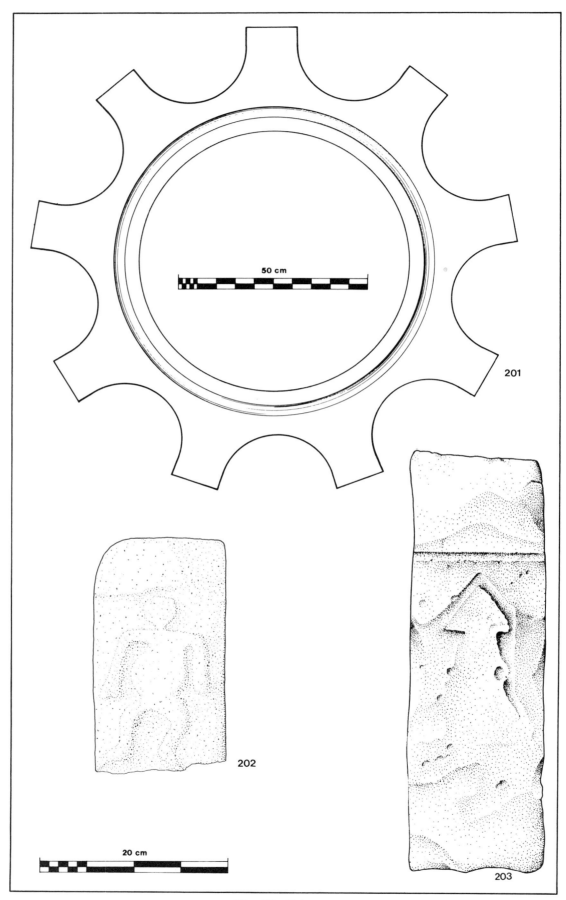

50 cm

201

20 cm

202

203

Fig. 88. Chimney

172

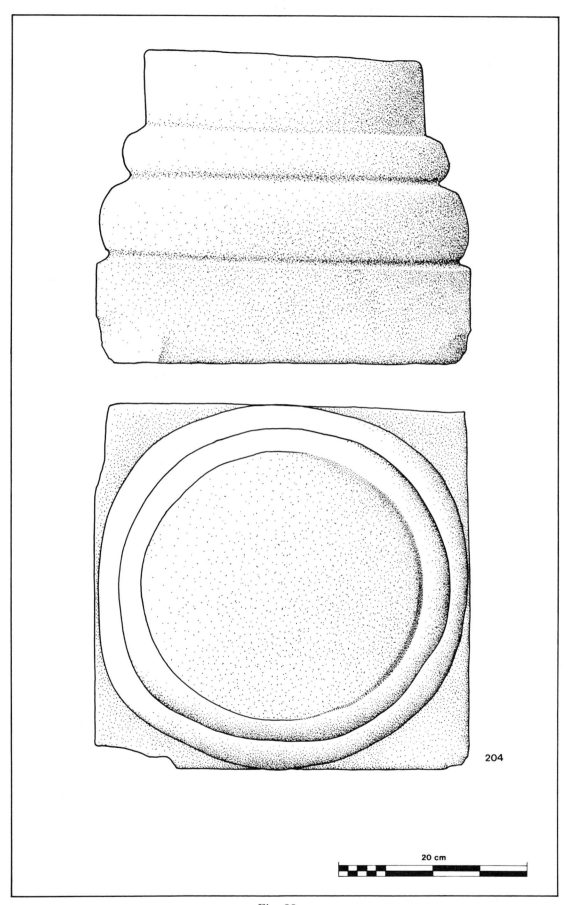

Fig. 89.

173

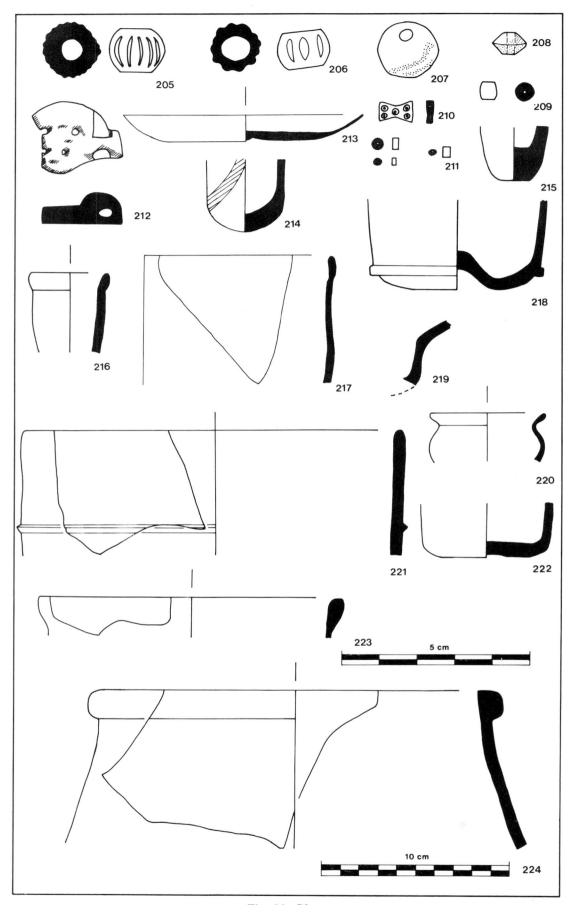

Fig. 90. Glass

174

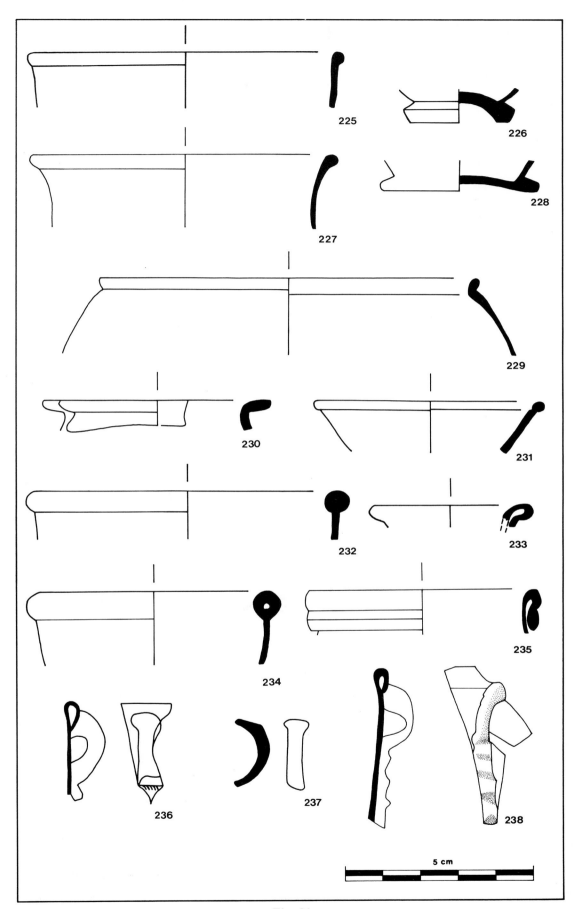

Fig. 91.

175

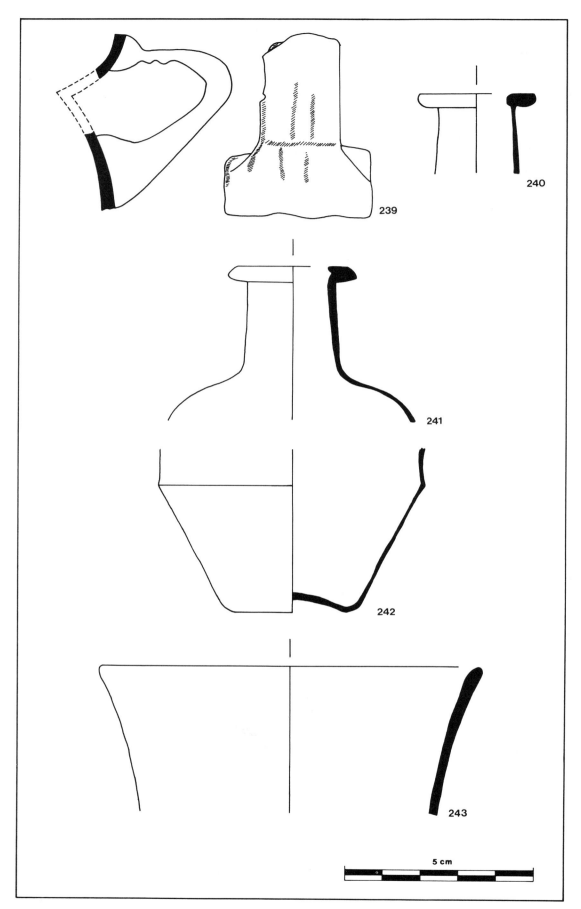

Fig. 92.

176

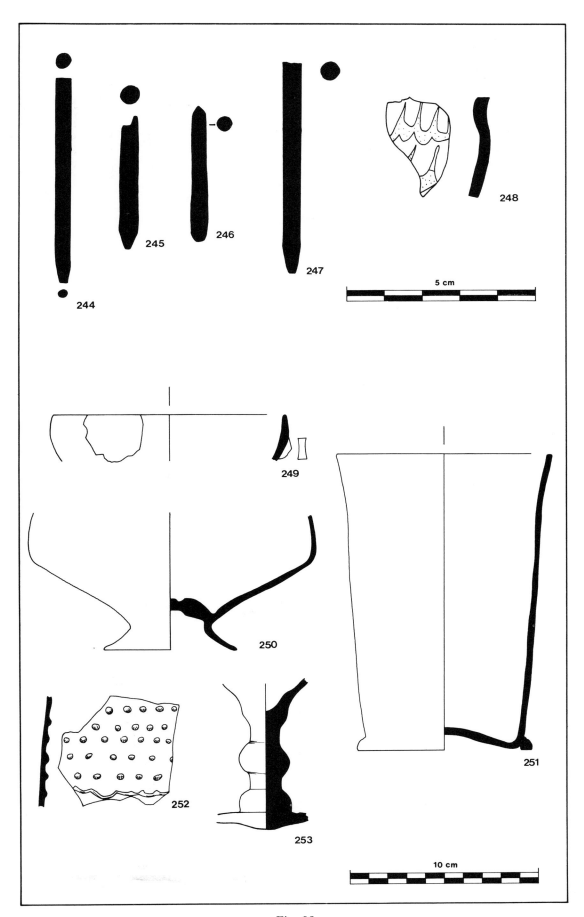

Fig. 93.

177

CHAPTER 8

The Coins

The following notes (on coins nos 1, 3-7) were kindly supplied by Simon Bendall. The Abbasid silver dirhem (coin no.2) was identified by Bay İsmail Galip of the Ankara Museum.

(1)   Venice, silver grosso

Register no.	TH/82/143
Excavation ref.	TH82.7757.015.30.003
Findspot	cistern (7757.053) (Figs 7, 19 and 20 and Pl.4b)
Date	Antonio Venier, AD 1382–1400
Comment	the cistern (7757.053) is one of the very latest features on the site and the back-fill of the cistern did not occur before Level 3.3.

(2)   Abbasid, silver dirhem

Register no.	TH/82/144
Excavation ref.	7858.162.30.003
Findspot	destruction debris of Level 1.2, used for make-up in Level 2.1
Date	AD 740 (H.123), Hisam b. Abd el-Melik; minted at Wasit (information of Bay İsmail Galip, Ankara Museum).
Comment	clearly a 'stray', but the coin is not worn.

(3)   French Provincial denier of Magueloone (Melgueil)

Register no.	TH/82/227
Excavation ref.	TH82.7556.152.30.005
Findspot	a pit (7556.153), pre-Level 1.1
Date	twelfth to thirteenth century
Comment	one of the commonest western coins found in the East. Struck in the name of William I Raymond (1190-1195, but possibly type fossilised for a short period? The coin may provide a possible terminus ante quem for Level 1.1.

(4)   Byzantine Anonymous Folles. Class D

Register no.	TH/83/306
Excavation ref.	TH81.7458.060.30.002
Findspot	pit fill, Level 1.1 (7458.061)
Date	c.AD 1050/6
Comment	worn.

(5)   Byzantine Anonymous Folles. Class A2.47

Register no.	TH/83/305
Excavation ref.	TH81.7858.076.30.002
Findspot	oven, Level 3.2
Date	c.AD 1065–1070
Comment	worn. Clearly a 'stray'.

(6)   Byzantine Anonymous Folles. Class G

Register no.	TH/83/308
Excavation ref.	TH81.7457.021.30.001
Findspot	pit fill, Level 1.3
Date	c.AD 1065–1070
Comment	worn.

(7)   Byzantine Anonymous Folles. Class C (Dumbarton Oaks C.1 - C.48)

Register no.	TH/83/307
Excavation ref.	TH81.7457.036.30.003
Findspot	(?)pit fill, Level 1.2
Date	c.AD 1042–1050
Comment	the commencing date for this type may be a little earlier. The coin is worn.

CHAPTER 9

The Early Medieval Finds

Two large (?)cess pits of an earlier period were discovered. The surface from which they had been dug had been destroyed by the late Medieval activity. Similar pottery is published in the Antioch reports (Waag 1948: Fig.96) where it has been given a 10th century date. The Abbasid coin (above, no.2) is dated to AD 741 (H.123),

some 150 years earlier. It is possible, on the basis of this one coin, that some of the early Medieval finds may be older than the tenth century although the coin shows no signs of wear. A broad date, c.AD 750–850, for the material from two early Medieval pits, may be tentatively suggested.

Catalogue of Early Medieval Objects

Objects are at scale 1:1 unless otherwise stated.

Fig. 94

1. 7758/323/42/019. Stone bowl. Grey to green. Micaceous. Double ring and dot decoration. Part of base found (not illustrated); flat. RD 0.30. Scale 1:2.
2. 7458/076/01/100. Stone bowl. Black. Double ring and dot decoration. RD ? Scale 1:2.
3. 7758/323/31/142. Iron knife. Simple blade. Back of blade: flat. Tang: simple, tapering, oblong in cross-section. Stop ridge slightly longer (in both planes) than blade; decorated with bead and reel below main part of ridge; the whole of the stop ridge is gilded. Point broken. L 0.147.
4. 7458/076/03/005. Part of (?)mould. Ceramic. Orange. D 0.20. Scale 1:2.
5. 7458/076/31/036. Copper alloy disc. Two incised rings on top. Part of edge, now slightly bent. (Top) D 0.031, Th 0.009; (point) L 0.0047 (broken).

Fig. 95

6. 7458/076/50/037. Olive-green tinge. RD 0.088.
7. 7458/076/50/037. Olive-green tinge. RD 0.08.
8. 7458/076/50/037. Pale green. RD 0.095.
9. 7458/076/50/037. Pale olive-green. RD 0.077.
10. 7458/076/50/037. Pale turquoise. RD 0.07.

Fig. 96

11. 7458/076/50/034. Pale green tinge. RD 0.08.

12. 7458/076/50/037. Pale green tinge. RD ?
13. 7458/076/50/037. Pinkish amber. RD c.102.
14. 7458/076/50/034. Ultramarine-blue. RD 0.082.
15. 7458/076/50/037. Yellowish green. RD 0.09.

Fig. 97

16. 7458/076/50/035. Very pale blue. RD 0.12.
17. 7458/076/50/037. Pale turquoise. RD 0.12.
18. 7458/076/50/037. Pale green. RD 0.074.
19. 7458/076/50/034. Ultramarine-blue. RD 0.08.
20. 7458/076/50/037. Light turquoise. RD 0.07.

Fig. 98

21. 7458/076/50/037. Dark turquoise. RD 0.05.
22. 7458/076/50/037. Light blue. RD 0.08.
23. 7458/076/50/037. Clear. RD 0.12.
24. 7458/076/50/037. Pale green. Fluted. RD 0.14. (?)Residual or (?)Hellenistic.
25. 7458/076/50/037. Pale turquoise. RD 0.17.

Fig.99

26. 7458/076/50/037. Clear. RD 0.03.
27. 7458/076/50/037. Light green to blue. RD 0.03
28. 7458/076/50/037. Pale green. RD 0.04.
29. 7458/076/50/037. Dark blue. RD 0.031.

30. 7458/076/50/037. Light turquoise. RD 0.022.
31. 7458/067/50/025. Clear. RD 0.02.
32. 7458/076/50/037. Light turquoise. RD 0.025.

Fig. 100

33. 7458/076/50/037. Pale turquoise. RD 0.02.
34. 7458/076/50/037. Pale green. RD 0.015.
35. 7458/076/50/037. Pale green. RD 0.036.
36. 7458/076/50/037. Pale green. RD 0.017.
37. 7458/067/50/022. Pale green. RD 0.032.
38. 7458/076/50/037. Clear. RD 0.011.
39. 7458/076/50/037. Pale green. RD 0.024.

Fig. 101

40. 7458/076/50/036. Pale green. BD 0.048.
41. 7458/076/50/036. Pale green. BD 0.05.
42. 7458/076/50/036. Pale green. BD 0.05.
43. 7458/076/50/036. Pale green. BD 0.058.
44. 7458/076/50/036. Pale green. BD 0.063.

Fig. 102

45. 7458/076/50/036. Pale turquoise. BD 0.065.
46. 7458/076/50/036. Pale green. BD 0.05.
47. 7458/076/50/036. Green. BD 0.05.
48. 7458/076/50/036. Light green. BD 0.025.
49. 7458/076/50/036. Pale green. BD 0.017.
50. 7458/076/50/036. Light blue. BD 0.051.
51. 7458/076/50/036. Light purple. BD 0.04.

Fig. 103

52. 7458/076/50/036. Pale green. Decorated on exterior. BD 0.03–0.035.
53. 7458/076/50/036. Amber. Interior decoration shown. Exterior is opposite i.e. bumps are hollows.
54. 7458/076/50/036. Dark green. BD 0.016.
55. 7458/076/50/036. Pale green. BD 0.06.

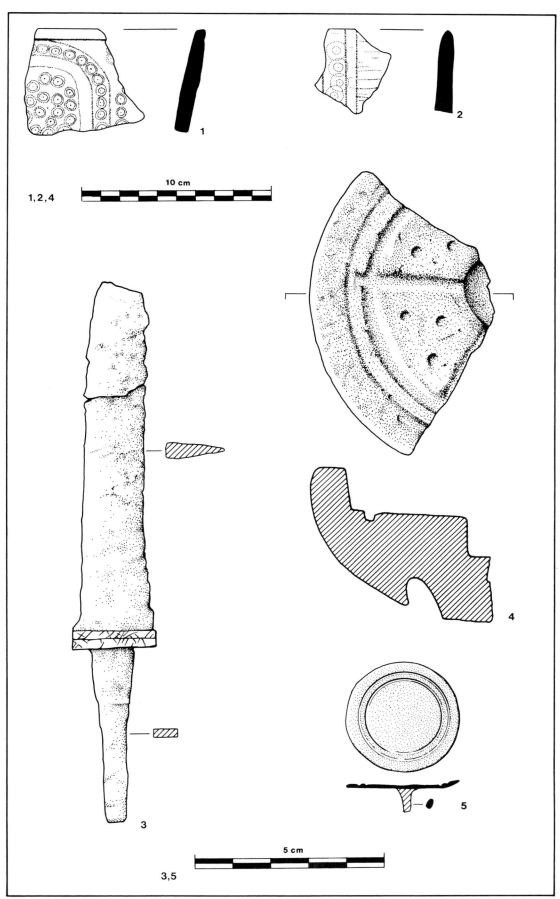

Fig. 94.

183

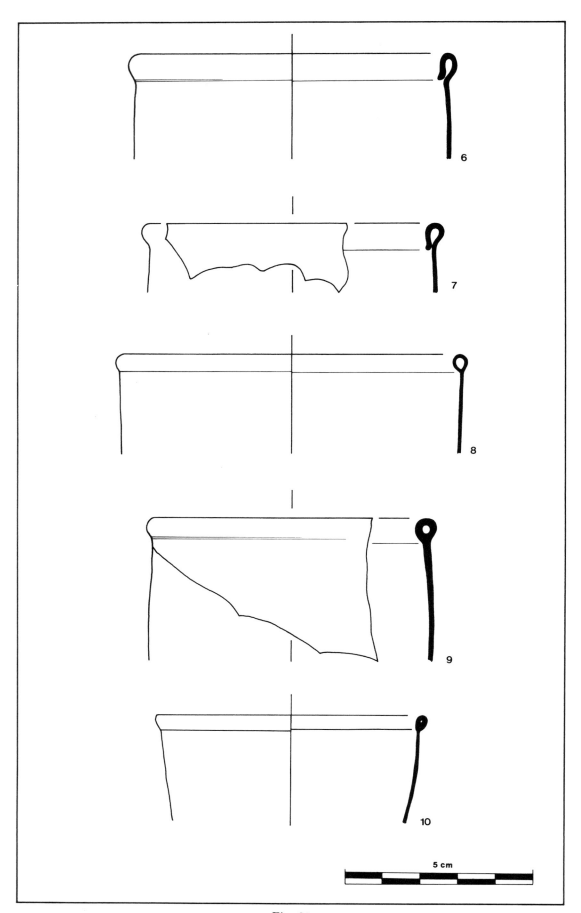

Fig. 95.

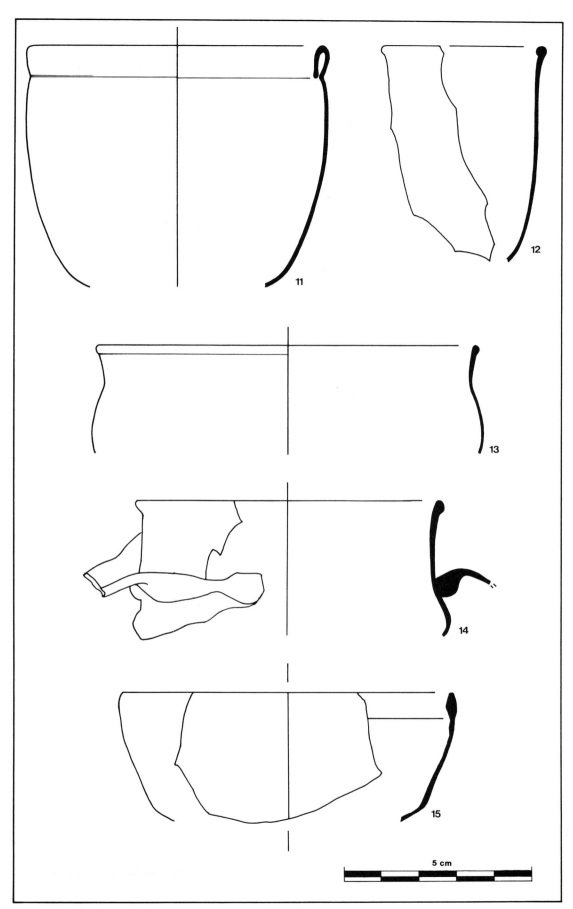

Fig. 96.

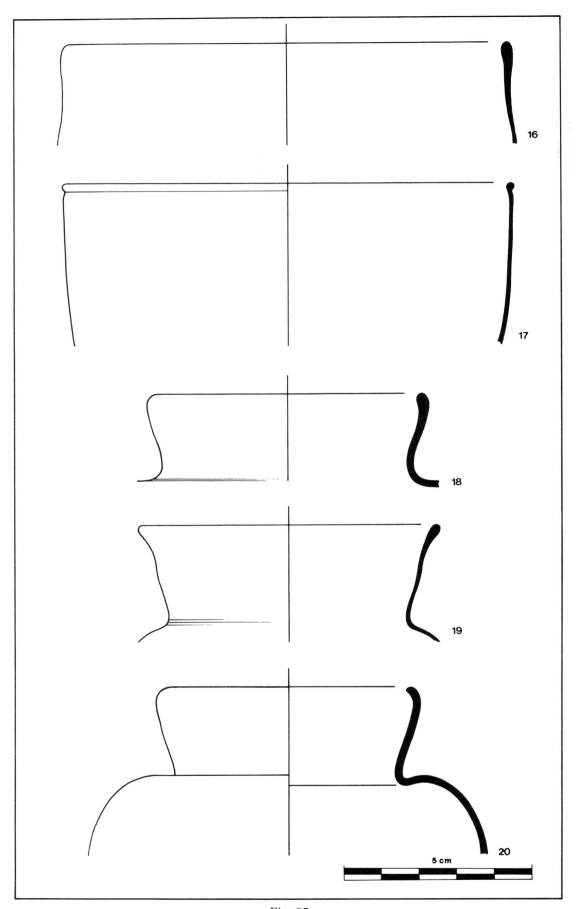

Fig. 97.

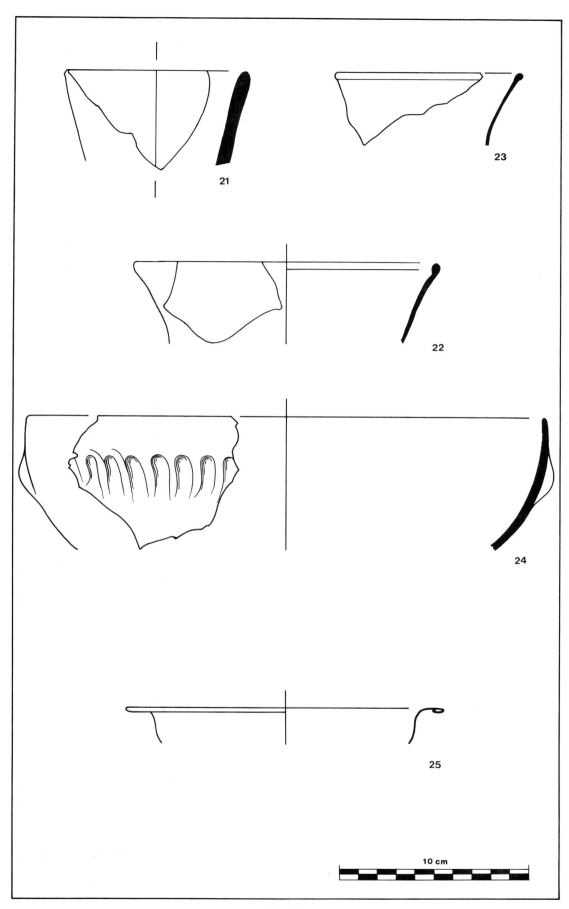

Fig. 98.

187

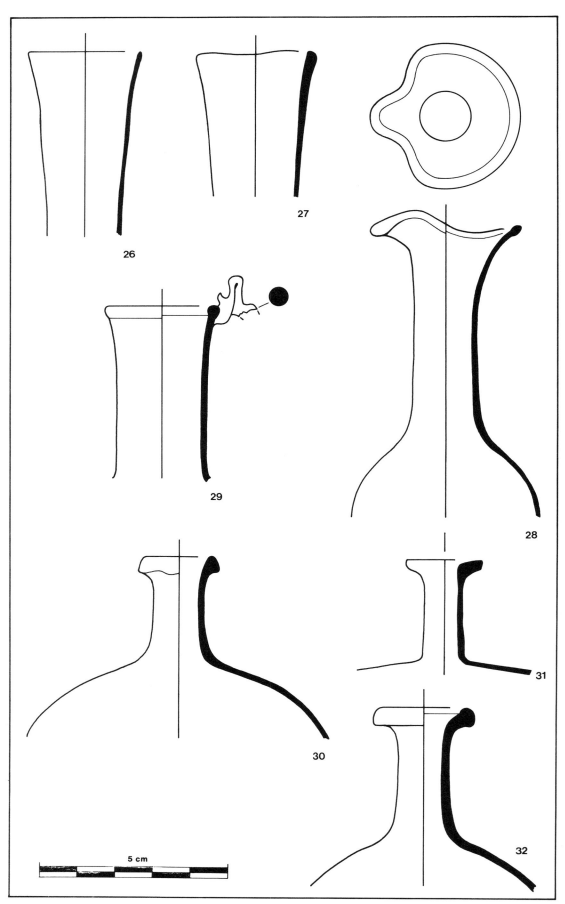

5 cm

Fig. 99.

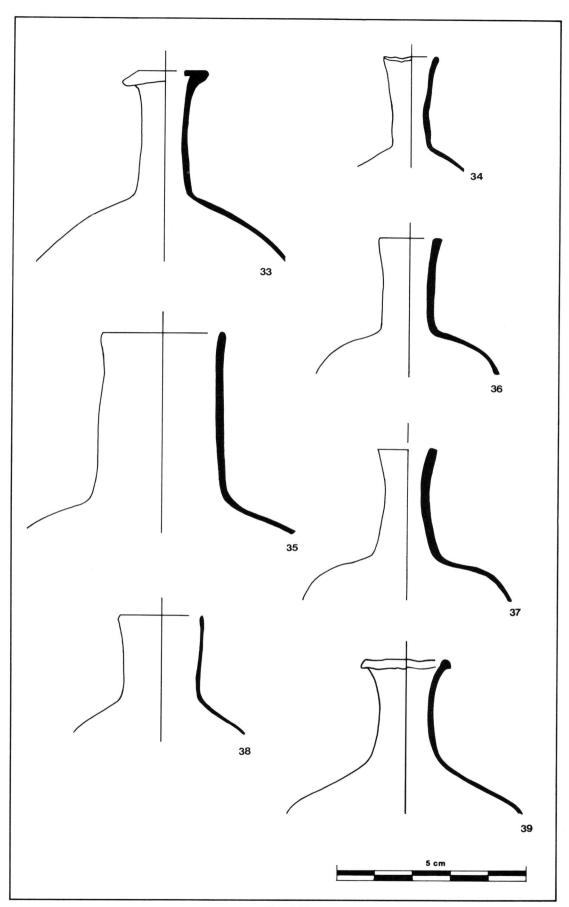

Fig. 100.

189

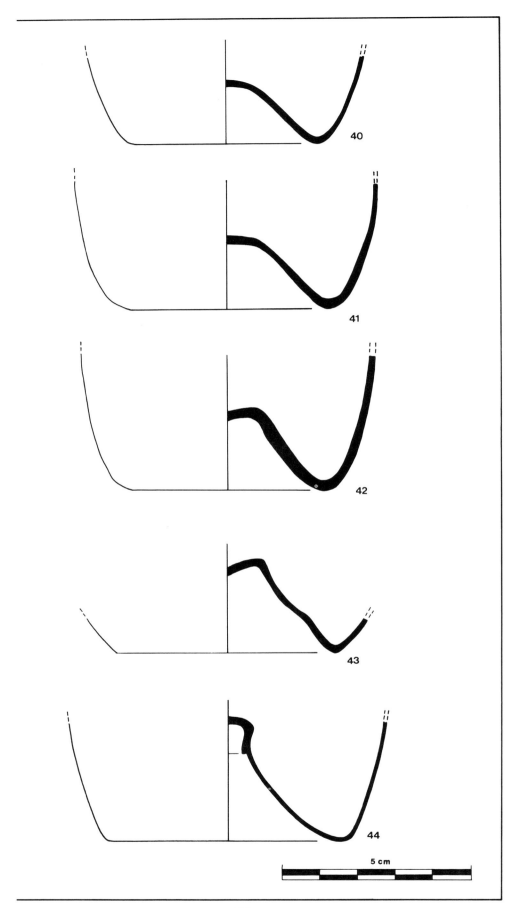

Fig. 101.

190

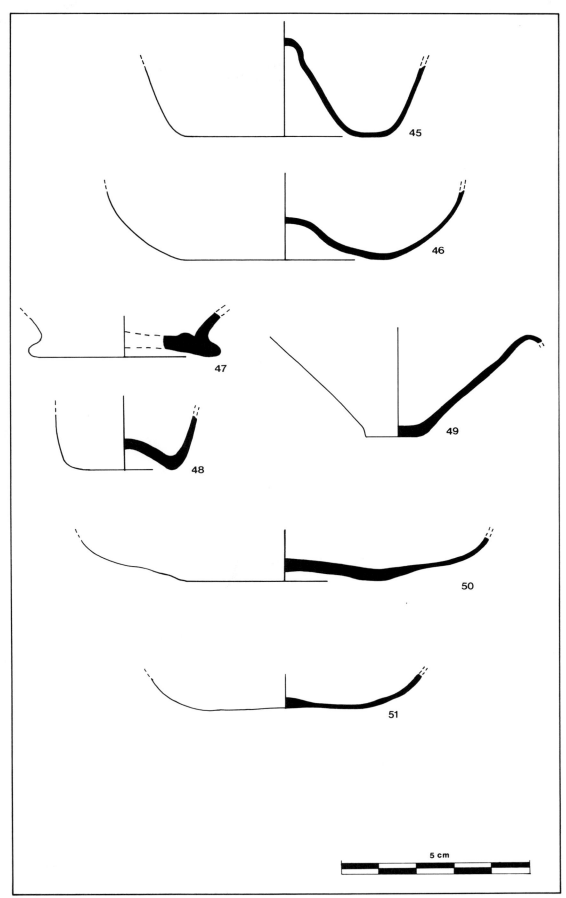

Fig. 102.

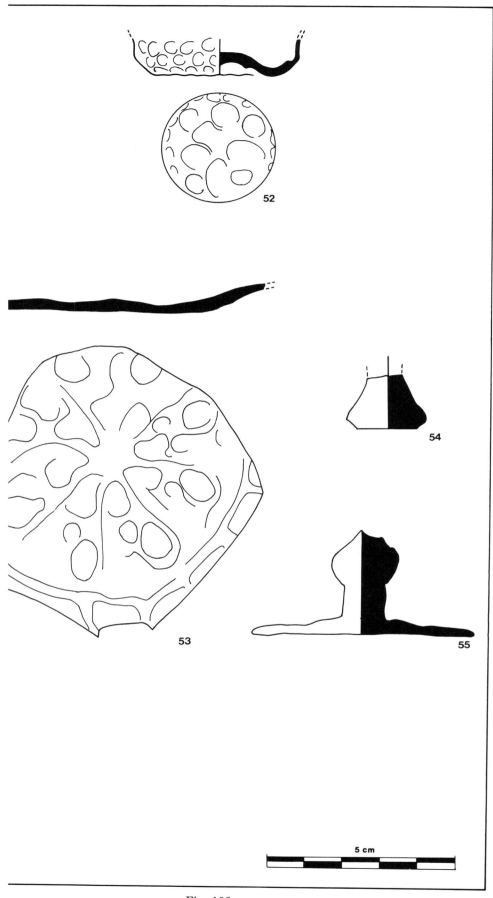

5 cm

Fig. 103.

Catalogue of Early Medieval Pottery

Fig. 104

1. 7458/076/01/097. One-handled jar. Orange to grey fabric with numerous grit, and occasional mica, inclusions. Incised lines on mid-body. Impressed mark on handle. Brittle. RD 0.12.

2. 7458/076/01/097. Jar. Greyish buff fabric with numerous grit, and occasional mica, inclusions. Brittle. RD. 0.12.

3. 7458/076/01/097. Jar. Orange red fabric, grey core with numerous grit, and occasional mica, inclusions. Brittle. RD 0.12.

4. 7458/076/01/100. One-handled jar. Grey core, orange exterior and interior. Numerous grit inclusions. Brittle. Brownish red paint in stripes. RD 0.19.

5. 7458/076/01/096. (?)Two-handled jar. Buff fabric with moderate amount of grit and mica inclusions.

6. 7458/076/01/096. Two-handled jar. Buff fabric with numerous grit and mica inclusions. Brownish red paint on exterior. RD 0.146.

7. 7458/076/01/096. One-handled jug. Greyish buff fabric with numerous grit and mica inclusions. Combed decoration on neck and shoulder. RD 0.12.

8. 7458/076/01/096. (?)Two-handled jar. Buff fabric with moderate amount grit and mica inclusions.

9. 7458/076/01/097. Two-handled jar. Black fabric. Surface smoothed. RD 0.15.

10. 7458/076/01/097. Jar. Red to grey fabric with numerous grit and mica inclusions. RD 0.14.

Fig. 105

11. 7458/076/02/015. Jug. Buff fabric with numerous white grit and mica inclusions. Surface smoothed. RD 0.105, BD 0.07, H 0.242.

12. 7758/323/01/281. Jar. Red fabric. Surface smoothed. RD 0.15.

13. 7758/323/01/280. Jar. Buff fabric with moderate amount of very fine grit inclusions. RD 0.12.

14. 7458/076/02/014. Flask. Pale greenish buff fabric with mica inclusions. Surface smoothed. Moulded relief decoration. Is bottom half of vessel made in sections? BD 0.115.

15. 7758/323/01/280. Bowl. Core grey, exterior and interior fabric buff with moderate amount grit and mica inclusions. RD 0.14, BD 0.064, H 0.045.

16. 7458/076/01/097. Bowl. Pinkish buff fabric with moderate amount of grit, and numerous mica, inclusions. RD 0.21.

17. 7458/076/01/097. Two-handled jar. Buff fabric. RD 0.072.

18. 7458/076/01/100. Flask. Yellow fabric with moderate amount of grit, and occasional mica, inclusions. RD 0.10.

19. 7758/323/01/280. Flask. Pale red fabric, pale grey core, with occasional grit inclusions. RD ?

20. 7458/076/01/097. (?)Flask. Buff fabric with occasional mica inclusions. RD 0.125.

21. 7659/001/01/106. Bowl. Grey fabric with occasional very fine grit inclusions. (?)Moulded decoration on rim. RD 0.16. From topsoil.

22. 7458/076/01/100. Bowl. Grey fabric with occasional fine inclusions. Incised decoration on rim. RD 0.13.

23. 7758/323/01/280. (?)Bowl. Buff fabric with moderate amount of grit inclusions. Incised decoration on rim. RD ?

24. 7458/076/01/100. Flask. Creamish buff fabric with chaff temper. Porous. RD 0.08.

25. 7458/076/01/097. Flask. Buff fabric with large amount of chaff temper. Porous. RD 0.05.

26. 7758/323/01/280. Flask. White fabric with moderate amount of grit inclusions. RD 0.065.

27. 7758/323/01/280. Neck or part of pedestal base. White fabric with occasional grit inclusions. Impressed decoration. One part of vessel made in sections.

28. 7758/323/01/280. Flask. Cream fabric with numerous grit inclusions. Neck part of vessel made in sections. RD 0.032.

29. 7758/323/01/280. (?)Flask. White fabric with moderate amount of grit inclusions. Applied pellets. Incised lines. RD 0.05.

30. 7458/076/01/100. One-handled (?)flask. Creamish buff fabric with fine grit inclusions and chaff temper. RD 0.06.

/100. Miniature jar. Creamish with large amount of chaff l occasional grit inclusions. 0.043, H 0.08.

/100. Miniature jar. Creamish with large amount of chaff)us. RD 0.04, H 0.088.

/100. Miniature jar. Creamish with large amount of chaff fine grit inclusions. Porous. RD

/100. Miniature jar. Pinkish vith many grit, and occasional ons, and chaff temper. Porous. ver motif decoration. RD 0.03.

/100. Miniature jar. Orange with large amount of chaff l numerous grit inclusions. :coration. RD 0.05.

/100. Miniature jar. Redish ic with moderate amount of and occasional grit inclusions.

'280. Miniature jar. Creamish with occasional very fine grit D 0.05.

'280. Base. White fabric with nount of grit inclusions. BD

39. 7458/07601/100. Base. Pinkish orange fabric with occasional grit and chaff inclusions. All-over green glaze with patches of blue. BD 0.035.

40. 7758/323/01/280. Base. White fabric with grit inclusions. BD 0.05.

41. 7458/076/02/016. Jug. Greenish buff fabric. Decoration: corrugations on middle and upper body; dimples around middle of body; fine incisions on neck; in three registers 1) (upper) cross-hatching, 2) diagonal hatching, 3) (lower) facing semi-circles; on outer edge of rim, three horizontal grooves; on top of handle, a knob. RD 0.059, BD 0.057, H 0.202.

42. 7758/323/01/280. Sherd. Fabric: exterior white, interior buff. Moulded decoration.

43. 7458/076/01/100. Sherd. Orange buff fabric with occasional chaff temper and occasional grit inclusions. Brownish red paint decoration.

44. 7458/076/01/100. Sherd. Pinkish cream fabric with numerous chaff and grit inclusions. Sepia paint decoration.

45. 7458/076/01/100. Rim. Light cream fabric. All-over olive-green glaze. Relief decoration.

46. 7458/076/01/100. Rim. Orange pink fabric. All-over green glaze. Relief decoration.

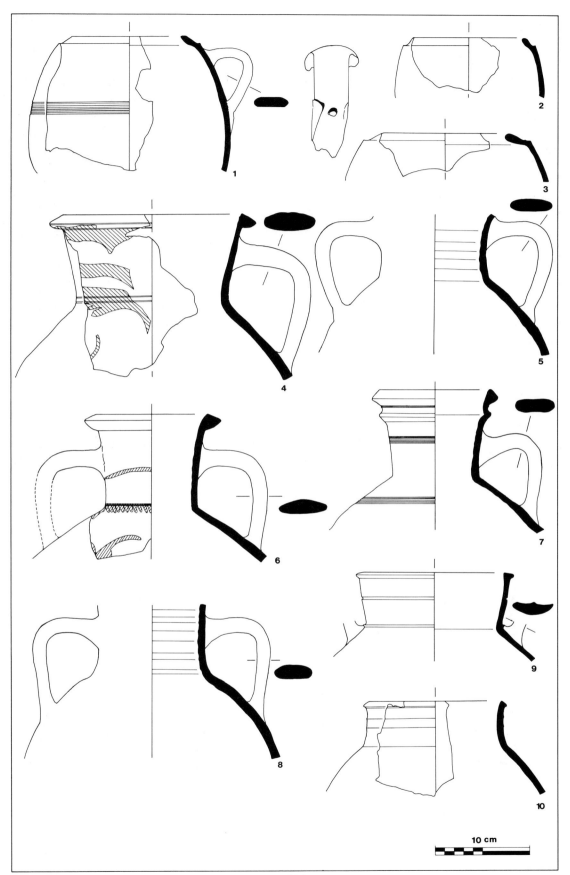

Fig. 104.

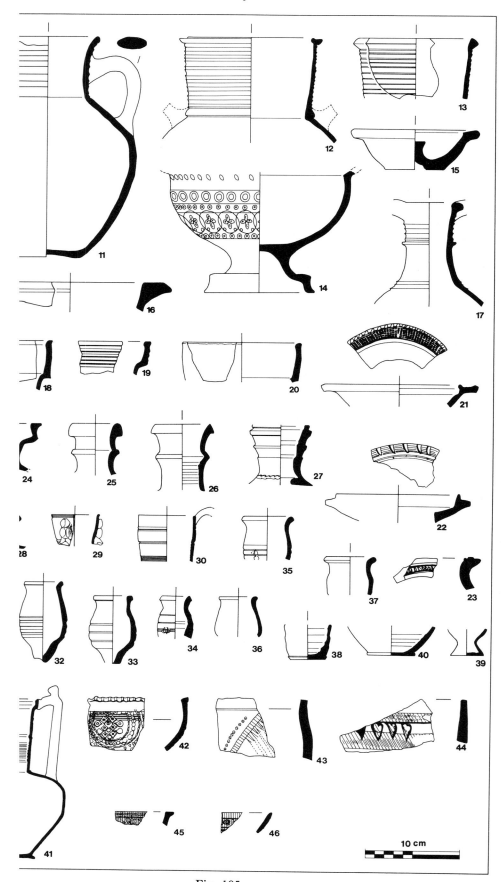

Fig. 105.

CHAPTER 10

Dating

The chronology of the Medieval settlement on the top of the mound must be based on the pottery, especially the fine glazed wares. Of the seven coins relevant to the period (many Roman coins were recovered), four are Anonymous Bronzes of the Byzantine period and one is Abbasid.

The Abbasid coin (no.2, above p.177) is a silver dirhem and is dated AD 740 (H.123). It was a stray: it came from Level 1.2 destruction debris/Level 2.1 make-up. On the other hand, the coin may be a chronological indicator for occupation on the site. The early Medieval finds at Tille, therefore, may in part belong to the eighth to ninth century AD.

No reliability can be given to the Anonymous Bronzes. One coin (no.5) came from pit fill Level 1.1. The second coin (no.6) came from pit fill Level 1.2. The third coin (no.7) is uncertain but probably came from pit fill Level 1.2. The fourth (no.4) came from oven fill Level 3.2. Nevertheless, all four provide an approximate terminus ante quem for Level 1.1, i.e. the earliest phase of Level 1 is not earlier than c. AD 1075–1100 (if one allows for circulation and use). All four coins are worn.

Even though the three coins (nos 4, 6 and 7), all from Level 1 contexts, are neatly grouped in the mid-eleventh century (the fourth coin, no.5, being a stray), the pottery evidence contradicts this date. As at Aşvan (Mitchell 1980) the Byzantine coins were probably in circulation for a century after they were struck.

I have suggested in the comments on the fine glaze wares that the bulk of the pottery came from Syria. The Raqqa wares certainly do not begin until AD 1171. This is the date given to the dispersion of the Fatimid potters (Lane 1947), although the Tell Minis wares may be dated slightly earlier (Porter 1981). The Tell Minis wares were found in Level 2.2 to 3.1 contexts and also in a Level 1.2 context (if one piece [no.302] is accepted as the Tell Minis style). Raqqa wares were found in Level 2.2, 3.1 and 3.4 contexts. The divided dish (no. 358) which I believe to be from Raqqa came from a Level 1.2 context.

If the fine glaze wares and the coarse wares are to be dated (mainly) by the Aşvan period II material, the late settlement on the mound at Tille would have started in the early twelfth century. The French Provincial denier (coin no.3) would, however, contradict this proposal. On the other hand, the majority of the Raqqa and Tell Minis wares coming from the late Level 2 strata at Tille would perhaps indicate a date of the mid-thirteenth century for this phase (Level 2). The Raqqa wares do not continue beyond AD 1259 when the city of Raqqa was sacked by the Mongols (Lane 1947).

Of the black-under-blue wares attributed to the second half of the thirteenth century or early fourteenth century (Porter 1981) all (with the exception of one piece) came from Level 3 contexts. Associated with these levels and with this type of ware is our seventh coin (no.1). It is silver and is pierced for suspension. The coin is one of Antonio Venier (Doge of Venice AD 1382–1400). It came from the back-fill of the cistern—an operation which was a deliberate act and did not occur before Level 3.3. This coin would give a date of c. mid-fifteenth century for the end of the settlement on the höyük.

The problems arising from the use of sherds rather than whole pots is well known. It is easy for sherds to move, both horizontally and vertically (i.e. through time), away from their true contemporary context. If one discounts the Byzantine Anonymous Bronzes (in circulation well after being struck?) because none of the pottery seems to be of eleventh century date, and further, if the life of the main settlement is presumed to have started near the very end of the twelfth century (coin no.3, c. 1190–1195, pre-1.1), a great deal of occupation must be squeezed into the next one hundred years or so. This 'squeeze' is a consequence of the mid-thirteenth century date indicated by the presence of the Raqqa and Tell Minis wares in the late Level 2. Level 3 must then be given a life-span of c. 150 years. It would seem slightly more balanced if the end of Level 2 was somewhat later, perhaps c. AD 1300. Hence the Raqqa and Tell Minis wares found in Levels 3.4 and 3.1 would then be residual, or strays, i.e. their original use was in late Level 1/early Level 2. Given that the late fourteenth century Venetian coin was found in the cistern back-fill, it would be reasonable to put the end of the settlement on the mound at c. AD 1450.

Although secure evidence for an accurate

: settlement was not found, it is ...at the main occupation took ...teenth century. The structures ...he time span indicated by the ... finds suggest that occupation ...ous and that there may well have been a period between Level 3.2 and 3.3 when the top of the mound was deserted. The main settlement at Tille during Level 3 would have been, it is proposed, at the foot of the mound where chance finds show similar, i.e. contemporary, pottery.

CHAPTER 11

Türkçe Özet

Giriş

Tille Höyük Kazısı, Aşağı Fırat Kurtarma Projesi çerçevesinde Atatürk Barajı inşaatı ile ilgili olarak sürdürülmüştür.

Yakın geçmişte birçok bilim adamı tarafından ziyaret edilmiş olan yerleşimin planı, Profesör F.K. Dörner başkanlığındaki Eski Kahta ekibi tarafından çizilmiştir. Ayrıca Özdoğan (1977) ve Serdaroğlu (1977) yerleşimle ilgili topografik ve arkeolojik notlar çıkarmışlardır. 1979–1981 yılları arasında sürdürülmüş olan çalışmaların raporları da Anatolian Studies'de 'The Years's Work' başlığı altında yayınlanmıştır. Yine Anatolian Studies'in 32. sayısında (French, Moore, Russell 1982) konuyla ilgili bir ara rapor yayınlanmıştır. Bunların yanı sıra II. III. IV. ve V. 'Kazı Sonuçları Toplantısı' bildirilerinde, yıllık çalışmalarla ilgili kısa özetler verilmiş bulunmaktadır.

Höyük üzerindeki Ortaçağ katlarının kaldırılması 1980–1984 yılları arasında yedi kazı sezonunda gerçekleştirilmiştir.

Konum

Tille Höyük Fırat nehrinin batı kıyısında, eski Adıyaman-Urfa/Diyarbakır karayolu üzerinde bulunan köprünün hemen yakınında yer almaktaydı (Şek. 1). Tille, günümüzdeki adıyla Geldibuldu Köyü, yolun kuzeyinde, Kahta'nın yaklaşık 30km doğusunda , höyüğün doğu, batı ve güney yamaçlarındaki onyedi haneden oluşan küçük bir yerleşimdi.

Fırat nehrine karışan bir akarsu tarafından oluşturulmuş dar ve derin bir dere yatağının kenarında yer alan Höyük yaklaşık 200 x 140m (doğu terası dahil olmak üzere) bir alanı kaplamakta olup ovadan yüksekliği 26 metreye ulaşmaktadır. Höyüğün konik kısmının taban çapı yaklaşık 130 metredir; kazının başlama-sından önce ise, düz tepe 40 x 33 m olarak ölçülmüştür. Korunagelmiş Ortaçağ yerleşi-minin en erken evresi ile kaplı olan alanın da 46 x 40m olduğu saptanmıştır. Höyüğün kenarları, özellikle kuzey kenarı oldukça diktir (Şek. 2).

Mimari

Üç yapı katı ve bu katlara ait çeşitli evrelerden oluşan bu dönemin oldukça karmaşık bir strati-grafisi vardır. 1. yapı katı en erken, 3. yapı katı ise, en geç dönemleri temsil etmektedir. Bu raporda her evreyle ilgili başlıca noktalar ve mekanların işlevleri üzerinde durulacaktır.

Höyük üzerindeki yerleşim inşa edilmeden önce höyüğün üzeri düzleştirilmiş, Helenistik Çağ'a ait korunagelmiş duvarlar yıkılmış ve Erken Ortaçağ katı ve ilişkili yapılar kaldırılmıştır. Erken Ortaçağ yerleşimine ait (7. ve 8. yy) tek kanıt iki büyük çukurdur.

1. Yapı Katı, 1. Evre (Şek. 7)

Bu dönemde Höyük üzerindeki yerleşim üç odası, kapalı bir avlusu ve ambarları olan bir evden ve Höyüğün kuzeybatısında yer alan bir seri ek yapıdan ve avlulardan oluşmaktaydı. Bu ek yapıların hayvan barınağı, tarımsal araç ve günlük gereksinim olmayan gıda malzemelerinin depolanması için kullanılmış olduğunu düşünmekteyiz.

Çevre duvarı taş temeller üzerine inşa edilmiş kerpiç bir dış duvardan ve yine kerpiç bir iç 'set' duvardan oluşmaktadır. Büyük bir olasılıkla bu set duvar üç amaçla kullanılmıştı: 1) yerleşimin, kuzey rüzgarlarıyla gelen yağmur ve nemden korunması 2) dış duvara bitişik olarak yapılmış ahşap çatıların desteklenmesi 3) yapılarla dış sur duvarı arasında seğirdim yolu olarak ör. siper olarak kullanılması. Çevre duvarı dışında ise, kullanım amaçları belli olmayan birçok küçük oda vardır.

I–IV no.lu odalardan oluşan ana birim, höyüğün kademeli kısmında sur duvarına bitişik olarak inşa edilmiştir. Avlunun batısında, başlıca üç oda vardır. I no.lu oda tabanının bir kısmı oldukça sıkı bir şekilde küçük çakıl taşlarıyla döşenmiştir. Bu oda tabanının diğer kısmıyla, II ve III no.lu odaların tabanları ise, saman katkılı ince bir kat çamur ile döşenmiş ve düzenli olarak yenilenmiştir. Bu nedenle bu odaların tabanları, günümüze ince tabakalardan oluşan bir seri halinde ulaşmıştır. III no.lu odanın arka avluya açılan bir kapısı vardır. Kapalı avlunun (IV) doğu duvarı üzerinde ise, bu avluya XXIII no.lu odadan girişi sağlayan kapıya bitişik bir merdiven vardır. Bu merdivene zemin kattaki XXXIII no.lu odadan ulaşılmaktadır. Sahanlıkta bulunan iki dikme avlunun orta kısmı üzerinde yer alan bir oday desteklemek

mış olmalıdırlar. II no.lu odada
: ise, I ve II no.lu odalar üzerinde
ın varlığını kanıtla-maktadır.
oğu köşesinde bulunan giriş ise,
arafında bulunan yapılara geçiş
alar ve avluların biraraya
şan küçük yapılar çoğunlukla
bir şekilde inşa edilmiş ve
k olarak kesişmeyen eğri
maktadırlar ve yer yer parçalar
lmişlerdir.

ey yarısında bulunan yapıların
ukla çakıltaşı ve taş parçaları
Hayvan barınağı olarak kulla-
ıası bu yapılar, kuzeyde bulu-
apıdan XXII ve XXI no.lu
naktadır. Bu alanlar üzerinde
, çukur, ocak ve tandır vardır.

uzeydoğu köşesinde bulunan
ki katlı olması gerekmektedir.
orunagelmiş olan yüzey planı
ı ifade edmeyecektir. Büyük
lar çalışma ve depolama ama-
mıştır. XXVII no.lu odanın
bitişik taş duvara ait kısım
diven temeliydi.

ırından geçen yolun ise, XVIII
şecek şekilde yukarıya doğru,
batısında bulunan ek yapılara
ere uzandığını tahmin etmek-

2. Evre (Şek. 9)

erleşim biriminin II no.lu orta
ış, avlunun kuzeyinde bulunan
ş ve II no.lu odanın güneybatı
erdiven inşa edilmiştir. Bu dö-
avlu tabanının çamurla kaplı
tedir. Bu çamur tabanın yağ-
rüklenmeden günümüze kadar
n, avlunun üzerinin kapalı old-
teyiz.

oldukça düzensiz alanlardan
güneyi, büyük olasılıkla arka
polama birimleri ve çalışma
şmaktaydı. Oturma amacı ile
ana yerleşim biriminin güney
olarak inşa edilmiş çatıları
vardır. Bunlar VII–IX no.lu
no.lu odada, odanın batıda
kısmı üzerinde bulunan damı
elere ait kaideler bulunmuştur.
· üzerine inşa edilmiş kerpiç
a görülmeyen bir özelliktir.
n bir köşesinde ise bir ocak yer
len taş yığını ile kaplı olan IX

no.lu oda ise, yapı malzemelerinin depolanması için kullanılmış olabilir.

1. kat 1. evrede, höyüğün kuzeyinde bulunan bir grup yapı ile höyüğün güneyinde bulunan yapılar arasında kalan dar, uzun ve açık alan, bu evrede birkaç oda ve bir avlu ile çevrilmiş olarak karşımıza çıkmaktadır. Höyüğün batısında bulunan birçok küçük yapı ve avlu ise yıkılmış ve yerlerini bir küçük yapı (XIII no.lu oda) ve çöplük olarak kullanılmış birçok çukurdan oluşan geniş bir alan almıştır.

XVI no.lu yeni yapı ile XVII no.lu yapılar diğer yapılarla kıyaslandıklarında oldukça iyi inşa edilmiş oldukları görülür. Kuzey odasında tabana inşa edilmiş üç adet ocak vardır. XVII no.lu odada ise, üç çukur ve iki ocak bulunmaktadır. Evin doğusu XVIII no.lu avlu ve XIX no.lu açık alan ile çevrilidir. Bu evrede ev ilk planına uygun olarak yeniden inşa edilmiş ve batısına bitişik bir başka yapı (XIV no.lu oda) eklenmiştir.

Bu yapıların XX–XXII no.lu odalardan oluşan güneydoğu kısmı oldukça sağlam bir şekilde inşa edilmiştir. XX no.lu odanın tabanı çamurdur. Odanın kuzeydoğu köşesine bir pithos, kuzeybatı köşesinde ise kabaca yapılmış bir çömlek kap yerleştirilmiştir. Bu odada ayrıca bir de ocak bulunmaktadır. XXI no.lu odanın güneydoğu köşesinde ise bacası ile birlikte bir fırın bulunmuştur.

Bu evrede bir giriş inşa edilmiştir. Yerleşime uzanan ve oldukça büyük kireçtaşı bloklarından yapılmış kaldırım taşları ile döşeli yol hafifçe basamaklıdır. Bu yolun batı uç noktasında iki sütun kaidesi vardır. Giriş bu iki sütun kaidesinin etrafına duvar çekilerek oluşturulmuştur. Yol bu girişten sonra kuzeybatıya doğru uzanır.

Bu evrede ana yapı genişletilmiş ve yerleşime depolama birimleri, avlular ve iki oturma ünitesi eklenmiştir. XVI ve XVII no.lu odalardan oluşan ilk ev, XVIII no.lu evle bağlantılı bir avludan ve XIX no.lu açık bir çalışma alanından oluşmaktadır. İkinci mekan yani XX no.lu oda ise, XXI ve XXII no.lu çalışma alanı ve avludan oluşmaktadır.

1. yapı katı yerleşimin kuzey kısmının önemli bir bölümünü etkileyen büyük bir yangınla son bulmuştur. I–VI, XI, XII, XXIV–XXVIII no.lu odalar, XVI no.lu küçük ev ve XVII no.lu mekan 0.20–0.50 metre arasında değişen kül, odun kömürü ve yanmış kerpiç birikintisi ile örtülü olarak bulunmuştur. XI ve XII no.lu odalarda bulunmuş olan oldukça kalın yanmış malzeme örtüsü, bu iki oda üzerinde ikinci bir kat olduğunu göstermektedir. XVI no.lu küçük evin ve XVII no.lu odanın da yanmış olmaları garip gözükmektedir; çünkü bu yapı ile en yakın

yangın geçirmiş oda olan XII no.lu oda arasında önemli bir uzaklık vardır. Bu durum, yangının asıl yapıların yıkılması amacıyla bilinçli olarak başlatılmış olabileceği şeklinde yorumlanabilir.

2. Yapı Katı, 1. Evre (Şek. 10)

1. kat 2. evrenin yangınla son bulmasından sonra ortaya çıkan bu ilk yapı katı tamamiyle yeniden inşa edilmiştir. Bazı duvarları bir önceki kata ait duvarların yönünde ya da çok yakın konumdadır. Odaların ve alanların sayısında belirgin bir artış olmuştur: 1. kat 2. evrede otuzbir olan bu sayı, 2. kat 1. evrede kırksekize ulaşmaktadır.

Tamamiyle yeniden inşa edilmiş olan dış çevre duvarının taş temelleri, 1. katta görülmüş olan ilk çevre duvarının kalıntıları üzerine inşa edilmiştir. Duvarın kuzeydoğusunda XXXV no.lu odaya açılan küçük bir giriş eklenmiştir.

I, II, III, IV? no.lu odalar ve üzerlerinde bulunan katdan oluşan asıl yaşama bölgesinin, yine yerleşimin kuzeybatı köşesinde yer aldığını görüyoruz. Bütün bu odaların tabanları saman katkılı çamurla kaplıdır ve I no.lu odanın kuzeydoğu köşesinde bir ocak vardır. VIII no.lu geçit ise, yerleşimin içinden geçerek asıl yerleşim alanını XLVII no.lu ana yola bağlamaktadır. Bu alanın güneyinde VII ve V no.lu avlular ve malzeme depolamak ve hayvanları barındırmak için kullanılmış olan VI no.lu oda bulunmaktadır. V no.lu avlunun güneyinde ise, tabanı çamurla kaplı ve kuzeybatı köşesinde ise küçük bir ocak olan X no.lu küçük oda vardır. Odanın güneyinde 1.30 metrelik bir kısım - uyuma alanı olarak?- odanın diğer tarafından bir sıra taş ile ayrılmıştır.

XI no.lu alan ise, kuzeydoğu ve güneydoğu köşelerinde bulunan XII ve XIII no.lu kapalı iki küçük odadan oluşan açık bir alan gibi gözükmektedir. XI no.lu bu alanın kuzey tarafında bulunan 2.00 metre karelik bir kısım taşla, diğer taraflar ise koyu renk toprakla kaplıdır. İçinde bir de tandır bulunan tabanı çamurla kaplı XII no.lu oda büyük olasılıkla ev işlerinin yapıldığı odaydı. Tabanı iyice basılmış koyu renk toprakla kaplı XIII no.lu oda ise, hayvanlar için kullanılmış olmalıdır.

XV no.lu oda yerleşime başlıca birimlerin inşaasının tamamlanmasından sonra eklenmiştir. Bu odada bir de oval biçimli fırın vardır (Şek. 11). Bu fırının güney ucunda ateşe kömür atmak için veya baca olarak kullanılan bir de delik mevcuttur.

XLVII no.lu ana yoldan girilen, XVI ve XVII no.lu mekanların merdiven olduğu sanılmaktadır. Bu merdivenin batı ucu 3.00 x 2.70 metre karelik bir alan oluşturacak şekilde dışarı

doğru genişletilmiştir. Burası XV, XXI ve XX no.lu odaların üzerinde bulunan ilk kata girişi sağlayan sahanlığı temsil etmektedir. XX ve XXI no.lu odaların giriş katı çamur ile kaplıdır. Bu oda tabanlarının çamurla kaplı olmasından, bu mekanların da ev işlerinin yapılmasında kullanılmış olduğunu tahmin etmekteyiz.

XVIII no.lu küçük yol, XIV no.lu geniş açık alanı ve XIX no.lu küçük alanı, XXII no.lu odaya ve XLI no.lu banyo alanına bağlar.

XXIII, XXIV, XXV ve XXVI no.lu uzun alan büyük bir olasılıkla bölümlere ayrılmış durumdaydı. Bu varsayımı batı duvarından çıkıntılar yapmış olan birçok ahşap bağ ve bulunmuş olan birkaç dikme kaidesine dayandırmaktayız.

Tabanı çamur ile kaplı XXVIII no.lu odanın kuzeydoğu köşesinde, XXVII ve XXX no.lu odalardan erişilen bir merdiven vardır. Küçük dikdörtgen bir birim ise, bir tandırı çevrelemektedir. XXX–XXXIII no.lu odaların tabanları saman katkılı çamur ile kaplıdır ve ev işlerinin yapıldığı yerler olarak kullanıldıkları tahmin edilmektedir. XXVII, XXX, XXXI, XXXIII ve XXXV no.lu odaların bu yerleşim evresinin sonunda yangın geçirmiş oldukları, zemin üzerinde bulunan yanık tabakasından anlaşılmaktadır.

XXIX no.lu mekan, sarnıç olduğu düşünülen oldukça geniş ve derin bir çukurdan oluşmaktadır. Yapımı iki evrede tamamlanmıştır. İkinci yapım evresinde (2.kat, 1.a evresi ve 3. kat, 2. evre arasında bir zaman) bir kat toprakla sıvanmış, kerpiç duvarları vardır. Oval olan bu çukur, taş temeller üzerine inşa edilmiş dikdörtgen bir duvarla çevrilidir.

Yerleşimin kuzeydoğu köşesi XXVI no.lu avlu, tabanı taş kaplı XXXV no.lu çalışma alanı, günlük işlerinin yapıldığı XXVI no.lu mekan ve XXXVII açık alandan oluşur.

Doğubatı yönünde uzanan ana yolun güneyinde, yerleşimin ise güneydoğu köşesinde banyo kompleksi yer almaktadır (Şek. 12). Banyo binasının batısı ve güneyi XLI no.lu avlu ile çevrilidir. Bu avlunun 5.50 metrelik güney kısmının tabanı taş döşeli ve sıvalıdır.

Banyo binası üç aşamada inşa edilmiştir: önce taş bir platform döşenmiş, daha sonra bu platformun üzerine kuzey odaları inşa edilmiş, son olarak da XLIII ve XLIV no.lu odaların karşısına güney odası eklenmiştir. XLII no.lu en yakın yuvarlak ateş yakma çukuru bazalt ile döşelidir ve yükseldikçe çapı daralmaktadır. Yukarıda sözü edilen tandırın iç dolgu tabakası içerisinde bir baca tepesine ait parçalara rastlanmıştır. Bacanın tepesinde dokuz adet çıkıntı vardır (Şek. 88, 201). Bulunmuş olan bazalt

;i kabartma bezelidir. Bu ka-
lerden bir tanesi hamile bir
: bir phallusdur? (Şek. 58, 202-
bir baca, XLIII no.lu odada
ısıtma bölümüne ulaşmaktadır.
IV no.lu odaların tabanları
 blokları ve silindirik kaplarla
ır (Şek. 46, no. 198). Bu kap-
ı çimento kalıplar üzerine
ızıları ise özel ayaklar üzerine
 46, 197). XLIV no.lu odanın
ine yapılmış olan dikey baca
entodan yapılmıştır. Bu baca
ların altında bulunan yeraltı
:ak havayı XLV no.lu yukarı
levini görmüş olmalıdır. XLV
ıbanı beyaz alçı ile kaplıdır.
güneyinde, doğusunda ve kuze-
ızeydoğu köşesinde birbirleriyle
 hendek vardır. Bu üç hendek,
ınayolun altında bulunan ve
larını ana girişten dışarı boşal-
ısyon sistemi ile birleşen bir su
<tadır. Üst kat oda planlarının
ın da planlarını yansıttığını
yet mantıklı olduğunu düşün-
<uzey kısımda iki oda vardı:
ık oda ve XLIV no.lu ılık oda.
n XLV no.lu oda giyinme odası
IV no.lu odanın tabanı altında
an çıkan havayla belli bir
ısıtılmış olmalıdır.
ı evresine ait XLVIII no.lu giriş
ılmaya devam edilmiş; fakat bu
ısmına bir su hendeği, güney
eki eklenmiştir. Bu evrede girişe
ılmıştır. Su hendeğinin kenar
ıan girinti, bu kapının açık
inde kullanılmış olmalıdır. İyi
ıtemi, geniş bir su sarnıcı ve
yerleşim tam bir bütündür. Bu
< bir aile tarafından kullanılmış
yüksektir. 1. kat, 2. evrede de
eşim üç ayrı yaşama alanından
tı köşede bulunan ana yaşama
eisi için?), toprak seviyesinde
o.lu odaları ve üst katlarını ve
 IV ve VI no.lu mekanları
yük olasılıkla merdiven II no.lu
o.lu oda girişinin batısı?) bir
şimin güneybatı kısmına yakın
n ise XX, XXI, XXV ve
no.lu odanın üst katlarından
çüncü alan yerleşimin kuzey-
lir ve XXX–XXXIII no.lu
 seviyesinde bulunan katlarını,
st katlarını ve aynı zamanda

XXIII–XXXV no.lu odaları kullanmaktadır.
Ayrıca yalnızca X no.lu odadan oluşan
dördüncü bir alan da, bu evrede yaşama
mekanı olarak kullanılmıştır.

2. Yapı Katı, 1a Evresi (Şek. 14)

Bu alt evrede çoğunluğu batı yarıda olmak üzere,
bazı küçük değişiklikler meydana gelmiştir. Her
ne kadar çevre duvarının sağlamlaştırılmasının,
bundan sonraki evrede, yani 2. kat 1b evresinde
yapılmış olma olasılığı varsa da, biz bu evrede
gerçekleşmiş olmasının daha olası olduğunu düşünmekteyiz.

Bu evrede dış çevre duvarına üç adet kule
benzeri yapı, savunmayı güçlendirme veya
dengeleme amacıyla eklenmişlerdir. Ancak her
iki amaca da yönelik olması daha güçlü bir
olasılıktır.

Bu evrede ana yaşama biriminde de bazı
değişiklikler meydana gelmiştir. Bu evrede 12.20
metre uzunluğunda olan I no.lu oda ile V no.lu
geniş avlu, kuzeylerine inşa edilmiş olan III no.lu
oda ile küçültülmüşlerdir. Bulunmuş olan birçok
destek kaidesinden bu dönemde V no.lu avlunun
üzerinin kapalı olduğu anlaşılmıştır. Avlunun
kuzeydoğu köşesinde büyük olasılıkla bir merdivene ait iki sıra destek vardır. Avluda geniş bir
ocak, üç çukur ve bir de fırın mevcuttur. V ve III
no.lu odaların yangın geçirmiş oldukları tabanın,
ocağın, fırının ve destek kaidelerinin üzerindeki
yanık tabakasından anlaşılmaktadır. Bu taba-
kanın incelenmesinden sonra V no.lu avlunun
ahşap ve toprak malzeme ile inşa edilen bir
damla örtülü olduğu; yani üzerinde başka bir
kat olmadığı anlaşılmıştır. Diğer taraftan III
no.lu odanın üzerinde çökmüş bir ikinci kat
olduğu saptanmıştır.

VIII no.lu patika, VII no.lu avludan yeni inşa
edilmiş bir duvarla ayrılmış ve VII no.lu avlunun
tabanı yeniden kaba taşlarla döşenmiştir. Bir evre
öncesine ait XI no.lu avlu XII ve XIII no.lu
alanlar olmak üzere ikiye ayrılmıştır. XI no.lu
odanın güneydoğu köşesindeki tanımlanan-
mayan alanda ise, bir merdivenin bulunma
olasılığı vardır. Buraya zemin seviyesinde olan
VIII no.lu patikadan girilmektedir. Sahanlık
büyük olasılıkla XII no.lu odanın üzerindeydi
ve XI, X ve muhtemelen IX no.lu batı odalarının ve VII, VI, III, II ve I no.lu kuzey
odalarının üzerinde bulunan yukarı katlara
girişi sağlıyordu.

2. yapı katı, 1. evreye ait XIV no.lu geniş açık
alan ise üç kısma bölünmüş ve XIV no.lu orta
bölüm düz kireçtaşı blokları ile döşenmiştir.
İçinde bir de fırın bulunan XV no.lu oda, doğu
kısmına eklenmiş XXIV no.lu oda ile

küçültülmüştür. Aynı şekilde XXI no.lu oda da iki küçük kısma ayrılmıştır. XXIV ve XLIX no.lu odaların garip şekilleri ve ölçüleri buradaki merdiven yerinin değiştirilmiş olabileceğini akla getirmektedir. XVII no.lu oda boyunca uzanıp, XVI no.lu odanın üst katında batıya ve kuzeye dönmesi gereken merdivenlerin, XXI no.lu odada başlayıp, XLIX no.lu odanın üzerinde devam edip, XVI no.lu oda üzerinde batıya ve XXIV no.lu oda üzerinde ise kuzeye döndüğünü tahmin ediyoruz.

XXX no.lu odanın tabanı bir kaç kat saman katkılı çamur ile döşenmiştir. XXXIV no.lu oda giriş kısmının tabanı ise taş ile döşelidir. XXX no.lu odanın 1.50 metrelik batı kısmı, odanın ortasında bulunan bir ocakla kaplıdır. Bu odada ayrıca bir de fırın vardır. Bu evrede tabanı saman katkılı çamurla kaplı olan XXXIV no.lu oda ile tandır ve fırınların bulunduğu odanın çeşitli öğeleri bu evre süresince çoğunlukla yenilenmişlerdir. XXXV ve XXVIII no.lu odaların tabanları da saman katkılı çamur ile kaplıdır. XXVIII no.lu odanın batı duvarı bir destekle sağlamlaştırılmıştır. Bu evrede XL no.lu odada bir küçük fırın ile iki çöp çukuru görülmektedir.

XLI no.lu avlunun banyo binası ile bağlantılı kısmı ile XLV no.lu mekanın güneyinde bulunan kısmın tabanları çakıltaşı ile yeniden döşenmiştir. Banyo dairesinin güney odasının (XLV) tabanı ise, küçük çakıl taşları ve sıva ile yeniden döşenmiştir.

2. Yapı Katı, 1b Evresi (Şek. 15)

Bu dönemde I no.lu oda tabanının üst kısmı düzleştirilmiş ve geniş kireçtaşı blokları ile özenle yeniden kaplanmıştır; fakat bu kaplama bütünüyle günümüze kadar ulaşamamıştır. Odanın doğusunda, düz kısmı doğuda olan D harfine benzeyen bir ocak vardır (Şek. 16).

Bu evrede V no.lu avlunun tabanı nehir yatağından çıkarılmış çakıl taşları, kemik parçaları ile karışık küçük taşlar ve kırık çanak çömlek parçaları ile gayet düzensiz bir şekilde döşenmiştir. Odada herhangi bir birime veya desteklere ait kanıt yoktur. Bu durumda, 2. yapı katı, 1a evresinde meydana gelen yangından sonra, bu odanın üzerinin büyük olasılıkla tekrar bir çatıyla örtülmediğini söyleyebiliriz.

Bu dönemde VI no.lu odanın kullanım amacı değiştirilmiş ve iki depo ve üç geniş fırın eklenmiştir (Şek. 17).

VIII no.lu yol, nehir yatağından çıkarılmış orta boy çakıltaşları üzerine yerleştirilmiş küçük çakıltaşları ile, VII ve V no.lu odalardaki gibi kaplanmıştır. XI ve XIII no.lu odalarda çok

küçük değişiklikler meydana gelmiştir. XVIII no.lu yol ise, nehirden alınmış küçük çakıltaşları ile oldukça sıkı bir şekilde döşenmiştir.

Yerleşimin güneybatısında bulunan ve merdivenle bağlantılı odaların planlarında yine değişiklikler meydana gelmiştir. Yerleşimin merkezinde de birçok değişiklikler yapılmıştır. 2. kat, 1a evresine ait XXV ve XXVI no.lu odalar ise küçük alanlara bölünmüşlerdir. Gayet küçük bölmelere ayrılmış bu iki alanın görünüşü, bu bölmelerin hayvanlar için kullanılmış olabileceklerini akla getirmektedir. XXX no.lu odada bulunan ocak artık kullanılmamaktadır ve XXIV no.lu odaya girişi sağlayan geçiş ise, kapatılmıştır. XXXIV no.lu odanın kuzeybatı köşesine alçak bir platform inşa edilmiş, bu odada bulunan fırın ve tandırlar XXXVI no.lu odaya taşınmışlardır.

Banyo dairesinin güney odasında küçük bir değişiklik yapılmış, güney ve batı duvarları genişletilmiştir. Bu dönemde bu odanın tabanı basılmış, koyu renkli, sert toprakla kaplıdır.

2. Yapı Katı, 2. Evre (Şek. 18)

Bu dönemde höyüğün üzerinde bulunan yapılarda ufak değişiklikler meydana gelmiş, höyüğün tepesinde bulunan yerleşimin genel görünümünde önemli bir değişiklik olmamıştır.

I no.lu odada bulunan fırının yerine, doğu duvarına bitişik taş platformun üzerine bir ocak yapılmıştır. II no.lu oda olarak adlandırılan koridor, yeni yapılan bir duvarla doğusundan kapatılmıştır. Odanın ortasına ise, uzunlamasına geniş bir taş dibek (Şek. 85 no. 198) yerleştirilmiştir.

Bu dönemde III no.lu oda daha küçüktür. Bunun nedeni bu odanın batı kısmının bölünerek, XII no.lu odanın meydana getirilmesi için yapılmış olan kavisli duvardır. V no.lu avlu ise iki büyük alana, merdiven olarak yorumlanacak bir birime ve daha küçük bir odaya bölünmüştür. VI no.lu oda ise 2. kat, 2. evrede tamamen şekil değiştirmiştir. Batı ve güney duvarları güçlendirilmiş, kapı girişi yer değiştirmiş ve doğu kısmına eklenen yeni bir odayla daha da küçülmüştür. Bu evrede XI no.lu odanın kuzey ve doğu duvarları da yenilenmiştir.

XIII, XIV, ve L no.lu mekanlar bu dönemde geniş açık alanlardır. XX no.lu oda daha önce XX, XXI, XLIX ve XVI no.lu odanın bir kısmının altında bulunan alanı kapsamaktaydı. Yerleşimdeki başlıca değişiklikler bu alanda meydana gelmiştir; merdiven kaldırılmıştır. Bu dönemde buradaki yapının tek katlı olduğu görülmektedir.

XXIII no.lu mekan bu evrede 2. yapı katı, 1b

II–XXV ve LIII–LV no.lu
ladığı alanı tanımlamak için
r. Bu alanın güney yarısında
erleri mevcuttur. Her ne kadar
ᵣerleri düzenli bir şekilde
da, oda üzerinin bu dönemde
u kanıtladıklarını varsaymakt-
ᵣ XXXI no.lu oda, bir önceki
XXII no.lu odayı da içine
ᵣapı katı, 1b evresinde XXXVI
lunan fırınlar, 2. yapı katı, 1a
ᵣu gibi XXXIV no.lu odaya
XXXVI, LII ve XXXIX no.lu
ufak değişiklikler meydana
no.lu banyo dairesine ait güney
düzgün kesilmiş düz kireçtaşı
ᵣmiş yeni bir tabanı vardır.
ᵣığlı olduğu yapı katı, yerleşimin
ᵣnı tahrip eden yangınla son
ᵣ II no.lu odalar oldukça yıkık
ᵣ yangın sonucunda ikinci kat,
ne çökmüştür. I no.lu odada
ı.40 metre yüksekliğe ulaşan
sı kazılarak araştırılmıştır.

1. Evre (Şek. 19)

ᵣğün üzerindeki yerleşim, az da
evreyle benzerlik göstermekte-
batı üçte ikisini kaplayan alanı-
la bulunan mekanların dağılımı,
ᵣn planına uymaktadır. Yalnız iki
ᵣe duvarının izlerine rastlanılır.
y ve güneydoğu kısmının büyük
katın görünen yüzeyi bir önceki
an yüzeyine, herhangi bir kanıtın
ᵣasını sağlayamayacak kadar ya-
ᵣöyüğün kuzey kenarında bulu-
ᵣ da, 11 x 5 metrelik bir alanı

m odalar, bir önceki dönem
olsalar bile yeniden numaralan-

nde küçük taşlar ve çakıl taşları
toprakla kaplı III ve V no.lu
ᵣ olduklarını düşünmekteyiz. Bu
ᵣarları 2. kat, 2. evreden koruna-
ve VII no.lu odalarda, taban-
ᵣniş olması dışında başka bir
ᵣmemektedir. VIII no.lu mekan,
diğer duvarlara oranla iki kat
ᵣası nedeniyle merdiven olarak
IX no.lu mekan, II no.lu
ᵣığün güney kısmında bulunan
ᵣ uzanan bir ana cadde meydana
ᵣ.lu mekan ise, yine bir avludur.
ᵣy ve batı duvarları yeniden inşa

edilmiş, tabanı küçük çakıl taşları, çanak çömlek
ve kiremit parçaları ile kaplanmıştır.

Kuzey yarısında altı adet dikme kaidesi
belirlenmiş olan XIII no.lu odan kısmen kapalı
bir alandır. Saptanmış olan bu kaideler bir bölme
duvarının temeli olarak tanımlanmıştır. XIV
no.lu odanın batı, XV no.lu odanın ise üç
duvarı yeniden inşa edilmişlerdir. XVII no.lu
sarnıç büyük olasılıkla bu evrede de kullanıl-
maktaydı. Tabanı saman katkılı çamurla gayet
özenli bir şekilde döşenmiş olan XIX no.lu oda,
dış çevre duvarına birleşen dar ve uzun bir
mekandır. Bu yapı büyük olasılıkla küçük bir
evdi. XX ve XXI no.lu odaların da dış çevre
duvarına bitişik oldukları tahmin edilmektedir.
XXII no.lu alan, XIX no.lu odanın güneydoğu
köşesinden başlayarak doğuya doğru uzanan sur
duvarının kuzeyinde bulunan düz alana çıkışı
sağlayan eğimli bir yoldur. Bu eğimli yolun
güney ucu 3. yapı katı, 2. evre yerleşim alanı
içine girmektedir. Batı kısmında bir sıra kenar
taşı vardır.

Höyüğün üzerinde büyük olasılıkla üç yerleşim
alanı vardı. Kuzeybatı köşede bulunan I ve II
no.lu odaların eskiden olduğu gibi ikamet
amacıyla, güneyde bulunan odaların ise avlu
olarak ve depolama amacıyla kullanılmış olması
olasıdır. VI no.lu oda ise, büyük olasılıkla doğu,
güney ve muhtemelen batısında (her ne kadar
bunlar günümüze kadar ulaşmamışsa da)
bulunan bağlantılı yapılarıyla oturma odası
olarak kullanılmıştır. Üçüncü ikamet bölgesi ise,
XIX no.lu oda ve höyüğün doğu yarısında
bulunan alanları ve beraberindeki yapılarıyla
XX no.lu odalardan oluşmaktadır.

3. Yapı Katı, 2. Evre (Şek. 20)

Bu yapı evresinde meydana gelen değişiklikler,
yerleşimin ana şeklini değiştirmeyecek kadar az-
dır. II no.lu oda ikiye bölünmüş, III ve V no.lu
odaların ise boyutları değişmiştir. 3. kat, 1. evrede mevcut olan VIII no.lu oda yok olmuştur.
XI ve XII no.lu odalar birleştirilerek bir oda
meydana getirilmiş ve XXIII no.lu oda da ikiye
ayrılmıştır. II ve VIII no.lu odalar, saman katkılı
çamur tabanları ve fırınları ile ev işleri için
kullanılmış gibi gözükmektedirler. Bu iki odanın
tabanları üzerinde yangınla tahrip olmuş olduklarını gösteren kül tabakası vardır. III, IV ve VII
no.lu odalar depolama ve çalışma alanları olarak
gözükmektedir. V no.lu avlu ise, genişletilmiştir.
XII no.lu mekanın merdiven olması ihtimali vardır; fakat ikinci katın hangi odalar üzerinde olabileceğini tahmin etmek güçtür. VI no.lu
odanın doğusunda büyük bir avlu vardır. XVI
no.lu mekanın tabanı kemik ve odunkömürü

parçaları, kırık çömlek ve cam parçaları ve çürümüş organik malzemeden oluşan bir çöp birikintisi ile kaplıdır. XXIII ve XXIV no.lu odaların batı duvarları, tehlikeli bir şekilde yana yatmış oldukları için yeniden inşa edilmişlerdir.

3. Yapı Katı, 3. Evre (Şek. 21)

Bu evrede korunagelmiş yapıların parçalar halinde olduğu gözlenmektedir. 3. kat, 3. evrede yerleşim iki ayrı alanda toplanmıştır. Batıda kalan alan, evin (II no.lu oda) ve bir giriş yoluna (III no.lu oda) sahip bağlantılı avlunun (I no.lu oda) etrafında toplanmıştır. Höyüğün kuzeydoğu köşesini kaplayan ikinci alan ise, yine bir ev (V no.lu oda) ve bitişik ek binalardan (VI-IX no.lu odalar) oluşmaktadır.

3. Yapı Katı, 4. Evre (Şek. 22)

Bu evrede ancak altı odanın varlığı kanıtlanmıştır. Yerleşim yine iki ayrı yapıdan oluşmaktadır ve bu yapılarda çok az değişiklik meydana gelmiştir.

3. Yapı Katı, 5. Evre (Şek. 23)

Höyüğün batısında bulunan yapı üzerinde bir değişiklik olmaması nedeniyle, bu dönemde kullanılmış olsa bile, bu evreye dahil edilmemiştir. IV no.lu mekan büyük olasılıkla I, II ve muhtemelen III no.lu odaların üzerinde bulunan üst kata çıkışı sağlayan merdivendir.

Çanak-Çömlek

Çalışma yaptığımız bu alan ve dönemle ilişkili yayınlanmış çok az malzeme vardır. Bununla beraber bazı buluntuların benzerlerine Aşvan, Hama ve Antioch'da rastlanılmaktadır. Kazıda bulmuş olduğumuz çanak çömleğin büyük bir kısmı Tille'de üretilmemiştir; fakat bölgesel kökenlidir. İthal edilmiş mallar ise olasılıkla yörenin en önemli merkezlerinden biri olan Samsat pazarından gelmiş olmalıdır; çünkü bu çanak çömleğin yakın benzerlerine bu merkezde rastlanılmaktadır.

Geniş, bir veya iki kulplu, uzun ve dar boyunlu kaplar (3–15 numaralar) oldukça yaygındır. Yemek pişirmek için çok yaygın olarak kullanılmış iki tür kap vardır: turuncu, kum katkılı hamurdan yapılmış olanlar (49, 54, 55, 58, 60, 80–84 numaralar) ve sert, perdahlanmadan fırınlanmış, oksidasyon veya redükleme yöntemi ile bezenmiş olanlar (85–96 numaralar). Çok yaygın olarak kullanılmış kaselerin cilaları da birbirlerinden farklıdır (245–265 numaralar). Bu cilalar içinde en çok koyu kahve/siyah kullanılmıştır. Bunların yanı sıra önemli miktarlarda türkuvaz veya yeşil cilalı olanlara da rastlanılmıştır. Diğer bir grup ise, renkli çizgi (açık gri, kızıl kahve, kahverengi) bezeli kaplardan oluşturmaktadır. Bezemesiz kaplara da sıklıkla rastlanılır.

Gayet ince bir şekilde özenle cilalanmış keramiklerin büyük çoğunluğunun Suriye'den ithal edilmiş olduğunu düşünmekteyiz. Tell Minis grubuna dahil keramikler 324–327 ve büyük olasılıkla 302 no.lu parçalarla, Raqqa grubu keramikler ise 328, 335, 339, 344 ve 358 *inter alia* ile temsil edilmektedirler. 308–317 arası siyah boyalı, mavi perdahlı keramik türü höyük üzerindeki yerleşimlerin sonuncusundan elde edilmiş ve 286–299 no.lu sgraffiato keramikleri ile birlikte bulunmuşlardır.

Tarihleme

Höyüğün tepesinde bulunan Ortaçağ'a ait yerleşimin tarihlendirilmesi çanak çömleğe, özellikle gayet ince cilalanmış buluntulara dayandırılmak zorundadır. In situ olarak bulunmamış olan 8 adet Ortaçağ sikkesinden 5'i hakkında kesin bir tarihleme yapmak olası değildir. Bunlardan biri Abbasi sikkesidir ve İ.S. 741 yılına tarihlendirilmiştir. Bu sikkenin bu tarihten sonra bir yüzyıl daha kullanıldığı tahmin edilmektedir. Bizans dönemine ait diğer dört imzasız, bronz sikke ise 11. yüzyılın ortalarına tarihlendirilmiştir. Bu sikkeler höyük üzerindeki Ortaçağ'a ait ana yerleşimden daha erken bir döneme ait olmalıdırlar; çünkü buluntuların hiçbiri 11. yüzyıla ait gibi gözükmemektedir.

Höyükte ele geçmiş olan keramik buluntuların ışığı altında, höyük üzerinde bulunan yerleşimin 12. yüzyıl ortalarında bir tarihte başlamış olabileceğini tahmin etmekteyiz. 1. yapı katının 2. evresinde yalnızca bir tane Tell Minis ve bir tane Raqqa mallarından bulunmuştur. Bu gruplara ait keramiklerin büyük çoğunluğu 2. yapı katının geç dönemlerinden elde edilmiştir. Buna göre bu katların 13. yüzyıl ortalarına tarihlendirilmesi gerekmektedir.

3. katın geç evrelerine ait olan siyah boyalı, mavi perdahlı kaplar 13. yüzyılın ikinci yarısına ve 14. yüzyılın başlarına tarihlendirilmişlerdir. Yine bu evrelere ait olan ve bu tip mallara örnek gösterilebilecek buluntu altıncı sikkedir. Bu Antonia Venier'e (1382–1400) ait gümüş bir sikkedir ve sarnıcın arkasında bulunan dolgunun içinde bulunmuştur. 3. yapı katı, 3. evreden önce bu tip yapay dolgulara rastlanılmamıştır. Bu buluntu höyük üzerindeki yerleşimin 15. yüzyıl ortalarında son bulduğunu göstermektedir.

Plate 1

a. Tille Höyük from the West (02.10.1981)

b. Tille village from the South (08.11.1983)

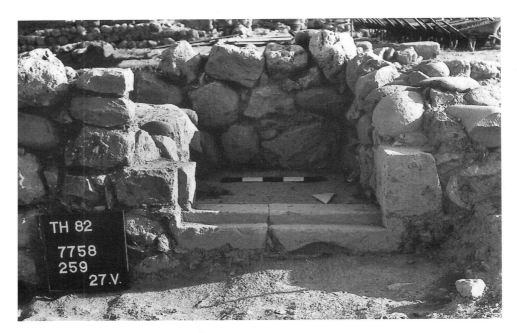

a. Courtyard IV Staircase entrance

b. Level 1 Phase 2 from the East

Plate 3

a. Bath-house from the North-West

b. Bath-house Furnace from the West

a. Level 2 Phase 1, Gateway from the West

b. Level 2 Phase 1, Cistern, Gateway, Bath-house from the West

Plate 5

a. Level 2 Phase 1a, Perimeter Wall, Rooms I and II from the West

b. Level 2, Phase 1b, Room VI from the South

a. Section 1 from the West, 065, 042, 067, 021, 066, 047, 043, 020

b. Section 1 from the West, 069, 024, 068, 048, 044, 022, 023

Plate 7

b. Tell Minis Ware = Fig. 52 no.325

d. Tell Minis Ware = Fig. 52 no.327

a. Tell Minis Ware = Fig. 52 no.324

c. Tell Minis Ware = Fig. 52 no.326

a. Under-glaze = Fig. 53 no.345

b. (?)Sandwich glaze, polychrome decoration, Fig. 53 no.346